Cognitive Therapy for Psychosis

Cognitive Therapy for Psychosis provides clinicians with a comprehensive cognitive model that can be applied to all patients with a diagnosis of schizophrenia, or related disorders, in order to aid the development of a formulation that will incorporate all relevant factors. It promotes an understanding of an individual's difficulties within a cognitive framework, illustrates the process of assessment, formulation and intervention and highlights potential difficulties arising from work with patients and how they can be overcome.

Experienced clinicians write assuming no prior knowledge of the area, covering all of the topics of necessary importance including:

- An introduction to Cognitive Theory and Therapy.
- Collaborative development of idiosyncratic case formulations.
- Deriving intervention strategies from the formulation.
- Difficulties in engagement and the therapeutic relationship.
- How best to utilise homework with people who experience psychosis.
- Working with people with negative systems.
- Relapse prevention and management.

Illustrated by excerpts from therapy sessions, this book digests scientific evidence and theory, but moreover provides clinicians with essential practical advice about how to best aid people with psychoses by reducing their distress and improving their quality of life.

Anthony P. Morrison is Reader of Clinical Psychology at the University of Manchester and co-ordinates a specialist early intervention programme for people with psychosis at Bolton, Salford and Trafford Mental Health Partnership. **Julia C. Renton** is a Clinical Psychologist who leads the provision of Cognitive Therapy within the early intervention programme. **Hazel Dunn** is a Consultant Cognitive Therapist who leads a Cognitive Therapy Service in Chorley. **Steve Williams** is Consultant Nurse in Psychosocial Interventions in West Wales. **Richard P. Bentall** is Professor of Experimental Clinical Psychology at the University of Manchester. All of the authors have published numerous papers in the area of cognitive theory and therapy for psychosis and have extensive clinical experience of delivering cognitive therapy to people with psychosis.

Cognitive Therapy for Psychosis

A formulation-based approach

Anthony P. Morrison,
Julia C. Renton, Hazel Dunn,
Steve Williams and
Richard P. Bentall

Routledge
Taylor & Francis Group

LONDON AND NEW YORK

First published 2004 by Routledge
27 Church Road, Hove, East Sussex BN3 2FA

Simultaneously published in the USA and Canada
by Routledge
711 Third Avenue, New York NY 10017

First issued in paperback 2015

Routledge is an imprint of the Taylor & Francis Group, an informa business

© 2004 Anthony P. Morrison, Julia C. Renton, Hazel Dunn, Steve Williams, Richard P. Bentall

Typeset in Times by Keystroke, Jacaranda Lodge, Wolverhampton

Cover design by Lisa Dynan

This publication has been produced with paper manufactured to strict environmental standards and with pulp derived from sustainable forests.

British Library Cataloguing in Publication Data
A catalogue record for this book is available from the British Library

Library of Congress Cataloging in Publication Data
Cognitive therapy for psychosis : a formulation-based approach /
Anthony Morrison . . . [et al.].--1st ed.
    p. ; cm.
Includes bibliographical references and index.
  ISBN 1-58391-9810-8 (hbk : alk. paper)
  1. Psychoses--Treatment. 2. Cognitive therapy.
  [DNLM: 1. Psychotic Disorders--therapy. 2. Cognitive
  Therapy--methods. WM 200 C6768 2004] I. Morrison, Anthony P., 1969–
  RC512.C558 2004
  616.89'142--dc22
                                                    2003017017

ISBN 13: 978-1-138-88146-4 (pbk)
ISBN 13: 978-1-5839-1810-4 (hbk)

This book is dedicated to the following people:

For my Dad, who inspired me in all sorts of ways, and for my Mum, who still does – Tony Morrison

For Mum and Dad, for all their support, and for my wonderful son, Thomas, for making me laugh – Julia Renton

For my husband, Martin – Hazel Dunn

For Helen, for all her support and patience over many years – Steve Williams

In memory of John Bentall and Pendril Bentall – Richard Bentall

Contents

Illustrations

Figures

Table

Preface

Since the early 1990s there has been a plethora of studies of cognitive approaches to emotional disorders. The studies have ranged from elucidation of the specific biases and interpretations to the underlying beliefs systems and to the examination of brain changes as a result of cognitive therapy. Elegant cognitive therapy strategies have been developed and applied successfully in clinical trials for the affective disorders, the anxiety spectrum, eating disorders and extending even to chronic pain and borderline personality disorder. The most innovative work since the early 1990s, however, has been the development of understanding and elaboration of cognitive therapy approaches to the treatment of schizophrenia. This work interestingly has been conducted predominantly in the United Kingdom.

The authors of this book constitute what is known in American football as "triple threats": they all are clinicians, researchers and theoreticians. Thus, the interdisciplinary research occurs in the minds of the authors as well as in their interaction with each other. In this instance, the research, theory-building and clinical applications are a synthesis of individual and group effort.

It is often difficult to know which comes first: theory, therapy or research? Theory serves as a roadmap for the clinician and informs the researcher regarding the important areas for investigation. On the other hand, the clinical work provides the data that generate the formulation of the theory and the ideas for research. Finally, research not only validates (or invalidates) the clinical and theoretical propositions but also provides new guidelines for therapy and ideas for theory building. The authors have drawn on the blend of theory, research and practice in developing the corpus of knowledge, formulating the basic assumptions, and adapting and refining appropriate strategies for the treatment of this difficult, perplexing disorder. The result is a landmark in the evolution of cognitive therapy for psychoses.

It is of interest that despite the widespread popularity of these approaches in the United Kingdom and their official recognition by the UK National Health Service, the work has not yet crossed to the other side of the Atlantic. I expect that the work of the current authors in this volume should be a stimulus to their North American colleagues to adapt to their approaches to severe mental illness.

Aaron T. Beck

Introduction

This book has been written in order to provide clinicians with a description of the approach that we take to the understanding of psychosis, and to illustrate how this understanding can determine which interventions will be helpful in reducing the distress of a person with psychotic experiences. It offers an approach that is based on Aaron T. Beck's cognitive therapy for emotional disorders, and assumes that the differences between people with psychosis and people with emotional disorders are largely about the kinds of interpretations they make for events. It is an approach that suggests that the experiences of people with psychosis are understandable, and that the distress they experience as a result is associated with the culturally unacceptable interpretations that they make about events, and is often maintained by counterproductive responses. We also recognise that psychotic experiences are often functional for a person, particularly when they develop; their present difficulties are frequently a result of using old survival strategies that have not changed to reflect the person's new environment. While it is likely that there are multiple pathways to psychosis, it would seem that changing the way people think and behave is a useful way of alleviating distress and improving quality of life. This book is designed to allow readers to gain a psychological perspective on psychosis, and a detailed understanding of the cognitive, behavioural, emotional, physiological and environmental factors that contribute to the development and maintenance of distressing psychotic experiences. It will also provide readers with knowledge regarding the process of cognitive therapy for psychosis, and equip readers with a variety of cognitive and behavioural methods for helping people with psychosis to change. It emphasises Beck's principles for cognitive therapy, particularly the collaborative nature of the endeavour and the need to be scientific in our efforts. It also examines specific issues in the implementation of cognitive therapy for psychosis, which our experiences of providing supervision and workshops suggest many clinicians struggle with. These include how best to utilise homework with people who experience psychosis, how to maximise chances of successfully delivering a psychological service within the wider mental healthcare setting, how to integrate with other services and how to deliver cognitive therapy when there are significant environmental factors that contribute to people's problems.

This book is divided into three parts. The first part examines how we understand psychosis, considering theory and case conceptualisation or formulation, and how this relates to the kind of assessment we should perform. The second part examines how to do therapy, focusing on the structure and principles of therapy, and intervention strategies that can help achieve change for both positive and negative symptoms. It also examines schema change issues. The third part examines issues that arise in the delivery of cognitive therapy to people with psychosis. In particular, it considers how to deal with co-morbid difficulties and relapse prevention, how to enhance patients' ability to do work between sessions (homework) and how to provide cognitive therapy within wider mental health services.

Part I starts with an overview of the rationale for an understanding of psychosis that incorporates psychological and social factors, rather than accepting the prevalent and dominant medical model (Chapter 1). Chapter 2 examines the development of cognitive theories of emotional disorders, showing the relevance of a view that sees thoughts as affecting the way people feel and behave, and looks at recent developments in the ways that emotional disorders are conceptualised, for example the maintaining effects of the behaviours people adopt to avert feared outcomes, and the ways that people allocate attention to things. Chapter 3 examines the development and maintenance of psychosis from a cognitive perspective, integrating existing work on the understanding of hallucinations and delusions with the lessons learnt from emotional disorders that are highlighted in the previous chapter. Chapter 4 outlines how to conduct a cognitive behavioural assessment that will collect the information that the theory from Chapter 3 suggests is important, and Chapter 5 illustrates how this information can be integrated into a psychological case conceptualisation that will determine what intervention strategies will be used.

Part II begins with an examination of the principles and structure of cognitive therapy, and how issues such as collaborative empiricism, guided discovery and agenda setting become even more important when encouraging people with psychosis to become their own therapists (Chapter 6). Chapter 7 examines the importance of the therapeutic relationship, and offers some advice regarding how best to engage people with psychosis in cognitive therapy. Chapter 8 examines the use of cognitive intervention strategies that are derived from a case conceptualisation, mainly in relation to reducing the distress associated with positive symptoms, and Chapter 9 examines how to utilise behavioural techniques within a cognitive framework. Chapter 10 examines schema change processes, and Chapter 11 focuses specifically on achieving change in relation to negative symptoms.

Part III begins with a consideration of the many problems that are commonly associated with psychosis, including depression, post-traumatic stress and substance use, and how cognitive therapy can help to address these (Chapter 12). Chapter 13 examines a cognitive approach to relapse prevention or management, and Chapter 14 examines how best to integrate the use of homework into cognitive therapy for psychosis. Finally Chapter 15 considers the many problems that can be encountered when attempting to implement cognitive therapy for psychosis within the wider healthcare system and in unhelpful social environments, and offers some tentative ideas for solutions to these.

The book has been written as a joint effort, although each author took lead responsibility for certain chapters. However, all authors take responsibility for the content of the book as a whole, since it has grown out of a shared team ethos. Tony Morrison took the lead on Chapters 3 and 4, and had significant input to all of the other chapters, except for Chapter 1. Julia Renton took the lead on Chapters 2, 5, 8, 9 and 10. Hazel Dunn took the lead on Chapters 6, 7, 13 and 14. Steve Williams took the lead on Chapters 12 and 15. Richard Bentall took the lead on Chapters 1 and 11. Tony Morrison also acted as editor for the book.

We would like to acknowledge the contribution that many of our colleagues have made to the development of our approach to psychosis. We have worked closely with a number of clinicians who have helped us with several research projects and participated in peer supervision with us. These are Jake Bowley, Paul French, David Glentworth, Warren Larkin, Ian Lowens and Graeme Reid. In addition, there are many researchers and clinicians, from the fields of both psychosis and emotional disorders, whose published work has clearly influenced our thinking. Those whose work on emotional disorders has been influential include Aaron T. Beck (who we would also like to thank for his interest and enthusiasm for understanding psychosis), David Clark, Anke Ehlers, Melanie Fennell, Anne Hackmann, Christine Padesky, Paul Salkovskis and Adrian Wells. People whose work on psychosis has influenced us include Max Birchwood, Paul Chadwick, Val Drury, David Fowler, Philippa Garety, Andrew Gumley, Gillian Haddock, David Kingdon, Rufus May, Emmanuelle Peters, Nick Tarrier and Douglas Turkington. Most of all, we would like to thank our patients, from whom we have learned a great deal.

Tony Morrison

Part I

Theory, assessment and formulation

Chapter 1

An overview of psychosis

The decade preceding the publication of this book has seen a remarkable turnaround in professional attitudes towards the psychological treatment of severe mental illness. Whereas, before, most psychologists and psychiatrists were pessimistic about the possibility of helping psychotic patients other than by drug treatment, the last few years have seen important innovations in the psychological treatment of delusions, hallucinations and other symptoms previously assumed to be the spasms of a disordered brain. The roots of these developments can be traced in earlier experiments – for example the simple behaviour modification programmes introduced by Skinnerian psychologists in the late 1960s (Ayllon & Azrin, 1968; Paul & Lenz, 1977) and the more sophisticated behavioural family therapy interventions pioneered during the late 1970s and later (Falloon et al., 1985; Leff, Kuipers, Berkowitz, Eberlein-Fries, & Sturgeon, 1982; Tarrier et al., 1988). Nonetheless, the idea that individual therapy might ameliorate the core symptoms of psychosis, rather than merely enable the patients to cope better with their illness, is a relatively new one. Of course, pessimists remain, notably in the United States of America, where the idea that schizophrenia and bipolar disorder are varieties of brain disease that have no substantial psychological component continues to hold sway (Bellack, 1992). However, in Britain and continental Europe, for the most part, individual psychological treatments are rapidly becoming seen as an indispensable part of the therapeutic armoury.

The new treatments, which go under the generic term of *cognitive behaviour therapy* (CBT), have been developed partly by pragmatic experiment, partly on the basis of educated guesswork about the psychological processes that influence symptoms, and partly by adapting therapeutic methods known to be effective for non-psychotic conditions such as anxiety and depression. In this book, we introduce the reader to some of these techniques, always bearing in mind that this process of innovation is incomplete – methods that are available today are no more likely to constitute the last word in the psychological treatment of psychosis than current drug treatments are likely to constitute the last word in psychopharmacology. The approach we advocate is formulation based, which is to say that we believe that individual therapy should begin with a detailed formulation or theory about the origins of each particular patient's symptoms and problems. In this first chapter, we provide some theoretical background to this approach, by briefly discussing recent developments in our understanding of the psychology of psychosis.

As a crude simplification, it is possible to discern two contrasting attitudes among those who research and practise CBT for psychosis. Some people in the field take a purely pragmatic approach to the development and delivery of new treatments. At its extreme, this attitude is exemplified in the belief that particular treatments can be devised for particular symptoms in such a way that new practitioners could just look up in a textbook the treatment recommended for their patient's symptoms and proceed according to instructions. According to this approach, CBT might be *prescribed* for severe psychiatric disorders such as schizophrenia or bipolar disorder in the same way that, say, a particular neuroleptic medication might be prescribed.

Others working in the field, by contrast, believe that treatment should proceed from a thorough understanding and appreciation of the psychology of the patients' symptoms and problems. In bringing together this understanding, therapists will base their therapeutic judgements on a careful appreciation of their patients' history and circumstances, and will look to the latest research for inspiration and ideas about how these symptoms and problems can be explained. Many of those who advocate this scientist-practitioner, formulation-based approach (and in this category we include ourselves), therefore, argue that the development of CBT for psychotic symptoms requires a radical reappraisal of our understanding of the psychology of psychosis. Since the early 1990s, such a radical reappraisal has begun to emerge, and many of those who have contributed to this development have also contributed to the development of the formulation-based approach that we are advocating in this book.

Rethinking the psychology of psychosis

In order to sketch out the new, emerging understanding of psychosis, it will be helpful to look back on the theoretical models that preceded it. In fact, three general paradigms are discernible in the psychiatric literature on madness. The first, which was outlined by Emil Kraepelin (1990) and which dominated research between the end of the nineteenth century and the mid-1970s, assumed that psychosis is best described by broad diagnostic concepts such as schizophrenia or bipolar disorder, and that these concepts describe brain diseases that are probably inherited. The task of psychology within this conceptual framework is to identify neuropsychological abnormalities in patients, in the hope that these might provide clues about the aetiology of the presumed brain pathology. Within this paradigm, there is little scope for psychological intervention, as it is assumed that brain diseases are unresponsive to this kind of treatment.

The second paradigm is exemplified by stress-vulnerability models of psychosis (Nuechterlein & Dawson, 1984; Zubin & Spring, 1977) and assumes that biologically vulnerable individuals become psychotic only when exposed to stressful life events. Although psychotic disorders are still held to fall into general disease categories such as schizophrenia and bipolar disorder, these diseases are hypothesised to lie along continua with ordinary behaviours and experiences, so that individuals can be more or less schizophrenic, or more or less manic-depressive. From the therapist's point of view, this approach is much more useful than the traditional disease model, because it points to environmental factors that may be manipulated in order to bring about therapeutic change. However, it leaves unchallenged the diagnostic concepts assumed by earlier investigators.

The third paradigm, which began to be developed in the late 1980s, focuses on *symptoms* (particular classes of behaviours, experiences or complaints) rather than broad diagnostic categories (Bentall, in press). According to this approach, the task of psychological research is to discover the psychological processes that give rise to these behaviours and experiences; once this has been achieved there will be no residual diseases such as schizophrenia or bipolar disorder that remain to be explained. This paradigm has been associated with renewed optimism about the value of individual psychological treatments for psychotic patients, as the processes responsible for each symptom have sometimes proven to be tractable to psychological intervention (Kuipers et al., 1997; Sensky et al., 2000; Tarrier, 1997; Tarrier, Beckett, Harwood, Baker, Yusupoff, & Ugarteburu, 1993). In the remaining sections of this chapter, we outline each of these paradigms in turn, and discuss their limitations and implications for treatment in more detail.

The disease paradigm

At the end of the nineteenth century, the German psychiatrist Emil Kraepelin (1899/1990) argued that many of the clinical problems he had encountered in the asylums of industrial Germany had a common characteristic, namely a progressively deteriorating course. This observation led him to suggest that many conditions previously considered to be different – for example hebephrenic, catatonic and paranoid states – were in fact caused by the same (unknown) morbid process and ought therefore to be considered as variants of the same disease, he named this disease dementia praecox, or senility of early life. It differed from neurological conditions such as cerebral syphilis because no obvious biological cause could be identified. On the other hand, it could be distinguished from manic depression (a term he used to encompass all conditions in which abnormal mood was the prominent symptom), which had a more favourable outcome. The progressive deterioration seen in dementia praecox patients was regarded as inevitable and unstoppable, leading to intellectual deterioration, poor judgement and the eventual destruction of the personality.

Kraepelin's distinction between dementia praecox and the affective psychoses has been described as a cornerstone of modern psychiatry (Kendell & Gourlay, 1970), and is evident in modern diagnostic manuals such as DSM-IV (American Psychiatric Association (APA), 1994) and ICD-10 (World Health Organization (WHO), 1992). However, his characterisation of these conditions has not gone unchallenged. Famously, Eugen Bleuler (1950) in Zurich observed a more varied outcome in patients diagnosed as suffering from dementia praecox. Rejecting Kraepelin's view that intellectual deterioration was a core feature of the disorder, Bleuler identified subtle emotional and intellectual characteristics as fundamental symptoms of the condition – inappropriate affect, emotional ambivalence, autism (a retreat into a preferred fantasy world) and loosening of associations. Intriguingly, he believed hallucinations and delusions to be mere accessory symptoms (by-products) of the morbid disease process. His more optimistic view ultimately led him to reject the term dementia praecox on the grounds that the disorder was neither a dementia (not everyone deteriorated) nor praecox (although onset was most common in early adulthood, it could strike people later in life). Arguably his substitute term *schizophrenia*, although more enduring, has caused at least as much confusion, leading lay people to confuse the shattering of personality that the term was meant to suggest with the type of Jekell and Hyde multiple personality sometimes portrayed in Hollywood movies.

Nearly fifty years later, Kurt Schneider (1959) brought about another seismic shift in thinking about schizophrenia, by trying to establish criteria for the diagnosis according to two ranks. In the first rank were signs of the disorder that were relatively easy for the clinician to detect – audible thoughts, delusional perceptions and the experiencing of outside influences on the body. In the second rank were all the other symptoms of schizophrenia. It is often assumed that he held the first rank symptoms to be fundamental features of the disorder, but this was not the case (Hoenig, 1982). Schneider was a pragmatist who simply wanted to make the process of diagnosis more transparent. However, English-speaking psychiatrists (many of whom had not read his original work, which was not widely available in English translation) took Schneider to mean that the first rank symptoms were those which were most important, and this view has prevailed in modern diagnostic manuals such as DSM-IV and ICD-10, which tend to highlight positive symptoms such as hallucinations and delusions.

Kraepelin's characterisation of manic depression has also been substantially revised by later psychiatrists. Most notably, Klaus Leonhard (1957/1979) argued that this broad diagnostic entity should be subdivided into unipolar disorders (in which only depression is evident) and bipolar disorders (in which the patient suffers from episodes of depression and episodes of mania), a distinction that is recognised in both the DSM and ICD diagnostic systems.

Mary Boyle (1990) has pointed out that the diagnostic concepts proposed and revised by Kraepelin and those who followed him were not derived from empirical research (although Kraepelin certainly collected and analysed symptom data from a large number of patients) but reflected particular assumptions about the nature of psychiatric disorder. These assumptions were spelt out over eighty years later by Gerald Klerman (1978), one of a group of American psychiatrists who dubbed themselves 'neoKraepelinians' and who were responsible for the highly influential third edition of the DSM. Klerman's neoKraepelinian manifesto had ten main points, but three are particularly important in the present context.

First, the neoKraepelians assumed that there is a clear dividing line between mental health and mental ill-health. Someone was either mentally sick or not sick. Second, it was assumed that there are a finite number of different psychiatric disorders: someone could be either manic depressive *or* schizophrenic. Third, it was assumed that mental disorders were brain diseases. Each of these assumptions merits close examination.

Bleuler challenged the assumption that there is a clear boundary between mentally healthy and mentally sick people, arguing that "There is also a latent schizophrenia, and I am convinced that this is the most frequent form, although admittedly these people hardly ever come for treatment. It is not necessary to give a detailed description of the various manifestations of latent schizophrenia. In this form we can see . . . all the symptoms, and the combinations of symptoms, which are present in the manifest types of the disease." This idea of a continuum between psychosis and normality was taken up by later investigators, notably Paul Meehl (1962) and Jean and Loren Chapman and their colleagues (Chapman, Chapman, & Raulin, 1976; Chapman, Edell, & Chapman, 1980) in the United States, and Gordon Claridge (1987) in Britain. Studies conducted by these researchers and others have established beyond doubt that psychotic symptoms, often transient and attenuated, are experienced by a sizeable minority of the "normal" population. These findings have been reinforced by the results of recent epidemiological studies, in which large population samples have been interviewed, which have confirmed that perhaps ten times as many people experience symptoms such as delusions and hallucinations as seek and receive psychiatric treatment (Tien, 1991; van Os, Hanssen, Bijl, & Ravelli, 2000). There are as yet few clues about why some people are able to live in the community as happy and well-adjusted psychotics, but it seems most likely that these people find ways of thinking about their experiences that minimise their distress. Later, we shall see that patients' reactions to their psychotic experiences may be more important in determining their long-term outcome and quality of life than the characteristics of the symptoms themselves (Morrison, 2001).

The idea that diagnoses such as schizophrenia and manic depression denote separate disorders has, of course, been the central methodological assumption made by researchers in the century following Kraepelin. Patients are allocated to groups and compared on the basis of these diagnoses. The poor reliability of psychiatric diagnoses (the tendency for different clinicians to give the same patients different diagnoses) was therefore a source of embarrassment to neo-Kraepelinians (Spitzer & Fliess, 1974). Their development of operational definitions of psychiatric disorders, contained in manuals such as DSM-IV (APA, 1994) was an attempt to overcome this problem. The classification of schizophrenia and bipolar disorder according to this system is made on the basis of a checklist of symptoms, social and occupational dysfunction and duration. For example, a person may be diagnosed as schizophrenic if he or she has two of the following symptoms: delusions, hallucinations, disorganised speech (derailment or incoherence), grossly disorganised/catatonic behaviour or negative symptoms such as affective flattening or is avolitional. However, for reasons that are not obvious, if a person has bizarre delusions, or a voice keeping up a running commentary, or two or more voices conversing, then a diagnosis can be made without any other symptom from this list. The criteria also require that a person's social/ occupational functioning must be markedly below what was achieved prior to the onset of the disorder, and that the person must have been experiencing difficulties for at least six months, which must include at least one month (less if treated successfully) of acute symptoms. However, again, exceptions to this rule are specified. For example, if a person has not been experiencing acute phase symptoms for the full six months, prodromal or residual symptoms may still be used to justify the diagnosis.

As in earlier versions of the manual, exclusion criteria specify that the individual must not meet the criteria for other diagnoses, for example bipolar disorder or psychotic depression. Of course, when we turn to the DSM criteria for these conditions, we find that schizophrenia must be excluded, giving a clue that these conditions may not be as separate as the manual implies. In fact, researchers in a large epidemiological study in the United States experimented by deliberately ignoring these exclusion criteria, and discovered that over half of the people who met the criteria for one DSM-III diagnosis met the criteria for at least one other (Robins & Locke, 1991). Some diagnoses appeared to be particularly closely related. For example, anyone meeting the DSM-III criteria for schizophrenia had a forty-six times greater than expected chance of also meeting the criteria for mania.

The many other lines of evidence that undermine the distinction between schizophrenia and bipolar disorder can only be briefly alluded to here (see Bentall, in press, for a detailed discussion of these issues). For example, statistical analyses of the symptoms reported by patients show that they do not fall into two distinct groups as the Kraepelinian model supposes (Brockington, 1992; Kendell & Gourlay, 1970). Indeed, the symptoms experienced by people who have become psychotic seem to fall into at least three distinct subgroups – positive symptoms (delusions and hallucinations), problems of cognitive disorganisation (including incoherent speech) and negative symptoms (social withdrawal, apathy and anhedonia) – that are common to (although experienced to varying degrees by) patients diagnosed as schizophrenic or manic depressive (Andreasen, Roy, & Flaum, 1995; Klimidis, Stuart, Minas, Copolov, & Singh, 1993; Liddle, 1987; Toomey, Faraone, Simpson, & Tsuang, 1998). Nor is it the case that the diagnoses of schizophrenia and bipolar disorder foretell different outcomes as assumed by Kraepelin and his followers; rather a range of overlapping outcomes seem to be experienced by patients in each group (Kendell & Brockington, 1980). Perhaps most tellingly of all, biological evidence also fails to support the Kraepelinian paradigm. Genetic findings have been interpreted as supporting a continuum from schizophrenic to bipolar symptomatology rather than two different disease entities (Crow, 1986) and drug response does not seem to be predictable from the diagnosis a patient receives (Johnstone, Crow, Frith, & Owens, 1988). Overall, the evidence does not suggest that there are a finite number of distinct psychotic disorders as Kraepelin and his neoKraepelinian followers supposed.

The neoKraepelinian assumption that psychotic conditions are brain diseases is more difficult to address and the relevant research is largely beyond the scope of this book. However, it is important to say something about this assumption here, as it seems to have been a major cause of pessimism about the value of psychological treatments for people with these kinds of difficulties. Perhaps a good starting point is to concede that there do appear to be detectable neuro-biological differences between people with psychotic symptoms and people without (McKenna, 1994; Trimble, 1996), and that there is also evidence from family, twin and adoption studies that these conditions are influenced by heredity (Barondes, 1998; Torrey, Bowler, Taylor, & Gottesman, 1994). (As an aside, we would like to add that we believe that biological researchers have systematically exaggerated the size of these associations. For realistic estimates of the magnitude of these effects, see, for example, the late Richard Marshall's (1990) review of the literature on the genetics of schizophrenia, and Walter Heinrichs' (2001) very readable systematic review of neurobiological data collected from schizophrenia patients.)

It is not these findings, in themselves, that are the source of pessimism, but the assumption that they preclude both the role of environmental influences on the development of psychosis, and the possibility of using psychological interventions to help psychotic people. Contrary to this assumption, research in the 1990s revealed that the central nervous system is much more plastic (mouldable by experience) than previously thought, so that environmental effects such as emotional deprivation (Suomi, 1997) or trauma in childhood (Stein, Koverola, Hanna, Torchia, & McClarty, 1997) or in later life (Bremmer et al., 1995) can lead to profound changes in the neurochemistry and structure of the brain. These discoveries have been made at the same time as schizophrenia researchers have begun to recognise that environmental influences such as early attachment difficulties (Myhrman, Rantakallio, Isohanni, Jones, & Partanen, 1996), trauma (Butler, Mueser, Sprock, & Braff, 1996; Goodman, Rosenberg, Mueser, & Drake, 1997) and growing up in an urban environment (Mortensen et al., 1999) or alien culture (Bhurgra, Mallett, & Leff, 1999) can markedly increase the risk of psychosis in later life. In an interesting attempt to integrate some of these findings, Read, Perry, Moskowitz, and Connolly (in press) have argued that many of the neurobiological abnormalities observed in schizophrenia patients are, in fact, more consistent with environmental influences than the intrinsic morbid process assumed by most researchers.

Recent discoveries in human genetics reinforce these conclusions. Because there are trillions of synapses in the human brain but only about 30,000 genes in the human genome, it is not possible for genes to predetermine specific neural circuits. Brain development is therefore determined by interactions between genes and the environment at every level (Elman et al., 1999). These kinds of gene–environment interactions mean that that the determinants of human characteristics cannot be simply parsed into genetic and environmental contributions. Even traits that are very highly influenced by genes – for example intelligence – can also be dramatically influenced by experience (Dickins & Flynn, 2001). An epidemiological study by Mortensen et al. (1999) highlighted the role of these kinds of interactions in the development of schizophrenic symptoms. Mortensen and his colleagues were able to calculate the "population attributable risk" (the proportion of cases that would be removed if a specific risk factor was eliminated) for schizophrenia in a large Danish population sample. They found that the population attributable risk associated with having a parent or sibling diagnosed as suffering from schizophrenia was just over 5 per cent whereas the population attributable risk associated with being born and growing up in an urban area was nearly 35 per cent! Therefore, although genetic background appears to be a source of high risk for schizophrenia on an individual level, at a population level environmental factors are far more powerful.

The stress-vulnerability paradigm

Stress-vulnerability models of psychosis emerged partly as an attempt to account for the confusing and unclear picture emerging from genetic studies. By the early 1960s it was becoming obvious that, although the emergence of psychotic conditions appeared to be strongly influenced by heredity, it was not possible to identify any simple pattern of genetic transmission. Paul Meehl's (1962) suggestion that states analogous to schizophrenia might exist in non-psychotic people followed from his assumption that it was therefore a *vulnerability* to schizophrenia, rather than schizophrenia itself, that was inherited. According to Meehl's model, individuals who inherited a *schizotaxic* nervous system have neurointegrative difficulties which cause them to suffer from cognitive slippage (loosening of associations) and anhedonia, but these characteristics alone do not lead to schizophrenia. Schizotaxic individuals who are exposed to certain unspecified environmental stressors decompensate and become schizophrenic whereas those who are not will lead healthy lives while showing *schizotypal personality characteristics*. On this view, perhaps 90 per cent of those who carry schizophrenia genes do not become acutely psychotic.

Meehl's theory had few implications for clinicians, although it inspired a still active programme of research on psychotic personality characteristics in ordinary people. However, the discovery by George Brown (1984) and his colleagues in London that stressful interpersonal relationships could influence the course of psychotic illness gave a new impetus for the development and application of stress-vulnerability models in the clinical domain. Briefly, Brown and others found that psychotic patients leaving hospital to live with relatives who were critical and/or over-protective (and who were therefore said to exhibit high expressed-emotion, or EE) had a much higher chance of relapsing and returning to hospital than those leaving to live in hostels or with friends or relatives who are more emotionally relaxed, a finding that has been replicated many times in different parts of the world (Bebbington & Kuipers, 1994). Although most researchers studying this effect were at pains to emphasise that "We consider that families do not exert a causal influence" on psychosis (Kuipers, Birchwood, & McCreadie, 1992), the implication was that the environment could at least have a dramatic effect on a psychotic illness that had already become established.

Perhaps the most influential stress-vulnerability model of psychosis published to date has been developed since the early 1980s by Keith Nuechterlein and his colleagues in the UCLA Schizophrenia Research Group. According to this model, the probability of someone experiencing psychotic symptoms is determined by the interaction of four factors: personal vulnerability factors (presumed to be biological, for example an abnormally functioning dopamine system, information processing deficits), personal protective factors (such as coping skills), environmental precipitants (such as stressful life events or exposure to a critical or emotionally over-involved family environment) and environmental protective factors (for example good family coping skills) (Nuechterlein, Parasuraman, & Jiang, 1983). Under certain conditions, when personal vulnerability factors and environmental precipitants cannot be compensated by personal and environmental protective factors, overloading of the individual's information processing system leads, first, to prodromal symptoms and then ultimately to the acute symptoms of a psychotic crisis.

The UCLA model has spawned, and in turn been influenced by, a rich programme of research into the cognitive deficits of schizophrenia patients. Consistent with Kraepelin's (1899/1990) early suggestion that dementia praecox patients were highly distractible, much of this research has focused on attentional processes. It has been repeatedly demonstrated, for example, that schizophrenia patients perform poorly on tasks sensitive to distraction (Oltmanns & Neale, 1978), on measures of vigilance (sustained attention over a period of time: Nuechterlein et al., 1983) and on measures of very early visual information processing (Saccuzzo & Braff, 1981). It is perhaps less well known that similar findings have been obtained from patients diagnosed as suffering from bipolar disorder (Fleming & Green, 1995; Oltmanns & Neale, 1978) and psychotic depression (Nelson, Saz, & Strakowski, 1998).

From the point of view of the clinician interested in psychosocial interventions, stress-vulnerability models have enormous advantages over the Kraepelinian disease model, because they point to opportunities for treatment. As we have already indicated, one obvious therapeutic strategy that follows directly from these models involves manipulating environmental precipitating factors. Family interventions, designed to reduce the level of expressed emotion in the close relatives of patients attempt to achieve precisely this end. In 2001 a meta-analysis of the outcomes of twenty-five trials of this and related family treatments found that they have a marked impact on relapse rates (Pitschel-Walz, Leucht, Bauml, Kissling, & Engel, 2001). A second strategy that follows from the stress-vulnerability paradigm involves trying to enhance patients' coping skills. This is the rationale sometimes given for providing social-skills training to schizophrenia patients, although the long-term effects of this type of intervention remain a matter of some debate. Some of the earliest cognitive-behavioural interventions designed for psychotic patients also focused on coping skills rather than on acute symptoms such as hallucinations and delusions (Tarrier et al., 1993).

However, despite the renewed optimism about psychosocial interventions encouraged by the emergence of the stress-vulnerability paradigm, from the point of view of the clinician it still has three important limitations. First, the psychological researchers who have developed this paradigm, like those working within the disease paradigm before them, have assumed that psychosis is caused by some kind of morbid biological process (for example an inherited abnormality in the dopamine system). They have therefore attempted to develop their models by measuring cognitive *deficits* (deficiencies in gross cognitive processes such as perception, attention and memory) in the assumption that these will indicate underlying brain dysfunction. However, we have already seen that these deficits do not seem to be specific to any particular group of psychotic symptoms. Indeed, in a review of the available evidence, Michael Foster Green (1998) (a member of the UCLA Schizophrenia Research Group) has pointed out that these deficits do not seem to correlate with positive symptoms at all. Green tries to resolve this paradox by arguing that the positive symptoms of psychosis (for example delusions and hallucination) should be downgraded in importance, and argues that researchers should focus more on social and occupational functioning, which do seem to be related to deficits. However, this advice is not likely to be comforting to either patients or their relatives, who often find positive symptoms baffling and extremely distressing.

A second, related limitation is that the stress-vulnerability paradigm ignores those types of psychological processes and abnormalities that are most likely to be implicated in positive symptoms. These symptoms – for example voices criticising, or paranoid or grandiose delusions – typically reflect the individual's anxiety about his or her position in the social universe (Bentall, 1990b). Cognitive-deficit theorists, however, typically ignore the content of the stimuli that they present to the psychotic patients who participate in their research studies. Indeed, for the most part, measures of these deficits employ stimuli that are relatively meaningless, such as isolated letters or strings of digits, which the participant is asked to attend to or memorise. Of course, some stimuli are much more salient to human beings than others. The human brain has evolved specific strategies for processing information about one type of stimulus above all others – namely, other human beings (Brothers, 1997; Dunbar, 1997). The implication of this argument is that *biases in social cognition* are likely to play an important role in psychotic symptoms. At later points in this book we shall see that this is indeed the case.

The final limitation is that, because cognitive deficits are highlighted and biases in social cognition are ignored, the stress-vulnerability paradigm offers no clues about how positive symptoms might be treated psychologically. Indeed, although stress-vulnerability theorists have advocated manipulating the environment and enhancing coping skills as strategies for *ameliorating* psychosis, many have been as pessimistic as their medical predecessors about the possibility of treating symptoms directly.

The symptom approach

It was probably the British psychologist Don Bannister (1968) who first recognised that research on particular symptoms of psychosis provided a strategy for avoiding the problems of psychiatric classification that had beset earlier paradigms. As later researchers came to recognise, by focusing on patients who have particular types of experiences or behaviours (for example auditory hallucinations, paranoid delusions or disordered speech) it is possible to avoid diagnostic conundrums such as how schizophrenia can be discriminated from manic depression, or whether there is just one type of schizophrenia or many. Some investigators advocated this approach largely for pragmatic reasons, believing that the essential features of schizophrenia would be revealed by identifying common mechanisms underlying different symptoms that were presumed to belong to the disorder (Frith, 1992). Others took a more radical view, arguing that symptom-orientated research might ultimately lead to a complete and satisfactory understanding of psychosis (Bentall, 1990b).

Some of the research that has been conducted into the psychological mechanisms underlying particular symptoms will be described in Chapter 3. However, it is worth noting here that substantial progress has been made in revealing the mechanisms responsible for auditory hallucinations, delusional beliefs and disordered speech. In the case of auditory hallucinations, there is fairly compelling evidence that these experiences occur when individuals misattribute their verbal thoughts or inner speech to sources external to themselves (Bentall, 2000). Put crudely, people who hear voices appear to be talking to themselves without realising that they are doing so. Delusions seem to be associated with a variety of reasoning biases, including a tendency to leap to conclusions (Garety, Hemsley, & Wessely, 1991) and, in the case of paranoid and grandiose patients at least, a tendency to construct unusual explanations for distressing events (Bentall, Corcoran, Howard, Blackwood, & Kinderman, 2001). Disordered speech seems to occur particularly when the patient is emotionally distressed (Docherty, Evans, Sledge, Seibyl, & Krystal, 1994) and seems to reflect an inability to take into account the needs of the listener, perhaps as a consequence of working memory limitations (Adler, Goldberg, Malhotra, Pickar, & Breier, 1998) or more fundamental semantic deficits (Spitzer, 1997). Other symptoms, for example passivity experiences and negative symptoms, have received comparatively little attention from psychologists, but (bright and ambitious PhD students please note!) there is no reason to suppose that they will fail to yield to psychological analysis.

The symptom approach has advantages for clinicians that extend well beyond the avoidance of diagnostic disputes. Whereas previous psychological researchers had focused almost exclusively on cognitive deficits – the failure to perform basic mental functions such as remembering or perceiving – much of the research on symptoms has focused on *biases* in perception and reasoning. Biases are often the product of faulty learning, and therefore may be much more modifiable than deficits. Indeed, cognitive therapy strategies that have proved to be so successful in the treatment of depression and anxiety disorders seem to work by challenging biases in the way that patients perceive, recall and reason about the events that have affected them.

As we progress through this book, we shall show that novel cognitive therapy techniques that have been designed specifically to address the needs of psychotic patients are consistent with the findings from recent psychological studies of symptoms. Indeed, some techniques have been directly inspired by the results of psychological investigations, although others have been developed pragmatically by imaginative therapists. However, this observation does not imply that the symptom approach is without its limitations. Two limitations are particularly important from the perspective of the clinician.

First, psychological models of psychotic symptoms offer *general* models of the cognitive processes involved, and sometimes of the aetiological factors that affect these processes. They have usually been developed by administering psychological tests to groups of patients experiencing the same symptom. However, the clinician has to deal with individuals, and no matter how good the cognitive model that is available, he or she will have to take into account aspects of the patient's history and personal idiosyncrasies that are not described in any particular model. From the clinician's point of view, therefore, the models serve as guides rather than as infallible prescriptions for therapeutic intervention.

The second limitation is that most models attempt to explain particular symptoms, whereas the many patients seen in psychiatric settings have multiple symptoms. Some symptom researchers have therefore proposed the need for higher level models that identify processes common to a range of psychotic experiences and behaviours (Garety, Kuipers, Fowler, Freeman, & Bebbington, 2001). Strong defenders of the symptom approach, on the other hand, argue that these kinds of models are usually very vague, that there are many different reasons why some patients experience multiple symptoms, and that there is no necessity to believe that common aetiological factors are always implicated (Bentall, in press). We shall not try to resolve this argument here but merely note that clinicians may need to be able to flexibly combine and adapt several cognitive models in order to account for the difficulties of a particular patient.

It is these limitations that necessitate the formulation-based approach to psychological intervention that will be described in the remaining chapters of this book.

Chapter 2

An introduction to cognitive theory and therapy

In order to appreciate how cognitive behaviour therapy can be used to help psychotic patients, it is first necessary to understand the generic cognitive model that has informed the development of psychological treatments for emotional disorders. Stated most simply, this model assumes that an individual's emotional reactions are determined by their perception of events. That is to say, it is not solely the situation *per se* which determines what a person feels, but rather the way in which the person *construes* a situation (Beck, 1964; Ellis, 1962). More specifically, this emotional response is said to be mediated by perception of the situation, which in turn is mediated by different *levels* of cognition.

Beck's model of emotional disorders suggests that experience leads people to form assumptions (conditional beliefs, e.g. "*If* others see what I am really like *then* they will reject me" or rules, e.g. "I must always do what other people ask me to") or schemata about themselves and the world. Schemata are sets of beliefs (unconditional beliefs, e.g. "I am worthless") and assumptions, which may be encoded alongside other emotive material. These are subsequently used to organise perception and to govern and evaluate behaviour (Beck, 1964). The individual's cognitions (automatic thoughts, images and memories) are therefore based on attitudes or assumptions, developed from previous experiences.

These attitudes and assumptions are triggered when the individual experiences an event which clashes with or matches one of their underlying assumptions, activating the schemas and giving rise to the production of negative automatic thoughts, images and memories. It is these cognitions which lead to behavioural, physiological and affective symptoms. Alongside further changes in cognitive processing such as changes in attention (e.g. noticing only the negative reactions of others in the environment), or memory (e.g. remembering only past failures rather than successes) and interpretation, these symptoms, and any environmental changes that are consequences of them, further help to maintain and exacerbate cognitive distortions and maintain the vicious cycle of an emotional disorder. Thus, it can be seen that a person's present difficulties are a product of prior experience, schema development and information processing, assumptions, external events and their interpretation, and behaviour. This model is illustrated in Figure 2.1.

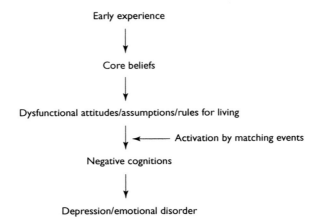

Figure 2.1 Beck's cognitive model of emotional disorders

Beck's original cognitive model of emotional disorder assumes three levels of cognition, namely automatic thoughts, underlying assumptions and core beliefs. *Core beliefs* are taken to be the most fundamental level of belief and are hypothesised to consist of beliefs about the self, world and others, which are global, rigid and may be over-generalised. An example of such beliefs may be "I am stupid", "Other people are untrustworthy" and "The world is cruel". These core beliefs influence the development of an intermediate class of belief or cognition which consists of attitudes, rules and assumptions. These are cross-situational beliefs or rules that guide our lives. They include "should" statements ("I should always put the wishes of other people first" and "The world should be fair") and conditional "if . . . then . . . " beliefs ("If I let people get close to me, they will find out what I'm really like and reject me" or "If I do not remain on guard at all times, then other people will take advantage of me"). These underlying assumptions, although often not articulated consciously, guide behaviour and expectations (for example, causing the individual to keep others at a distance, or to maintain a watchful and untrusting eye on others).

The final level of cognition is that of automatic thoughts, which are the moment-to-moment, unplanned thoughts that flow through our minds during the day. These are automatic, that is they arise, as if by reflex, rather than being the result of conscious reasoning processes or the result of any deliberate attempt to assess a situation and reach a conclusion through careful reasoning (Beck, 1964). Beck et al. (1972, pp. 12–13) define these cognitions as "any ideation with verbal or pictorial content" and outlines three important features of such thoughts, namely their automatic nature, their apparent plausibility to the individual, and their involuntary nature. It is important to remember that such thoughts are not peculiar to people experiencing psychological distress, but are common to us all. However, it appears that automatic reality testing of negative automatic thoughts is a common experience in ordinary people, whereas those who are in distress may not engage in this kind of critical examination of their own cognitive processes. The three levels of cognition are obviously interconnected. Core beliefs or schemas (e.g. "I'm worthless") give birth to underlying assumptions ("If I don't put everyone before myself, they will reject me"). This intermediate level of cognition tends to develop in ways that allow individuals to deal with discrepancies between expectations and experience and which allow them to function effectively in some situations despite their core beliefs. For example, a child who remains neglected at home and consequently develops a core belief that "I am worthless and unlovable" may, on beginning school, be treated kindly by the teachers as a valued member of the class. In order to make sense of this "discrepancy" (the child believes herself worthless but is seemingly ascribed some value), she may develop a rule to account for it. This rule may operate, not by changing the core belief, but by finding another way of explaining the teachers' behaviour. For example, the child might come to believe that "If I do what others require at all times, they won't know what I'm really like and won't reject me". It is important to remember that, at the time of their development, these assumptions may have been helpful, but translated into different situations they become unhelpful; thus, they have sometimes been called dysfunctional assumptions but are now more often known as underlying assumptions.

Core beliefs and underlying assumptions determine the types of automatic thoughts that will be produced in any given situation (e.g. If a person held the belief "I am stupid", and the underlying assumption that "If I allow others to get close to me, they will find out how stupid I am", when considering complaining about an injustice at work, the person is likely to generate the negative automatic thought, "If I complain, they will look at my work more closely, they'll find out how stupid I am and I'll be fired").

Rainfall provides a useful metaphor for understanding the relationships between the three types of cognitions we have considered in this section: core beliefs can be thought of as the seas, lakes and rivers; these give rise to the clouds (under-lying assumptions) which, in turn, give rise to the raindrops (negative automatic thoughts).

Cognitive therapy

Cognitive therapy was devised by Aaron T. Beck in the early 1960s as a structured, short-term, problem and present-orientated psychotherapy for depression. It is described by Beck, Rush, Shaw, and Emery (1979) as "an active, directive, time-limited, structured approach used to treat a variety of psychiatric disorders (for example, depression, anxiety, phobias, pain problems, etc.)" (p. 3).

Beck began his psychiatric career as a psychoanalyst and developed his theory while using dream analysis to validate the notion that depression was caused by self-directed hostility arising from wish fulfilment, namely the wish of degradation. While working on this project, Beck began to doubt Freud's premise that particular behaviour has its roots in the unconscious, and that any irrationalities observed on the conscious level are only manifestations of the underlying unconscious drives. From observation of his patients, he hypothesised that irrationality could be understood in terms of inadequacies in organising and interpreting reality. In a paper published in 1963, Beck noted that the schizophrenic excels in his tendency to misconstrue the world that is presented (Beck, 1963). While the validity of this statement had been supported by numerous clinical and experimental studies, it had not generally been acknowledged that misconstructions of reality may also be a characteristic of other psychiatric disorders. Based on his clinical experience, he expounded the view that psychological problems were not necessarily the product of "mysterious, impenetrable forces" but rather the result of faulty learning, making incorrect inferences on the basis of inadequate or incorrect information, and a failure to adequately distinguish between imagination and reality.

As mentioned previously, cognitive therapy is based on the theoretical rationale that an individual's affect and behaviour are largely determined by the way in which they think about the world (Beck, 1964). Cognitions (verbal or pictorial events in his stream of consciousness) are based on attitudes or assumptions (schemas) that are developed from previous experiences. Therefore, Beck (1976) suggested that psychological processes can be mastered by sharpening discriminations, correcting misconceptions, and learning more adaptive attitudes. He commented that since introspection, insight, reality testing, and learning are basically cognitive processes, this approach to the neuroses has been labelled cognitive therapy.

However, it is important to note that, while the *means* of cognitive therapy is focusing on the patient's misinterpretations, self-defeating behaviour and underlying attitudes, the *goal* is the relief of emotional distress and other symptoms of emotional disorder. The therapeutic techniques of cognitive therapy are designed to identify, reality-test and correct distorted conceptualisations and the beliefs underlying these cognitions. Patients learn to master problems and situations which they previously considered insuperable by re-evaluating and correcting their thinking. The cognitive therapist helps patients to think and act more realistically and adaptively about their psychological problems and thus reduces symptomatology.

Cognitive therapy and its applications

Beck originally expounded his cognitive theory with relation to depression, describing the *negative cognitive triad* of depressive cognitions relating to the self, the world and the future. Although initially used as a basis for treating depression, the model was rapidly adapted for use with anxiety disorders and phobias.

However, while schema theory presents a general theoretical framework for exploring and formulating factors maintaining certain types of psychopathology, many authors have highlighted the need for specific models of cognitive-behavioural factors associated with vulnerability and problem maintenance. This has led to attempts to integrate schema theory with theoretical models of other psychological constructs considered to be important in the development and maintenance of specific disorders. Already the resulting models have been remarkably helpful in improving the efficacy of cognitive therapy. These include Clark and Well's (1995) model of social phobia, Clark's (1986) model of the aetiology and maintenance of panic disorder, Wells' (1995) model of generalised anxiety disorder, Warwick and Salkovskis' (1990) model of health anxiety, and models of obsessional thinking devised by Salkovskis (1990), Rachman (1997) and Wells and Matthews (1994).

Since 1990, cognitive therapy has also been adapted for use with inpatients (Wright, Thase, & Beck, 1993), people with diagnoses of personality disorders (Beck, Freeman, & Associates, 1990) and those misusing alcohol or other substances (Beck, Wright, Newman, & Liese, 1993). In his original works, Beck (1952) expounded his cognitive theory with respect to a case example of a man with a delusional belief, who believed that fifty members of the Federal Bureau of Investigation had been employed to investigate him, were recording his every move and were able to record his thoughts. Later, it became accepted that, by their very definition, delusional beliefs were not amenable to rational argument or evidence, and so Beck's early lead in the cognitive behavioural analysis of psychotic symptoms was ignored. However, as will be discussed later, in recent years investigators such as Bentall, Birchwood, Chadwick, Fowler, Garety, Gumley, Kingdon, Morrison, Tarrier and Turkington have shown the successful application of the cognitive model to working with individuals experiencing psychosis.

The validity of cognitive theory

Beck (1976) proposed that a psychological treatment approach can qualify as a system of psychotherapy only if it provides "(a) a comprehensive theory or model of psychopathology, and (b) a detailed description of and guide to therapeutic techniques related to this model" (p. 307). In accordance to this, Beck and other authors have repeatedly emphasised the need for close links between cognitive theory and practice in research and the development of new theories. Clark and Steer (1996) comment that empirical research about the cognitive processes underlying psychopathology is important for the practice of cognitive therapy for two main reasons. First, they say that "the distinctiveness of cognitive therapy as a system of psychotherapy does not depend on the particular therapeutic techniques . . . , but upon the fundamental cognitive constructs and propositions that guide the implementation of therapy" (p. 75), and second, that "research on the cognitive model may help to elucidate possible change mechanisms that may account for the effectiveness of cognitive therapy" (p. 75) and that "Understanding such mechanisms may, in turn, lead to improvements in the cognitive treatment of various disorders" (p. 76). The application of these principles to the understanding of psychosis will be outlined in Chapter 3.

Without attempting a comprehensive review of the literature, some of the questions about the efficacy of cognitive therapy that have been investigated will be outlined. Gelder (1996) divides the research in this area into three main types: studies designed to characterise key cognitions in psychiatric disorders, make predictions about the role of these cognitions, and study factors that maintain cognitions.

With respect to the first of these areas, that of characterising key cognitions, investigations have focused on thinking, attention, memory, visual imagery, worry and metacognition. Studies of thinking have aimed to elucidate the role that cognitions play in the various disorders and measures such as the automatic thoughts questionnaire (Hollon & Kendall, 1980) have broadly confirmed Beck's original clinical observations. Within the field of attentional research, studies such as that done by Ehlers and Breuer (1995) have demonstrated that attentional bias towards specific cues plays an important role in the maintenance of different anxiety disorders. Likewise, researchers such as Clark and Teasdale (1982) have shown the effect of mood on recall and recognition memory for positive and negative stimuli. Another subcategory of thinking that has been studied is that of metacognition, a term used to describe an individual's set of beliefs and thoughts pertaining to his or her own cognitions. There has been comparatively little systematic work in this area. However, some studies, such as that of Ehlers and Steil (1995), have provided support for the general proposition that an individual's interpretations of his or her own cognitions affect both the magnitude of distress experienced and its persistence. Wells and Matthews' (1994) S-REF model, which implicates metacognition, is discussed later.

Stronger evidence in favour of the cognitive model has been obtained by testing various predictions that can be derived from its main assumptions. For example, Gelder (1996) reports a study by Teasdale and Fennel (1982) in which two sessions during the process of cognitive therapy were compared. In one session the patient talked about cognitions but no attempt was made to change them, whereas in the other session cognitive therapy techniques were used to change the target cognitions. As predicted, cognitions changed more in the latter sessions and consequently, mood also improved more in these sessions.

The third area of research into the validity of cognitive theories involves examining the factors that maintain cognitions. Within this area of study, researchers and authors have wondered why abnormal cognitions are so resistant to change and remain unmodified despite information incongruent with patients' beliefs. This has led to the development of theories about the roles of avoidance and safety behaviours, both of which have the long-term effect of maintaining dysfunctional beliefs and assumptions (Salkovskis, 1991; Salkovskis, 1996b; Wells et al., 1995). Similarly, it has been found that neutralising behaviours and thought suppression maintain the frequency of intrusive thoughts and the distress they cause (Salkovskis et al., 1998).

The efficacy of cognitive therapy

It is difficult to provide a brief outline of the literature on the efficacy of cognitive therapy. New models and interventions have been developed over time, leading to constant efforts to update the evidence on "what works". However, a few key trials within the main diagnostic groups will be outlined as such studies have provided the motivation for research into cognitive therapy within the field of psychosis.

In the field of *panic disorder*, Clark et al. (1994) compared cognitive therapy with imipramine, applied relaxation or a waiting-list control. While the superiority of cognitive therapy to imipramine at three months was lost at six months, follow-up data showed far fewer relapses in the cognitive therapy group. Arntz and van den Hout (1996) reported another study that showed that a significantly greater proportion of cognitive therapy patients achieved panic-free status at the end of treatment and that this superiority was maintained at follow-up. Studies working in *obsessive-compulsive disorder* include those by Freeston et al.(1997), who compared cognitive therapy to a waiting-list control group, and found a significant reduction in symptomatology in the therapy group with gains maintained at six months follow-up. With respect to *depression*, Beck's cognitive therapy has been evaluated in several well-controlled treatment trials. Rush, Beck, Kovacs, and Hollon (1977) undertook one of the first randomised control trials, comparing cognitive-behaviour therapy, imipramine and weekly supportive visits. The results showed that improvements in the cognitive-behaviour therapy group were greater than in the medication group. Other studies such as those by Blackburn, Bishop, Whalley, and Christie (1981) and Beck, Emery, and Greenberg (1985a) have also found cognitive therapy to be effective in both the treatment of and the prevention of relapse in depression. For other studies, readers are directed to general texts in the area of cognitive therapy, or such edited texts as *Frontiers of cognitive therapy* (Salkovskis, 1996a) and *The science and practice of cognitive behaviour therapy* (Clark & Fairburn, 1997).

The importance of individual formulation in cognitive therapy

Persons (1989) describes a case formulation as "a hypothesis about the nature of the psychological difficulty (or difficulties)" underlying the problems on the patient's problem list. A formulation should show how presenting problems such as unwanted cognitions, emotions and behaviour not only are caused by underlying psychological mechanisms but also support or maintain these mechanisms. She outlines the two levels at which the model conceptualises psychological problems as occurring. Because direct, objective measures of these underlying mechanisms are not usually available, the therapist's ideas about these can be viewed as a hypothesis that can be tested during the course of therapy.

Persons (1989) argued that the case formulation has several important roles in clinical work. First, the therapist's understanding of the overt components of a patient's problem and their underlying psychological mechanisms will guide the choice of intervention strategies. Second, the case formulation will allow the clinician to treat and understand unusual problems that the therapist has not encountered before. Finally, the formulation also helps the therapist to understand and manage difficulties that arise *within* the therapy. This includes the client's failure to do homework, problems in timekeeping for sessions, difficulties in the therapeutic relationship and treatment failure. Case formulation will be examined in more detail in Chapter 5.

Difficulties with the cognitive model

Despite widespread agreement about the general utility of Beck's model of emotional disorders, since the early 1990s there has been increasing debate about the extent to which it explains much of the phenomena encountered in clinical practice. Indeed Aaron T. Beck (1996) has acknowledged that, although the clinical formulation of emotional disorders has been useful in understanding and treating psychopathology over the years, recent research has shown that it does not fully explain many clinical observations and experimental findings. He has pointed out that a number of psychological problems are not well enough addressed by a model of linear schematic processing. These include:

- the multiplicity of related symptoms encompassing the cognitive, affective, motivational and behavioural domains in a psychopathological condition
- evidence of systematic bias across many domains suggesting that a more global and complex organisation of schemas is involved in intense psychological reactions
- the findings of a specific vulnerability (or diathesis) to specific stressors that are congruent with a particular disorder
- the great variety of "normal" psychological reactions evoked by myriad life circumstances
- the relation of content, structure and function in personality
- observations of the variations in the intensity of an individual's specific reactions to a given set of circumstances over time
- the phenomenon of sensitisation: successive recurrences of a disorder triggered by progressively less intense experiences
- the remission of symptoms by either pharmacotherapy or psychotherapy
- the apparent continuity of many psychopathological phenomena with personality
- the relevance of the model to normal moods
- the relationship between conscious and non-conscious processing of information.

Beck (1996) suggests that "although the current model of schematic processing still seems valid and useful for clinical interventions, it is apparent that these and related problems call for more global constructs and additional refinements related to progress in the field" (p. 2). He comments that there have been difficulties in accommodating many psychological and psychopathological phenomena into the simple schematic model of

stimulus ⇒ *cognitive schema* ⇒ *motivation, affect and behaviour.*

In response to this dilemma, Beck outlines what he calls a model of modal processing rather than the simple schematic processing. Modes can be thought of as structural and operational units of personality that serve to adapt an individual to changing circumstances. They consist of a composite of cognitive, affective, motivational and behavioural systems. The relevant components of these systems are unified within the mode and function synchronously as adaptational strategies. Beck argues that this notion can provide a more complete explanation of the "complexity, predictability, regularity, and uniqueness of normal and abnormal reactions" (p. 19). He continues that the concept of a mode represents "a global expansion of simple schema theory and provides the scaffolding for an integrated theory of personality and psychopathology" (p. 19). It can account for a variety of functions ranging from the relatively brief reactions in emergency situations to the more diverse and enduring phenomena such as affection, clinical depression and prejudice.

The "scientific validity" of cognitive therapy: links between cognitive therapy and cognitive science

Although cognitive therapy was devised during a time in which psychology as a whole was moving strongly in the direction of cognitive explanations of behaviour, there was a curious gap between these movements. The early claims of connections between cognitive behaviour therapy and cognitive psychology were statements of hope rather than facts. Teasdale (1996) has suggested that the development of cognitive therapy for depression has proceeded in relative isolation from basic cognitive science.

Criticisms of the cognitive model of psychopathology

Teasdale (1983) commented that one of the major difficulties involved in evaluating Beck's cognitive model stems from the fact that it is a clinical theory. Consequently, presentations of the model have tended to be relatively imprecise, to have varied from one statement to another, and have shifted in their emphasis over time. He pointed out that the cognitive model views the other signs and symptoms of the depressive syndrome as consequences of the activation of the negative cognitive patterns. For example, if patients incorrectly think they are being rejected, they will react with the same negative affect that occurs with actual rejection. This view suggests that negative cognitions produce depressed affect.

Some work has speculated that emotion has been ascribed too narrow a role in cognitive therapy and that future research must combine the study of cognitive psychology and cognitive therapy to fully understand and utilise the multi-directional effects of both cognition and affect. As we have already seen, Beck's model of emotional disorders hypothesises that early experience leads to the formation of dysfunctional assumptions, core beliefs and schemata. These can then be activated by matching environmental event, giving rise to the negative cognitions and the resulting mood and associated physiological, cognitive and behavioural symptomatology. However, Beck et al. (1979) also suggest that there may be multiple pathways to depression, but argue that cognition may be a useful focus of intervention.

Teasdale and Barnard (1993) suggest that, although this idea appears clear and straightforward and has proved extremely useful and valid in treatment, it must be elaborated and qualified in many ways. They point out that the simple assumption that certain types of cognition are the *antecedents* to emotional reactions has to be elaborated to include recognition of the fact that those same cognitions may be also powerfully influenced by affective state; that is, that cognitions often appear to be a *consequence* of emotional state. This assertion is supported by considerable experimental data, which demonstrate that depressed mood states can powerfully influence cognitive processes (Blaney, 1986). Consequently, once depressed, a powerful influence affecting the production of the negative interpretations that, it is suggested, are antecedents to depression, will be the depressed state itself. Much of the work of cognitive psychologists has shown that mood affects memory, attentional processes and the interpretation of ambiguous material. Beck's model supposes that vulnerability to depression depends on possessing enduring traits of characteristic underlying assumptions, attitudes and beliefs. However, contrary to expectations, experimental evidence shows that these underlying assumptions also return to "normal" with recovery.

Teasdale (1996) suggests that Beck's cognitive model recognises only one level of meaning, and for that reason has considerable difficulties with the distinction between intellectual and emotional belief, or more generally between hot and cold cognition. So when a patient says "I know that I'm not worthless, but I don't believe it emotionally", Beck suggests that this reflects a *quantitative* variation in a single level of meaning, namely degree of belief. Teasdale (1996) points out that many clinicians have found this to be unconvincing, regarding emotional belief as *qualitatively* different from intellectual belief. Teasdale (1996) also suggests that there is a reciprocal relationship between affect and cognition, and hypothesises that an explanatory account of emotional disorders is needed which recognises qualitatively different types of information, includes emotion and allows accounts of cognitive–affective interaction to be incorporated into a more general, comprehensive account of information processing.

Interactive cognitive subsystems

In an attempt to overcome some of these criticisms, Teasdale and Barnard (1993) have proposed the interactive cognitive subsystems model (ICS), which emphasises the importance of higher level meanings associated with the processing of affect-related schematic models. These models integrate sensory contributions, particularly those derived from bodily experiences, with patterns of lower level meanings. The processing of schematic models is marked by the subjective experience of "felt senses" with implicit meaning content.

First described by Barnard (1985), ICS claims to offer a theoretical scheme within which, in principle, accounts of any aspect of information processing can be developed. ICS explicitly recognises qualitatively different kinds of information, or mental codes, each corresponding to a different aspect of experience. Each different kind of information is transformed and stored by processes that are specialised for dealing with that particular kind of mental code and no other. These specialised processes are arranged in distinct subsystems, each subsystem storing and transforming only one kind of information. Information processing depends on information flowing from one subsystem to another. Each subsystem generates, from the patterns in the single information code that it takes as input, new patterns in the information codes that it creates as output. Within the ICS model, different aspects of experience are represented in patterns of qualitatively different kinds of information or mental codes. At the most superficial level there are three codes representing basic features of visual, acoustic and proprioceptive sensory input. At a deeper level, regularities in patterns of sensory codes are represented in intermediate codes. At an even deeper level are mental codes related to meaning. ICS recognises two distinct types of meanings.

Some meanings can be grasped fairly easily because there is a reasonably direct relationship between language and concepts, that is a sentence conveys one or more specific meanings. Patterns of implicational code represent a more general holistic level of meaning. This generic level represents deep recurring regularities across all other information codes. Meaning at this level is difficult to convey because it is not directly related to language. ICS proposes that only this generic level of meaning is directly linked to emotion. Teasdale (1996) suggests that the level of analysis represented by implicational meaning can be illustrated by the analogy between a sentence and a poem. Whereas a sentence conveys specific meaning by appropriate arrangement of letters or phonemes, a poem conveys holistic meanings that cannot be conveyed by single sentences.

Emotion-related schematic models encode the prototypical features extracted from previous situations, eliciting a given emotion. The ICS model proposes that generic level meanings can directly produce emotional responses, but specific level meanings cannot. Thus this model catches the distinction between emotional, gut level, hot meanings and intellectual, rational, cold meanings. Obviously, this has many implications for treatment and cognitive therapy.

The S-REF model

Other theorists have also worked to develop integrative models that better incorporate information processing research with Beck's schema theory. Wells and Matthews (1994, 1996) outlined what they call the S-REF (self-regulatory executive function) model which they claim advances the understanding of the roles of stimulus driven and voluntary control of cognition, procedural knowledge (beliefs) and of the interactions between different levels of information processing. The S-REF model is based upon a multilevel cognitive architecture comprised of three interacting levels: a level of automatic and reflexively driven processing units, a level of attentionally demanding, voluntary processing and a level of stored operations available to the individual.

In the S-REF model, stimuli initially undergo some automatic or low-level processing, which may generate intrusions, which activate the S-REF. It is then the S-REF that performs the appraisal of intrusions from lower level processing and initiates and regulates action aimed at reducing discrepancies between current state and goals. Aside from influencing the immediate focus of attention, and longer term changes in belief structures, it affects the sensitivity of the processing system to particular types of information in the lower network. The S-REF model thus offers a new way of conceptualising the influence of generic self-knowledge on a variety of indices of emotional distress as the severity of distress (and other symptoms of clinical affective disorder) is critically dependent on the extent of dynamic maintenance of S-REF activity.

The authors argue that, as in Beck's (1967) work, emotional disorder is intimately related to negative self-knowledge, which, in the S-REF model, serves to maintain S-REF activity, and to focus attention on negative aspects of the self. The model, however, expands on Beck's view of the maintenance of emotional disorder by emphasising that self-knowledge is, to a large degree, expressed indirectly, through its influence on the real-time processing associated with the S-REF process, which is the more proximal cause of dysfunctional cognition and emotion.

The S-REF model also suggests that there is a cognitive attentional syndrome that characterises all psychological dysfunction, and that self-focused attention is a marker for this. It also specifically implicates metacognitive beliefs as an important aspect of self-knowledge. For example, Wells (1995) suggests that positive beliefs about worry processes are centrally involved in the development of worry, and that pathological worry seen in generalised anxiety disorders occurs as the result of a co-occurrence of positive and negative beliefs about worry. The S-REF model also makes a distinction between declarative beliefs (e.g. "I am vulnerable") and procedural beliefs that guide information-processing strategy selection (e.g. "Worrying is a useful way of solving problems").

What lessons can be learned for the conceptualisation of psychosis?

Cognitive studies that have focused on the understanding and treatment of emotional disorders (and, particularly, anxiety disorders) highlight a number of key messages for clinicians and patients. For clinicians, the main lesson seems to be that, in order to have an effective treatment, we require an empirically validated cognitive model from which to derive our therapies. For patients, the important messages that are present in cognitive therapy for anxiety disorders seem to be as follows:

- You are not mad – the difficulties you are experiencing are understandable.
- Either your concerns are real or you believe them to be real (and both possibilities explain the way you feel).
- The way you interpret events affects how you feel.
- It is important to evaluate your beliefs by testing them out with changes in behaviour.
- What you attend to, and how you pay attention, can affect how you feel and what you believe.

These messages would seem to have potential to help normalise psychotic experiences and reduce distress in people with psychosis.

Summary

It can be seen that the cognitive model of emotional disorders suggests that the way we interpret events affects how we feel and the way we behave. It also suggests that the beliefs that we hold (and, therefore, our life experiences that lead to such beliefs) determine the way we interpret events. More recent refinements of the model have highlighted other processes that are important, such as the way we allocate attention, the beliefs that guide the strategies we adopt for information processing and the behaviours that maintain unhelpful beliefs. It is also important to recognise that there appears to be more than one level of meaning that is important in the development and maintenance of distress. The next chapter will apply some of these concepts to the understanding of psychosis.

Chapter 3

An integrative cognitive approach to understanding psychosis

As discussed in Chapter 1, the heterogeneity of symptoms associated with the diagnosis of schizophrenia, and the difficulties concerning the reliability and validity of the diagnosis, have led a number of authors to suggest that research examining the aetiology and treatment of psychosis should focus on the individual symptoms rather than broadly defined clinical syndromes. Positive symptoms are often viewed as the defining symptoms of the syndrome of schizophrenia, particularly within diagnostic schemes that emphasise the Schneiderian concept of first rank symptoms (Schneider, 1959). These symptoms include auditory hallucinations (audible thoughts, a discussion or argument about the patient or voices describing the patient's ongoing activity), somatic passivity experiences (the patient experiences bodily sensations as being caused by an external agent), thought insertion (the patient experiences thoughts as being put in his or her mind by an external agent), thought withdrawal (the patient experiences thoughts being removed by an external agent) and thought broadcast (the patient experiences thoughts as being transmitted to other people). Delusional perception (a normal perception is interpreted as having special, highly personal significance) was also considered a first rank symptom by Schneider, along with delusions that the patient's actions, impulses or feelings are being imposed or controlled by an external agent. However, other types of delusions, for example delusions of persecution, are considered to be positive symptoms within most modern diagnostic schemes. The status of thought disorder (or speech/language disorder, including tangential thinking and word salad) is more ambiguous. Most factor analytic studies have shown that this type of symptom belongs to a disorganisation factor that also includes subjective cognitive impairment, and which is quite independent of the positive symptoms (Liddle, 1987). However, some researchers have argued that psychotic speech and language disorders can be divided into two types – positive thought, language and communication disorder (mainly evidenced by incoherence) and negative thought, language and communication disorder (mainly evidenced by poverty of speech and poverty of content of speech) which belongs to the negative symptoms (Andreasen, 1979b).

Negative symptoms (which also consist of social withdrawal, flat affect and apathy) will be examined only briefly in this chapter, and will be considered in greater detail in Chapter 11. It will be useful to consider what is known about the psychology of positive symptoms, before examining an integrative model that will aid case formulation and selection of treatment strategies.

The psychology of auditory hallucinations

It has been estimated that as many as 60 per cent of schizophrenia patients experience auditory hallucinations (Slade & Bentall, 1988); the World Health Organization (1973) found that they were the most common symptom seen in patients with this diagnosis. Auditory hallucinations are defined in DSM-IV as being "a sensory perception that has the compelling sense of reality of a true perception but that occurs without external stimulation of the relevant sensory organ" (APA, 1994, p. 767).

It has been shown that auditory hallucinations are accompanied by sub-vocalisation or covert movements of the speech musculature (Gould, 1948; Inouye & Shimizu, 1970). In addition, verbal tasks that block subvocalisation also inhibit the occurrence of auditory hallucinations (Gallagher, Dinan, & Baker, 1994; Margo, Hemsley, & Slade, 1981). This has led many researchers to conclude that auditory hallucinations are externally attributed internal mental events (verbal thoughts or inner speech). However, there is some disagreement as to whether this external attribution arises as the result of a cognitive deficit of some kind, as is argued by David (1994), Frith (1992) and Hemsley (1993), or as the result of a bias in normal psychological processes. Bentall (1990a) and Morrison, Haddock, and Tarrier (1995) have argued that hallucinations are a consequence of a bias towards making external attributions for mental events (although they differ in their explanation of why this bias is present). Bentall (1990a) argues that auditory hallucinations result from a failure of source monitoring (the skill of identifying the source of an experience) that is affected by top-down processes (such as beliefs about causal agents, mental events), stress and environmental noise, and can be maintained by anxiety reduction. Morrison et al., (1995) suggest that auditory hallucinations may result from misattribution of intrusive thoughts because they are incompatible with metacognitive beliefs (their thoughts about thinking), and that they are maintained by a reduction in cognitive dissonance and cognitive, behavioural, affective and physiological responses.

There is a considerable body of evidence to support these accounts. Bentall and Slade (1985), using a signal detection task, found that people experiencing hallucinations showed a greater bias towards detecting signals when none were present. Heilbrun (1980) showed that people experiencing hallucinations are poorer than controls at recognising their own thoughts, and Bentall, Baker, and Havers (1991) found that people experiencing hallucinations exhibited an external attributional bias (a tendency to assume that ambiguously sourced information is generated externally) on a source monitoring test. Similarly, Morrison and Haddock (1997b) and Baker and Morrison (1998), using a type of word association test in which individuals had to describe their experience of generating associates, found that individuals experiencing auditory hallucinations, when compared with other patients and non-patients, had a bias towards externally attributing their thoughts. In the second of these studies, it was also demonstrated that this bias is associated with abnormal metacognitive beliefs. More recently, Johns and McGuire (1999) played back participants' speech in distorted form, and found that people experiencing hallucinations were less likely than controls to recognise it as their own. Taken together, these studies provide powerful evidence that hallucinations occur when people mistake their thoughts and memories for external stimuli. Theories about the occurrence of auditory hallucinations usually focus on the cognitive mechanisms involved in hearing voices, which may be of limited interest to clinicians. It may be more important to consider what causes people to be distressed or disabled by their voices. As cognitive therapy traditionally focuses on reducing the distress associated with unwanted thoughts, the emotional consequences of hallucinations may be the most appropriate focus when working with patients.

The psychology of delusions

Delusions are also a very common symptom of schizophrenia, the most common being delusions of reference, delusions of persecution and delusions of control (Garety & Hemsley, 1994). The work of Garety and her colleagues has shown that, contrary to popular belief, delusions are not held with absolute conviction and vary on many dimensions (see Garety & Hemsley, 1994).

Several different theories of delusions have been proposed. Maher (1974, 1988) suggested that abnormal beliefs arise as a consequence of rational attempts to explain anomalous perceptions, and therefore proposed that perceptual abnormalities drive all delusional beliefs. This account seems to be a good explanation of the so-called Capgras delusion in which the individual believes that a loved one has been replaced by a doppelgänger or impostor, as this kind of delusion is usually accompanied by subtle perceptual deficits that specifically affect the ability to recognise faces (Ellis & Young, 1990). However, as a general theory of delusions Maher's account is inadequate because most delusional systems arise in the absence of perceptual abnormalities (Chapman & Chapman, 1988) and because, contrary to Maher's assumption that reasoning abnormalities are absent in delusional patients, they have been quite easy to demonstrate

Garety and her colleagues have shown that patients experiencing delusions jump to conclusions, and have a rapid, overconfident reasoning style (Huq, Garety, & Hemsley, 1988)). Although this finding has been well replicated (see Garety & Freeman, 1999), Garety's more puzzling observation that, under some circumstances, deluded people may be more willing to *change* their hypotheses in the light of new information than other people (Garety et al., 1991) has yet to be adequately explained. However, her findings overall have obvious implications for cognitive behaviour therapists, suggesting that deluded patients might benefit from opportunities to learn how to better evaluate competing hypotheses

Bentall and colleagues have shown that persecutory delusions, in particular, are associated with the generation of external, personalising attributions for negative events (a tendency to explain such events in terms of the intentional actions of others: Kaney & Bentall, 1989; Kinderman & Bentall, 1997) and have argued that this bias may reflect the overactivity of cognitive mechanisms that serve to protect against low self-esteem in normal individuals (Bentall et al., 2001). It has sometimes been argued that the observation of low self-esteem in paranoid patients is inconsistent with this theory (Garety & Freeman, 1999); in fact, data on the relationship between self-esteem and paranoid ideation are spectacularly inconsistent, with some studies reporting high self-esteem (Lyon, Kaney, & Bentall, 1994), some reporting high self-esteem but only in the absence of depression (Candido & Romney, 1990), some reporting low self-esteem (Freeman et al., 1998) and some reporting no relationship at all (Drake, Pickles, Bentall, Kinderman & Lewis, in press). One possible explanation for this inconsistency suggested by Bentall et al. (2001) is that self-esteem may be highly variable or unstable over time in paranoid patients. However, Chadwick and Trower (1997) have suggested that there may be two types of paranoia – "poor me" or undeserved paranoia and "bad me" or punishment paranoia. It is likely that the former may correspond to the processes described by Bentall and colleagues, in which the attribution of negative events to an external cause can defend against self-blame and low self-esteem, whereas the patients with punishment paranoia would be expected to exhibit many of the characteristics of depressed patients, including low self-esteem.

The psychology of thought, language and communication disorders

Thought disorder has rarely been considered a target for psychological treatment. This may be partly because those who have researched cognitive behavioural interventions have assumed that the structure of thought is unlikely to be amenable to any kind of talking therapy. If this is so, they may have been misled by Bleuler's (1950) assumption that loosening of the associations is a fundamental feature of schizophrenia, and that thought disorder is therefore a disorder of thinking.

Some researchers have argued that thought disorder might better be understood as a disorder of communication (Rochester & Martin, 1979). Indeed, Andreasen (1979b) has suggested that the awkward term "thought, language and communication disorder" more accurately captures the phenomenon. Studies mainly conducted in the United States have shown that this symptom is associated with deficits in working memory (Grove & Andreasen, 1985) and also with disorganisation of the semantic memory system (the component of memory responsible for storing information about meanings: Spitzer, 1997). However, it is important to recognise that thought-disordered patients are rarely thought disordered all of the time, so that they are often able to communicate adequately.

Moreover, when asked to retrospectively explain thought-disordered passages of speech, they are often able to do so (Harrow & Prosen, 1978).

A number of investigators (Docherty et al., 1994; Docherty, Hall, & Gordenier, 1998; Haddock, Wolfenden, Lowens, Tarrier, & Bentall, 1995) have shown that patients with a history of thought, language and communication disorder become more incoherent when discussing emotionally salient, personal topics. This finding is consistent with Harrow and Prosen's (1978) observation that the content of incoherent speech often reflects the intrusion or intermingling of highly salient personal information into the ongoing conversation. While there may be no obvious cognitive behaviour therapy strategies for dealing with the mechanisms underlying these kinds of intrusions, an important implication of these observations is that strategies to improve patients' abilities to regulate their emotions may have important therapeutic effects.

Towards a cognitive model of the maintenance of psychosis

One central feature of psychosis is generally thought to be the inability to distinguish reality from unreality. However, it has always struck us that there is an inability to distinguish reality from unreality present in many other psychological disorders. For example, a patient with anorexia who weighs 6 stone but believes "I am fat", a depressed patient who believes "I am worthless" but manages to cope with the demands of motherhood in adverse social circumstances, a patient with obsessive-compulsive disorder (OCD) who believes that "I must pull my socks on and off ten times in order to stop my family dying", or a patient with panic attacks who believes "I am dying of a heart attack", all could be said to have lost contact with reality. However, such disorders are seen as less "mad" by psychiatric services and the general population, and as a result are far less stigmatising. There are two important implications of this. First, normalising psychotic experiences should impact directly on a person's distress by reducing stigma (as has been advocated by Kingdon and Turkington's pioneering work), as the patient's fear of madness is often more distressing than the psychotic experience itself (for example, would *you* rather be being talked about on the radio, or be considered schizophrenic and be at risk of being detained against your will?). Second, if the other disorders are not terribly different from psychosis, and there are cognitive therapies that work for them, it follows that these or similar approaches may be effective for psychotic symptoms.

Beck's (1976) cognitive model of emotional disorders has been influential in both the psychological formulation and treatment of mental distress, particularly in anxious and depressed patients (see Chapter 2 for further details). A number of similarities between Beck's cognitive therapy for the emotional disorders and current psychological interventions for schizophrenic symptoms are clearly evident (Chadwick, Birchwood, & Trower, 1996; Fowler, Garety, & Kuipers, 1995; Kingdon and Turkington, 1994). In the remaining sections of this chapter we shall outline an integrative cognitive model of schizophrenia, clearly based on Beck's cognitive theory of emotional disorders, and subsequent developments – notably Wells & Matthews' (1994) S-REF model – that is consistent with the findings we have already considered. This model clearly draws upon the current models of anxiety disorders and psychotic symptoms, and attempts to elaborate upon and integrate these theories, and earlier versions of this work, have been published elsewhere (Morrison, 1998a, Morrison, 2001).

Interpretation and intrusions in anxiety and psychosis

The cognitive model of panic (Clark, 1986) states that panic attacks result from an enduring tendency to misinterpret certain bodily sensations (usually normal anxiety responses) in a catastrophic manner (perceiving them as being indicative of an immediate disaster). It is hypothesised that this tendency to make catastrophic misinterpretations is maintained in two ways: selective attention or hypervigilance to idiosyncratic threat cues such as monitoring the body for signs of danger (Clark, 1988; Salkovskis, 1988), and avoidance, including safety-seeking behaviours that prevent spontaneous disconfirmation of threat (Salkovskis, 1991). The cognitive approach to hypochondriasis outlined by Warwick and Salkovskis (1990) also relies on a misinterpretation model; they suggest that patients experience health anxiety because they misinterpret unexpected physical symptoms as evidence of serious physical illness, and that these misinterpretations are maintained by processes such as selective attention, bodily checking and reassurance seeking (which are also consistent with Salkovskis' conceptualisation of safety behaviours). Similarly, some cognitive models of obsessive-compulsive disorder (Salkovskis, 1985; Wells, 1997) suggest that it is the appraisal or interpretation of intrusive thoughts that is the major source of distress and that these beliefs about intrusions may be maintained by neutralising behaviour designed to reduce perceived responsibility or to prevent unwanted consequences of thoughts. Again, these cognitive conceptualisations of OCD include selective attention as a maintaining factor. Thus, it can be seen that many of the current approaches to anxiety disorders involve the misinterpretation of intrusions, and suggest that these misinterpretations are maintained by safety behaviours (including selective attention) designed to reduce the likelihood of the feared outcome.

Morrison (1998a) has applied a similar analysis to the maintenance of auditory hallucinations. He has suggested that, when an internal or external trigger results in an auditory hallucination, it may be interpreted as threatening the physical or psychological integrity of the individual (for example "I must be mad", "The Devil is talking to me" and "If I do not obey the voices they will hurt me"). These interpretations result in an increase in negative mood and physiological arousal, which leads to more hallucinations and so to a vicious circle. Simultaneously, the interpretation of the hallucination as threatening elicits safety-seeking behaviours (including hypervigilance), which can both increase the future frequency of

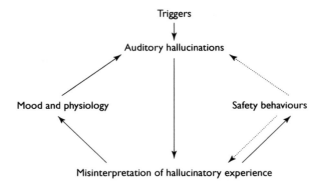

Figure 3.1 A cognitive model of auditory hallucinations (reproduced from Morrison, 1998a). With permission from Cambridge University Press.

auditory hallucinations and and also prevent the disconfirmation of the interpretation (therefore maintaining it). This model is represented in Figure 3.1.

Morrison (1998a) argues that voices may be a normal psychological phenomenon, and can potentially be experienced by anyone. Kingdon and Turkington (1994) have noted that hallucinations can occur in organic confusional states such as those induced by drugs (such as LSD and cocaine) and alcohol withdrawal. Other authors have suggested links between sexual abuse and auditory hallucinations (e.g. Read & Argyle, 1999), and a study of bereaved older adults found that 82 per cent experienced hallucinations and/or illusions one month following bereavement (Grimby, 1993). Other examples of situations (cited in Kingdon & Turkington, 1994) that can induce psychotic symptoms such as auditory hallucinations include being held hostage (Siegel, 1984), sleep deprivation (Oswald, 1974), sensory deprivation (Vernon, 1963) and solitary confinement (Grassian, 1983). In addition, studies assessing the occurrence of verbal hallucinations in college students have consistently found that a large minority (37–39 per cent) report experiencing such phenomena (Barrett & Etheridge, 1992; Posey & Losch, 1983). Surveys of hallucinatory experiences suggest that 10–25 per cent of the general population have had such experiences at least once (Slade & Bentall, 1988). Additional support for the notion of auditory hallucinations as normal phenomena comes from the pioneering work of Marius Romme in the Netherlands; for example, Romme, Honig, Noorthoorn, and Escher (1992) found that of the 173 subjects experiencing auditory hallucinations who had responded to a request on television, 39 per cent were not in psychiatric care.

Metacognition in anxiety and psychosis

Another development in the cognitive conceptualisation of anxiety disorders is the increasing recognition that metacognition is an important factor. Wells and Matthews (1994) have proposed a self-regulatory executive function model of emotional disorders, and several specific cognitive models of anxiety disorders have been developed incorporating elements of this. The S-REF model suggests that vulnerability to psychological dysfunctions is associated with a cognitive-attentional syndrome characterised by heightened self-focused attention, attentional bias, ruminative processing and activation of dysfunctional beliefs. In this model, cognitive-attentional experiences such as biased information processing and executive processes, which are directed by patients' beliefs, mediate cognitive intrusions. Some beliefs are metacognitive in nature and are linked to the interpretation, selection and execution of particular thought processes. Wells (1995) states that such metacognitive beliefs include beliefs about thought processes (e.g. "I have a poor memory"), the advantages and disadvantages of various types of thinking (e.g. "My worrying could make me go mad"), and beliefs about the content of thoughts (e.g. "It is bad to think about death"). Discussing such beliefs with reference to generalised anxiety disorder and obsessive-compulsive disorder, Wells (1995) argues that in these patients, it is their *appraisal* of and *response* to their cognitive processes which distinguishes them from non-clinical samples, as opposed to the *content* of their cognitions.

Interpretations of intrusions in psychosis: an integrative model

Applying the components of these models of anxiety to the phenomenology of psychotic symptoms suggests that intrusions (including hallucinations, which are assumed to be essentially normal intrusions within this approach) that are misinterpreted in certain ways will be viewed as psychotic phenomena. These misinterpretations will be maintained by safety behaviours (including selective attention), plans for processing, faulty self-knowledge (metacognition) and social knowledge and mood and physiology. This is summarised in Figure 3.2.

We would argue that it is the cultural unacceptability of the interpretation made that determines whether or not someone receives a diagnosis of a psychotic disorder. Examples of such interpretations would include an individual perceiving intrusive thoughts as evidence of alien thought insertion; perceiving self-critical thoughts as a malevolent voice; perceiving intrusive impulses as evidence of alien control over one's body; perceiving auditory hallucinations as evidence that the devil is trying to make one kill one's neighbour; perceiving a tight feeling around one's head as evidence of a halo; perceiving a memory of a dream as evidence that one is the Messiah; perceiving the mention of one's first name on television as evidence that everyone is talking about you or that the media are communicating directly with you; or perceiving a visit from a television licence inspector as evidence of a government conspiracy against you.

The main difference that appears to constitute the classification of such interpretations as psychotic symptoms, as opposed to a non-psychotic disorder, seems to be their cultural unacceptability (Morrison, 2001). For instance, if someone misinterprets racing thoughts or palpitations as a sign of alien control

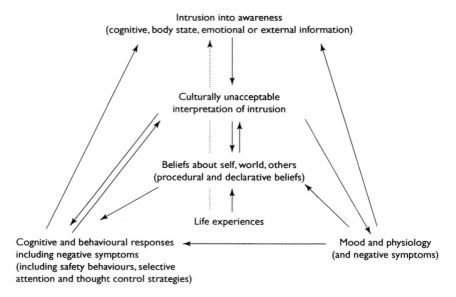

Intrusion into awareness
(cognitive, body state, emotional or external information)

Culturally unacceptable
interpretation of intrusion

Beliefs about self, world, others
(procedural and declarative beliefs)

Life experiences

Cognitive and behavioural responses
including negative symptoms
(including safety behaviours, selective
attention and thought control strategies)

Mood and physiology
(and negative symptoms)

Figure 3.2 A cognitive model of psychosis (reproduced from Morrison, 2001)

or persecution via telekinesis, he or she will be classified as delusional, whereas misinterpretation of the same sensations as a sign of impending madness or a heart attack would be regarded as indicative of panic disorder. Similarly, a benign lump in one's skin may be misinterpreted as a sign of cancer by a hypochondriacal patient, but the misinterpretation of the same stimuli as being a transmitter installed by the secret police would be more likely to result in a patient being regarded as psychotic. However, as will be examined later, it is evident that people often have good reasons for jumping to their culturally unacceptable interpretations (just as anxious patients have a reason for making their catastrophic interpretations). As has been noted by Bentall (1990b), many psychotic interpretations are characterised by being external in nature. Garety et al. (2001) go further, suggesting that all psychotic symptoms are the result of a combination of basic cognitive dysfunction and external appraisal. However, it should be noted that many psychotic interpretations are not external (e.g. "I'm God", "I'm special", "I'm royalty", and "the television is talking about me" are all internal appraisals). Similarly, many non-psychotic interpretations are external. For example, "people think I'm foolish", "others hate me", "others have harmed me", "my life has been destroyed by having been assaulted", "people will reject me" and "others think I'm boring" are all appraisals that are commonly found in anxiety disorders. Most importantly, it would seem that much of the distress in relation to psychotic interpretations is caused by the cultural unacceptability of the appraisal as opposed to whether it is external (both for the individuals concerned and for those in their social network).

Intrusions

Can psychotic symptoms or their triggers be conceptualised as normal intrusions? As mentioned earlier, Morrison (1998a) has argued that hallucinations may be normal responses to certain events or triggers, and conceptualises them as being similar to body sensations in panic disorder. Thus, it may be possible to view such experiences as intrusions. Morrison et al. (1995) suggested that intrusive thoughts, images and impulses are likely to be implicated in the development of psychotic symptoms, and that voices may be misattributed intrusive thoughts. Chadwick and Birchwood (1994) and Chadwick, Birchwood, and Trower (1996) have used an ABC (antecedent–belief–consequence) framework for understanding and intervening with psychotic symptoms. Within this model, they conceptualise voices as antecedents to the beliefs about voices and triggering stimuli for delusional beliefs as antecedents, which is also compatible with a role for intrusions in the development and maintenance of psychosis.

With reference to delusional beliefs, Verdoux et al. (1998) and Peters, Joseph, and Garety (1999) have shown that large proportions of people with no psychiatric history endorse items examining delusional ideas. Van Os et al. (1999) reported that over 60 per cent of non-GHQ (General Health Questionnaire) cases, and over 80 per cent of people who met GHQ caseness but had no history of psychosis, endorsed some items of delusional ideation. Peters et al. (1999) found that an average of 30 per cent of a large normal sample (n = 470) endorsed individual items of delusional ideation, and found that a sample of people belonging to religious cults scored significantly higher.

In addition, the well-documented links between drugs such as amphetamine and cocaine and psychotic symptoms are consistent with an account that incorporates intrusions into awareness. Kingdon and Turkington (1994) have noted that hallucinations can occur in organic confusional states such as those induced by drugs (such as LSD and cocaine) and alcohol withdrawal, and it is widely recognised that such drugs can cause paranoia. It is possible that such drugs induce an increase in the frequency of intrusions into awareness (including anomalous experiences), making a psychotic interpretation more likely (in a similar way to Clark's (1986) explanation of the cognitive mediation of sodium lactate induced panic).

As discussed earlier, Maher (1974) has suggested that delusions are the result of normal reasoning processes that lead to abnormal explanations for anomalous perceptual experiences. Fowler (2000) states that "most people with psychotic disorder have periods in which they have anomalous conscious experiences (e.g. thoughts being experienced as voices, alterations in the experience of thoughts; disordered or heightened sensory perception)", and appears to argue that such anomalies are central to the development of psychosis and are qualitatively different to the experiences of people without psychosis. As has been mentioned earlier, Garety et al. (2001) also suggest that basic cognitive dysfunction or anomalous experience is present in the majority of psychoses (and for all people with a diagnosis of schizophrenia). However, anomalous experiences are neither necessary nor sufficient for psychotic experiences (just as physiological abnormalities are not for panic attacks). Nor are such experiences specific to psychosis, and the evidence that they are qualitatively different from those experienced by non-psychotic people is far from convincing. As mentioned earlier, thoughts experienced as voices is a common experience in the general population (particularly following certain life events), and alterations in the experience of thoughts are present in most patients with anxiety disorders, as the work on metacognition demonstrates (see Wells (2000) for a review). Dissociative experiences are very common in patients with anxiety disorders – and post-traumatic stress disorder (PTSD) in particular – and approximately 50 per cent of adolescents experience at least one prodromal sign of schizophrenia (McGorry et al., 1995). Disordered or heightened sensory perception is easily induced in most people (for example taking certain substances will produce perceptual changes, as will sleep deprivation). Similarly, it has been shown that psychotic experiences are normally distributed in the general population (Johns & van Os, 2001).

Thus, it does seem plausible to suggest that some psychotic symptoms and the triggers for other psychotic symptoms could be viewed as normal intrusions into awareness, using Wells and Matthews' (1994) broad definition of intrusion which encompasses external stimulus information, cognitive state information and body state information. This would also be compatible with the notion of biological vulnerabilities for psychosis as structural or chemical factors could affect the rate and type of intrusions or ambiguous stimuli experienced (although such vulnerabilities are neither necessary nor sufficient).

Interpretations of intrusions

There is considerable evidence that suggests that the interpretation of intrusions is central to the understanding of psychotic symptoms. Kingdon and Turkington (1994) state that "the meaning invested in hallucinations may also be of impor-tance – whether a person says to himself, 'The devil is talking to me' or 'I must be going crazy', or dismissively; 'That was a strange sensation, I must have been overtired'" (p. 78). It has been proposed by several authors that the appraisals of positive symptoms (including auditory hallucinations) are likely to determine the cognitive, behavioural, affective and physiological responses or consequences (Chadwick & Birchwood, 1994; Morrison, 1998a; Morrison et al., 1995; Tarrier, 1987). A study utilising the beliefs about voices questionnaire (BAVQ: Chadwick & Birchwood, 1995) found a strong positive relationship between appraisals of malevolence and resistance of the voices and between appraisals of benevolence and engagement with the voices. More recently, Morrison and Baker (2000) found that patients' interpretations of their voices were associated with the measures of distress in relation to them, and that such interpretations were superior to frequency of voices as a predictor of distress. It has also been shown that appraisals regarding stigmatisation and the need for social containment of the mentally ill are associated with depression in patients with schizophrenia (Birchwood, Mason, MacMillan, & Healy, 1993), suggesting that social meanings may contribute to the development and maintenance of misinterpretations regarding ambiguous or anomolous experiences.

Peters et al. (1999), in their study of delusional ideation, found that it was not the content of beliefs that distinguished between delusional patients on a psychiatric ward and the general population, but rather the degree of conviction, distress and preoccupation; this is parallel to the differentiation between individuals with obsessive-compulsive disorder from normal individuals who have intrusive thoughts with very similar content (Rachman & De Silva, 1978; Salkovskis & Harrison, 1984). This suggests that it is how such thoughts are interpreted that is the difference between psychotic patients and the general population. Jakes and Hemsley (1996) reported that patients with obsessional thoughts were more likely to resist their thoughts, view them as senseless and seek reassurance in relation to them than patients with delusions, again suggesting that how people interpret their thoughts may distinguish diagnostic groups.

It is suggested here that the initial interpretation of an intrusion will determine the individual's choice of cognitive and behavioural responses or coping strategies, which will affect the subsequent occurrence of similar intrusions (as discussed later). Thus, if individuals interpret an auditory hallucination as the result of stress or sleep deprivation, they may reduce arousal or get some sleep but not give the hallucination any further thought. However, if they were to interpret it as being a sign of madness or indicative of their neighbours' attempts to harm them, they may engage in hypervigilance for similar experiences, attempt to suppress the experience, punish themselves for it or adopt safety behaviours to prevent the feared outcome, all of which may contribute to the maintenance of further hallucinations. The same processes appear to apply to how people interpret seeing 666 in a number plate, hearing clicks on their telephone line or having a thought that seems unusual.

Beliefs about self (including metacognition)

There are several groups of researchers that have identified beliefs about aspects of the self as being important in psychosis. As mentioned earlier, Chadwick and Birchwood (1994) have demonstrated that beliefs about voices are meaningfully related to their emotional and behavioural consequences and Morrison (1998a) has suggested that interpretations of voices determine the associated distress and disability.

It is evident that patients experiencing auditory hallucinations can hold positive and negative beliefs about their voices. Positive beliefs may be associated with efforts to engage and maintain particular hallucinatory experiences; indeed, Chadwick and Birchwood (1994) found that voices believed to be benevolent were engaged. In a study examining the attitudes of fifty psychiatric inpatients to their hallucinations, it was found that over 50 per cent reported some positive effects of hallucinating, with the most commonly cited benefits being that the hallucinations were relaxing or soothing and that they provided companionship (Miller, O'Connor, & DiPasquale, 1993). Morrison, Wells, and Nothard (2000) found that positive beliefs about unusual perceptual experiences were the best predictor of predisposition to auditory and visual hallucinations in normal subjects. On the other hand, negative beliefs about hallucinations may be associated with unhelpful coping strategies. Chadwick and Birchwood (1994) found that patients resisted voices believed to be malevolent and it has been suggested that the deliberate suppression of auditory hallucinations may be counterproductive (Morrison et al., 1995). It has been suggested by Morrison et al. (2000) that it may be the co-occurrence of positive and negative beliefs about voices that distinguish patients from non-patients who hear voices, and that hallucinations may be partially motivated and become distressing only when appraised as uncontrollable and dangerous. It is also common to find patients with delusional ideas who hold positive beliefs about their delusions, particularly in the earlier stages; for example, persecutory ideas may add meaning to the person's life, making them special; may provide excitement (something often lacking from a psychiatric patients' existence); or may defend against self-blame (as suggested by Bentall, Kinderman, & Kaney, 1994). In other words, positive beliefs about unusual experiences or beliefs may be implicated specifically in the development of psychotic symptoms; for example a patient may take substances to induce such phenomena, deliberately allocate attention to such phenomena, or such phenomena may occur as a coping response, as suggested by Romme and Escher (1989). Therefore, psychotic experiences may develop as functional survival strategies. It would only be when such experiences or strategies are appraised as uncontrollable or dangerous, or lead to negative environmental consequences (such as problems with occupational and social functioning, which may occur when the environment changes), that they become problematic. To take a specific example, if you develop a paranoid mode of operating in a prison environment or an abusive children's home, this may be very useful and help you avoid all kinds of unpleasantness. If, however, you are not flexible enough to stop using that strategy and adopt another when your circumstances change, then the strategy may become dysfunctional and cause you, or those around you, distress. It is also important to note that, for some patients, their psychotic experiences or beliefs may still be functional as survival strategies; for example, paranoia may still be useful if you are living in an area of severe urban deprivation with a high rate of interpersonal crime.

Positive and negative beliefs about thoughts may also be implicated in the development and maintenance of hallucinations. Baker and Morrison (1998) found that patients experiencing auditory hallucinations scored higher on metacognitive beliefs concerning both positive beliefs about worry and negative beliefs about uncontrollability and danger associated with thoughts. They also found that both groups of patients with a diagnosis of schizophrenia (with and without hallucinations) scored higher than non-patients on beliefs about metacognitive efficiency and beliefs about punishment, responsibility and superstition, and that subjects who scored higher on predisposition to hallucination had different metacognitive beliefs in comparison with subjects of low predisposition. In addition, Freeman and Garety (1999) found that the majority of a sample of people with persecutory delusions experienced meta-worry concerning the control of delusion-relevant thoughts.

Another theoretical approach that has placed great emphasis on another type of self-knowledge is that of Bentall et al. (1994). As described earlier, they state that paranoid thinking is functional or defensive in that it can reduce discrepancies between perception of the self as it is and ideals, and thus protect self-esteem. Several experiments have found support for both the hypothesised external attributional bias (Kaney and Bentall, 1989; Kinderman and Bentall, 1996) and an implicit negative self-concept (Lyon et al., 1994).

Frith (1992) has also suggested that positive psychotic symptoms, such as hallucinations and delusions, result from an impairment in the ability to represent mental states. In particular, thought insertion and passivity phenomena (delusions of control) are associated with an inability to represent a patient's own intentions to act (Frith and Done, 1989; Mlakar, Jensterle, & Frith, 1994).

Thus it appears that there are many ways in which different types of faulty self-knowledge, including positive and negative beliefs, may be involved in the development or maintenance of psychotic symptoms.

Beliefs about others and the world

While there has been less emphasis placed on examining the social and real world understanding of psychotic patients, there are some studies documenting deficits in social knowledge. Cutting and Murphy (1990) have demonstrated an impaired ability of patients with a diagnosis of schizophrenia to appreciate social knowledge about their culture in comparison with depressed and manic patients, and argue that decreased competence in social judgements is an intrinsic feature of schizophrenia. Further evidence for the involvement of impaired social knowledge in psychotic symptoms can be found in the work of Frith and colleagues examining theory of mind in schizophrenia. Corcoran, Mercer, and Frith (1995) found that psychotic patients had difficulty interpreting the intentions behind indirect speech. Frith and Corcoran (1996) showed that acutely ill psychotic patients performed worse than controls on false-belief tasks and concluded that psychotic symptoms reflect an impaired ability to infer the mental states of others. However, it is not clear whether these deficits are associated with any particular psychotic symptom (Drury, Robinson, & Birchwood, 1998) and Frith's own work suggests that they are state characteristics that are present only during acute illness.

More recently, a number of studies have examined the role of beliefs about others and the world in people predisposed to psychosis. Studies have shown that negative beliefs about others predispose non-patients to experiencing delusional ideas (Morrison, Sharkey, & Johnson, 2002a). Similarly, dysfunctional assumptions about the likelihood of rejection by others have been shown to be elevated in people at high risk of developing psychosis (Morrison et al., 2002a). On the basis of these findings, it is clear that faulty social knowledge is likely to be a vulnerability factor for psychosis, and has certainly been implicated in the development or maintenance of certain psychotic symptoms.

Procedural beliefs (plans for processing) and information processing bias

Within the S-REF model, Wells and Matthews (1994) distinguish between procedural and declarative beliefs (the latter guide the selection and execution of strategies for the processing of information such as reasoning strategies, thought control techniques and allocation of attention). While little research has directly examined plans for processing, there are a large number of studies that have focused on the nature of processing itself in psychotic patients. However, the above studies of metacognition give some indication that people with psychosis exhibit dysfunctional plans for processing (e.g. positive beliefs about worry).

Possibly the most frequently studied aspect of information processing in schizophrenia is that of attentional bias. Bentall and his colleagues (Bentall & Kaney, 1989; Kaney, Wolfenden, Dewey, & Bentall, 1992; Kinderman, 1994) have demonstrated that patients experiencing persecutory delusions have biases in information processing, and have suggested that these processes may be involved in the maintenance of delusions. Bentall and Kaney (1989) found that, using the emotional Stroop task, deluded patients exhibited selective attention to paranoia-related words, and Kaney et al. (1992) found that deluded patients showed biased recall towards threatening propositions. In addition, Leafhead, Young, and Szulecka (1996) found that a patient with delusional beliefs selectively attended to material related to her delusions (indicated by slower colour naming times on a modified Stroop task) and that this bias was not present when the patient had recovered.

A significant body of research has examined the role of self-awareness (or self-focused attention) in schizophrenia. Frith (1979) has argued that the symptoms of schizophrenia can be interpreted as the result of excessive self-awareness, and Ingram (1990) has suggested that an over-reliance on self-focused attention may be an important component of schizophrenia. This would certainly be consistent with the finding that increased private self-consciousness (a measure of self-focused attention; Fenigstein, Scheier, & Buss, 1975) was associated with an increased tendency to perceive oneself as the target (Fenigstein, 1984, study 4), suggesting a relation to persecutory delusions. Similarly, Smari, Stefansson, and Thorgilsson (1994) found that paranoia was associated with private self-consciousness in male schizophrenics, and Morrison and Haddock (1997a) have shown that patients experiencing auditory hallucinations exhibit higher levels of private self-consciousness than psychiatric and normal control subjects. In addition, a recent experimental study suggests that reducing internal focus of attention decreases the external attributional bias found in patients experiencing auditory hallucinations (Ensum & Morrison, in press).

Garety and Hemsley (1994) suggested that the normal tendency to perceive more support for a belief than is actually in evidence (or confirmation bias) is involved in delusion formation and maintenance. Bentall and Young (1996) have shown that delusional patients exhibited a confirmation strategy for positive outcomes and a disconfirmation strategy for negative outcomes (just as normal controls did) in a study examining their hypothesis testing. Finally, Bentall et al.'s (1994) model of persecutory delusions would also seem consistent with a conceptualisation that incorporates plans for processing, as it is possible that such procedural beliefs may influence the selection and execution of the external attribution that is hypothesised to reduce self-discrepancies. As already mentioned, there is also a significant body of work that has demonstrated that patients who experience auditory hallucinations make external attributions for internal mental events (e.g. Baker & Morrison, 1998; Bentall et al., 1991; Heilbrun, 1980; Morrison & Haddock, 1997b).

It therefore appears that there are information-processing biases that have been demonstrated in psychotic patients, and there are some initial indications that such biases may be associated with procedural beliefs.

Attempts to control and safety behaviours

There are initial indications that dysfunctional or counterproductive attempts at control are involved in psychosis. Morrison et al. (2000) found that subjects who scored higher on predisposition to hallucination used different thought control strategies in comparison with subjects of low predisposition. Freeman and Garety (1999) compared thought control strategies in patients with persecutory delusions and patients with generalised anxiety disorder and found that no significant differences between the two groups in strategies used. In addition, Morrison and Wells (2000) found that patients with a diagnosis of schizophrenia used significantly more punishment and worry-based control strategies and significantly less distraction-based control strategies than normal subjects.

Is there any evidence that safety behaviours may be operating in the maintenance of psychotic phenomena? Morrison (1998b) has suggested that, in the same way that people with anxiety disorders adopt certain behaviours in order to prevent some feared catastrophe (Clark, 1996; Salkovskis, 1991, 1996b; Wells et al., 1995), patients with distressing delusional beliefs initiate attempts to avert any negative outcomes that are implied in the delusional belief. An example is a patient who believes that he is being followed by a terrorist organisation and who attempts to lose his trackers by taking varying routes to the shops, hiding behind cars and changing clothes regularly or going out in disguise. These strategies may inhibit cognitive change as they are preventing disconfirmation of the delusional belief.

Morrison (1998a) has also argued that safety-seeking behaviours that are designed to prevent a threat to the individual's physical or psychological integrity that is attributed to the experience of auditory hallucinations (e.g. shouting back at a voice in order to avoid doing what the voice says or attempting to distract oneself from the voice to avoid going mad) may be removing the possibility for disconfirmation of the interpretation of the hallucination (in this case, that the patient must obey an omnipotent voice or will go mad as a result of hearing the voice). There is evidence that patients do engage in safety behaviours of the sort that *may* maintain their negative appraisals regarding their hallucinations (e.g. lying down, drinking alcohol, breathing exercises, jogging, shouting at or talking to the voices, seeking interaction; see Frederick & Cotanch, 1995; Nayani & David, 1996; Romme et al., 1992). Nothard, Morrison, and Wells (2002) used a semi-structured interview to elicit interpretations of voices and corresponding safety behaviours, and found that eleven of twelve patients reported clearly identifiable safety behaviours. Similarly, Freeman, Garety, and Kuipers (2001) have shown that patients with persecutory delusions exhibit safety behaviours. It would seem that patients with psychosis do adopt safety behaviours if they experience anxiety in relation to their psychotic experiences (i.e. if they have something that they fear will happen, they will try to prevent it).

In addition to preventing disconfirmation of the interpretation of an intrusion, it is also possible that some safety behaviours may directly increase the frequency of the intrusion itself. Patients experiencing auditory hallucinations have been reliably shown to adopt certain strategies in an effort to cope with their voices (Falloon & Talbot, 1981; Frederick & Cotanch, 1995; Tarrier, 1987). Romme et al. (1992) found that subjects use of distraction as a coping strategy was associated with perceived inability to cope with their voices; Nayani and David (1996) found that the use of watching television and listening to the radio as coping strategies were often cited as making hallucinations worse. Thus, it is possible that the use of certain safety behaviours may increase auditory hallucinations directly in a similar manner to that proposed by Salkovskis (1996b) in anxiety. Similarly, the evidence discussed above in relation to selective attention and heightened self-focus in psychotic patients may increase the actual frequency or perceived frequency of intrusions in same way that hypervigilance to threat can increase intrusions in anxiety.

Mood and physiology

Experimental and phenomenological findings, in relation to hallucinations in particular, suggest that mood and physiology are implicated in the maintenance of such phenomena, as the onset of hallucinatory episodes is associated with psychophysiological arousal (Allen & Argus, 1968; Cooklin, Sturgeon, & Leff, 1983) and emotional experiences such as anxiety (Slade, 1972), sadness and anger (Nayani & David, 1996) have also been shown to be associated with increases in the experiencing of hallucinations. In their model of delusional formation, Garety and Hemsley (1994) implicate both high affective loading of stimuli and high physiological arousal in the development and maintenance of delusional beliefs, and Kemp, Chua, McKenna, and David (1997) found that deluded patients' reasoning worsened in problems containing emotive material. Gumley, White, and Power's (1999) application of interacting cognitive subsystems theory to understanding psychotic relapse suggests that body state information and emotional inputs may directly affect implicational meaning (and hence, within this model, beliefs about self and others), which in turn is likely to affect ongoing interpretations of intrusions into awareness. It is also likely that the physiological effects of sleep deprivation and drug use will be involved in the development and maintenance of psychosis.

Such a model is also compatible with the findings regarding biological factors in psychosis (such as structural, chemical and genetic differences) as these could result in increased intrusions or anomalous experiences.

The role of early experiences, life events and the environment

While some would argue that the reason for the unusual interpretations that characterise psychosis is biological in origin, it is likely that early experiences (and, as demonstrated earlier, the beliefs formed as a result of them) have an important role in their development. Schizophrenia has been the subject of much research from geneticists over the past century because of the high risk associated with a family history of the disorder (e.g. Gottesman & Shields, 1982). It is possible, however, that a large part of this effect may be accounted for by the environmental factors that are in common within families (such as poverty, unemployment, low self-esteem, degrading life experiences and social isolation: Marshall, 1990), or as a direct result of learning experiences a child may be exposed to because of proximity with schizophrenic parents. Marshall (1990) has also noted that there is often a discrepancy between the actual evidence found in adoption studies searching for a genetic cause for schizophrenia and the inferences drawn and reported from such data.

It is well demonstrated that cultural or contextual factors have an effect on the presentation of positive symptoms in schizophrenia, as well as what is defined as such. DSM-IV (APA, 1994) includes in its definition of delusions the criterion that the belief is not one ordinarily accepted by other members of the person's subculture, and Mullen (1979) includes the characteristic that the beliefs are not shared by those of a common social or cultural background in his definition. It has been found that there is considerable cultural and geographical variation in the prevalence and modality of hallucinatory experiences, in addition to how such phenomena are interpreted (Al-Issa, 1978; Bourgignon, 1970). Also, Nayani and David (1996) found that, in a study of the phenomenology of auditory hallucinations, when regional accents of the voices differed from the patients' own, this was in a manner which reflected their original cultural milieu (e.g. British-born

African Carribean subjects with London accents heard voices with Jamaican accents).

There is a growing body of opinion that suggests that psychosis may emerge as a reaction to trauma (e.g. Ellason & Ross, 1997; Read, 1997). There is much speculation about the relationship between traumatic life events and the development of psychosis, particularly its association with childhood sexual abuse, physical abuse or interpersonal violence. In a seminal study, Romme and Escher (1989) found that 70 per cent of voice hearers developed their hallucinations following a traumatic event, and they suggested that hearing voices may be part of a coping process. Honig, Romme, Ensink, Escher, Pennings, and DeVries (1998) compared the form and content of chronic auditory hallucinations in three cohorts (patients with schizophrenia, patients with a dissociative disorder and non-patient voice-hearers). They found that, in most patients, the onset of auditory hallucinations was preceded by either a traumatic event or an event that activated the memory of earlier trauma, and that the disability incurred by hearing voices was associated with the reactivation of previous trauma and abuse.

Many studies have examined the links between sexual abuse and psychosis (see Read (1997) for a comprehensive review). Ross, Anderson, and Clark (1994) found that patients who report childhood abuse are more likely to report positive psychotic symptoms, and suggest that there are at least two pathways to schizophrenia: an endogenously driven pathway characterised by negative symptoms and a pathway determined by childhood trauma characterised by a predominance of positive symptoms. Read (1997) states that "it seems reasonable to conclude that there may indeed be relationships between childhood abuse and adult psychosis, and, more specifically, between childhood abuse and schizophrenia" (p. 450).

Mueser et al. (1998) examined the lifetime incidence of trauma in a large sample of people (n = 275) with serious mental illness and found that 98 per cent had experienced at least one traumatic event. An analogue study has also examined the links between childhood maltreatment and abnormal perceptions and beliefs. In a sample of 458 undergraduates, Berenbaum (1999) found that reported childhood maltreatment was associated with higher levels of unusual perceptions and beliefs.

Some authors have suggested that there is a link between the content of abusive experiences and the content of psychotic symptoms. Read and Argyle (1999) examined the relationship between three positive symptoms of schizophrenia (hallucinations, delusions and thought disorder) and childhood physical and sexual abuse among psychiatric inpatients. They found seventeen of the twenty-two patients with an abuse history exhibited one or more of these three symptoms and that half of the symptoms for which content was recorded appeared to be related to the abuse. This congruence between the nature of traumatic experiences and the form and content of psychotic symptoms suggests that there may be a causal link.

Ellason and Ross (1997) have suggested that a type of schizophrenia characterised by positive symptoms is trauma-induced, and Kingdon and Turkington (1999) have suggested a subtype of schizophrenia that they term obsessional psychosis, which they argue includes patients with repetitive and distressing hallucinations that are "associated with trauma, e.g. sexual abuse; the voice of the perpetrator may be heard and resisted because of the associated distress" (p. 69). Morrison, Frame, and Larkin (in press) suggest that both psychosis and PTSD may form a spectrum of responses to trauma (at least for some people), and that it is cognitive and behavioural factors that determine which pathway is followed.

It would appear that there is a significant amount of evidence to support the links between early experiences and adult life events (particularly of a traumatic nature) and the development of psychosis.

Negative symptoms

Negative symptoms are commonly thought to include apathy, anhedonia, avolition, flat or blunted affect and poverty of speech. It is highly likely that research focused on individual negative symptoms, as with positive symptoms, will lead to a better understanding of them (this will be discussed further in Chapter 11). It is also likely that there will be multiple pathways, even when considering the same negative symptom. However, there are some common themes that recur in the presentation of negative symptoms, and these can be incorporated within the model outlined above. The example of flat or blunted affect will be used to illustrate this point.

Mood (in particular, depression and anxiety) may contribute to the development of negative symptoms. For example, depression, which is a common response to a psychotic episode (Birchwood, Iqbal, Chadwick & Trower, 2000), could lead to somebody showing flat affect, as could the reduced emotional responding commonly seen in trauma victims (see Morrison et al., in press). Physiological factors such as over-medication or cannabis use could also result in flat affect. The role of life experience, beliefs and safety behaviours can also be illustrated in relation to flat affect. It may be that negative symptoms (as with positive symptoms) have been functional in the past, or the present. For example, as a consequence of being brought up in a household where expressions of emotion were punished with physical violence (with a family rule of "Boys don't cry" and where exceptions to this rule were met with a beating), a person may develop flat affect as a survival strategy. Similarly, it may still be functional for people to restrict their expression of emotions if they have learnt that exhibiting distress in front of mental health professionals can lead to unwanted increases in medication or admission to psychiatric hospital. This clearly overlaps with the concept of safety behaviours. Another common feared outcome is the catastrophic fear of relapse, and many negative symptoms may be attempts to avoid positive symptoms or the consequences of relapse (such as admission to hospital or stigmatisation).

Summary

It has been argued that many positive psychotic symptoms can be conceptualised as intrusions into awareness (e.g. auditory hallucinations) or the culturally unacceptable interpretations of such intrusions (e.g. delusional beliefs), and that it is the interpretation of these intrusions that causes the associated distress and disability. It is also argued that these culturally unacceptable interpretations are determined by beliefs about self, world and others. These beliefs include positive and negative beliefs about the nature of psychotic experience. These beliefs are determined by life experiences. The intrusions and their interpretations are maintained by mood, physiology (including the effects of sleep deprivation and drug use), and the way in which people respond to their experiences (including selective attention, safety behaviours and counterproductive control strategies), which may be guided by procedural beliefs (or beliefs about coping). It is also suggested that negative symptoms may evolve as ways of coping or as safety behaviours, and be determined by beliefs in the same manner, or be produced by mood and/or physiology.

Chapter 4

Cognitive assessment of psychotic patients

As the model outlined in Chapter 3 would suggest, the psychological assessment of psychotic patients is very similar to that of other patients. Therefore, this chapter begins by examining the purposes of assessment, then provides an introduction to the basic elements of a cognitive behavioural interview, and finally provide more detailed information regarding specific measures and methods of gathering information that can be used to produce a formulation that will guide intervention.

Aims of assessment

There are several reasons to conduct a cognitive behavioural assessment with patients.

Identification of problems

In cognitive therapy in particular, it is extremely important for the patient and therapist to have a shared understanding of what the problems that are being targeted for change are. Without a shared idea of what is being worked on, the patient is unlikely to engage fully with treatment and will be understandably reluctant to attempt homework tasks. Without such agreement, the therapist will be unable to proceed with problem-focused formulation and intervention and would have to rely on non-specific factors (such as empathy, professionalism and acceptance) for bringing about therapeutic change; in fact, agreement about what problems should be addressed will probably increase or enhance such non-specific factors and engagement. Once a comprehensive list of problems has been identified, it is important to collaboratively prioritise such problems and set goals in relation to these.

Problems highlighted by the problem list should be prioritised according to patients' wishes, the amenability of the problems to change (and therefore the likelihood of early success in therapy) and the impact that change in one problem may have on other difficulties. Goals that are set in relation to these problems should be measurable, specific and proximal.

Information gathering to guide formulation

Possibly the most important aim of assessment is to gather data to inform the development of a psychological formulation. If the right questions are not asked, it is unlikely that the right answers will be found. It is extremely important to conduct a thorough assessment of a patient's presenting problems in such a way as to ensure that the information required to construct a cognitive formulation can be obtained. Without this information, an accurate (or even partially accurate) formulation cannot be generated and therefore the appropriate and necessary intervention strategies will not be selected.

Hypothesis testing

The use of standardised assessment measures, idiosyncratic self-monitoring methods and behavioural tests can be used to gather information for hypothesis testing purposes as well. Thus, a formulation of the factors maintaining a specific symptom can be examined for its accuracy by retrospectively reviewing variations in the frequency or intensity of the symptom. Furthermore, predictions can be made on the basis of a formulation and then information can then be gathered and interpreted in order to test them. For example, the therapist and patient may agree to examine the role of selective attention in the maintenance of a symptom by attempting to modify the patient's attentional focus. They might decide to review the relationship between alcohol intake and voices in order to consider whether stress, associated with alcohol consumption, plays a role in voices.

Assessment as a form of intervention

Assessment can be an important first step in establishing the necessary foundations for therapeutic change and it can engender change in itself. The process of assessment involves questioning a patient in a manner that can contribute to socialising patients to the cognitive model. Thus, asking patients to describe what thoughts go through their mind, how this makes them feel and how it makes them behave can assist them in making the links between these factors for themselves (indeed, this is largely what the process of guided discovery is about).

In addition, assessment can help to establish rapport with the patient and develop the therapeutic relationship that is required to facilitate therapeutic change. Assessment is also an ideal opportunity to share normalising information about a patient's symptoms as they are elicited. For instance, providing information about the prevalence of hearing voices or unusual beliefs or famous celebrities who have experienced such symptoms can be extremely helpful, reducing patients' distress by destigmatising their experiences.

Assessment may also be a therapeutic mechanism in itself. There is some evidence that self-monitoring symptoms of certain psychological disorders using diaries and rating scales can reduce the frequency of such symptoms; for instance, PTSD patients who self-monitored intrusions experienced a significant decrease in intrusive symptomatology (Reynolds & Tarrier, 1996). Focusing approaches to auditory hallucinations could also be viewed as a therapeutic application of self-monitoring (see Haddock, Slade, Bentall, & Faragher, 1998), although the evidence for the effectiveness of this strategy is equivocal.

Monitoring

The monitoring of symptoms is also a very important part of cognitive therapy. The structured monitoring of specific symptoms can be useful as a way of gathering information, of testing hypotheses and of socialising patients as described earlier. In addition, monitoring symptoms is important to ensure that therapy is being effective (or if it is not, to highlight this so that the formulation can be re-examined and interventions modified accordingly). The administration of standardised or idiosyncratic measures pre- and post-therapy should be a minimum requirement for cognitive therapy to audit its effectiveness, but a more routine administration of such measures on a weekly basis or at regular review sessions should be encouraged. Similarly, self-monitoring using diary measures in relation to patients' concerns can be extremely useful for monitoring progress. Examples of self-monitoring forms can be seen in the appendix.

Common therapist assumptions

As the cognitive model suggests that our beliefs affect how we behave, a brief discussion regarding common therapist's assumptions about working with psychotic patients will be addressed here. Traditional psychiatric approaches to psychosis suggest that staff should not discuss the content of psychotic symptoms with the patient as this may reinforce delusional conviction. This is unlikely to be the case, and cognitive therapy in particular adopts a questioning approach in which patients are encouraged to view their delusions as one possible explanation for events, and to consider whether there are any other possible explanations. It is possible that patients may feel worse emotionally after discussing their difficulties, but this happens on surprisingly infrequent occasions. Given that this is possible, it is important to warn patients (and other staff involved in the patient's care) of this possibility, but also to point out that people sometimes feel better for having been able to discuss concerns that are important to them.

Introduction to cognitive behavioural assessment

As already outlined, the main purpose of cognitive behavioural assessment is to provide therapist and patient with a shared understanding of what the pertinent problems are, what has been involved in the development of these problems, what is involved in the maintenance of these problems and what will need to be measured in order to monitor progress. Clearly, for this to be possible, a very detailed description of the presenting problem will need to be made.

Current difficulties

The major focus of a cognitive behavioural assessment is the verbal interview that examines people's presenting problems in terms of the five systems model (Greenberger & Padesky 1995; this is really a memory aid rather than a cognitive model), which integrates cognitive, behavioural, emotional and physiological processes with the environment. This approach suggests that each difficulty should be examined in terms of cognitive components (what a person thinks and believes, what he or she pays attention to, whether there are any information processing biases involved), behavioural components (what a person does before, during and after a difficult situation, whether there are any safety behaviours designed to avert feared outcomes, avoidance, etc.), affective components (how a person feels emotionally before, during and after a situation), physiological components (how a person responds physically) and the environment in which the person lives. Assessment should examine each area in detail, and can begin to overlap with formulation by looking for thought–emotion–behaviour links or repetitive cycles. This will also aid socialisation to the cognitive model. Each of these elements will be described in further detail.

Cognitive components

Cognitive intrusions

These can include intrusive thoughts, negative automatic thoughts, worries or memories. These can be assessed using questions such as:

- "What was going through your mind at the time?"
- "What was the first thing that you thought?"
- "Did anything trigger the way you were feeling?"

Wells (1997) has identified ten ways of eliciting relevant negative automatic thoughts. These are asking what the worst is that could happen, recounting specific episodes in detail, following affect shifts, asking about imagery, manipulation of safety behaviours and use of dysfunctional thought records (DTRs), exposure tasks, role-plays, audio or video feedback and symptom induction tasks.

Appraisals and interpretations of intrusions

Cognitive intrusions are often interpreted in a manner that can increase the distress associated with them and may increase the frequency of the intrusions. Such appraisals can be assessed using questions such as:

- "Did you have any negative thoughts about the intrusion?"
- "What did having that thought mean to you?"

- "Could anything happen as a result of having such a thought?"
- "Is it normal/okay/acceptable to have such thoughts? If not, why not?"
- "What would happen if you could not stop these thoughts?"
- "Does having such thoughts say anything about you?"
- "Are there any advantages of having such thoughts?"

Attention

It is important to assess what attentional factors may be implicated in the development or maintenance of a problem. These factors can be assessed using questions such as:

- "When you were in that situation, what were you (most) aware of?"
- "What did you notice first?"
- "Were you on the look out for such thoughts/feelings/behaviours?"
- "When you felt scared/sad/angry what were you most conscious of?"
- "How do you think you seemed to other people?"
- "Once you noticed that, were you able to focus on anything else?"

For further discussion of the assessment of attentional processes, see Wells' (1997) or Wells and Matthews' (1994) description of metacognitive profiling.

Cognitive distortions

Beck's (1976) concept of thinking errors can be important to assess. These include jumping to conclusions, mind reading, personalisation, catastrophising, all-or-nothing thinking, magnification and minimisation. For a detailed discussion of thinking errors see Beck (1976), Burns (1980) or Fennell (1989).

Imagery

Beck's (1976) theory of emotional disorders states that appraisals are meanings sufficient to account for the strength of emotion, and that these meanings are accessible through images and memories in addition to verbal thoughts. A study by Morrison et al. (2002b) has shown that the majority of psychotic patients experience recurrent images in relation to their psychotic symptoms (for example, having an image of the person whose voice they hear, or having an image of being attacked if they are paranoid). Such images can be useful in identifying underlying assumptions and core beliefs and important events from the past (as the images often remind people of real events).

In Morrison et al.'s (2002b) study, a semi-structured interview was used to explore the content and meaning of the images. This involved an initial question regarding whether patients could identify images in relation to their psychotic symptoms. If patients were able to do so, then they were asked about the content of the images, whether the images were recurrent, and whether the images were associated with particular emotions and beliefs (the latter being investigated using the downward arrow technique). In addition, patients were asked when they first remembered feeling the way that experiencing the image makes them feel now (from Hackmann, Clark, & McManus, 2000) and whether the images were associated with any particular memories. If images were not readily identified, patients were given some training in the identification of images using positive memories (e.g. think of a time when you have been very happy or excited . . . dwell on this time . . . do you have an image or picture of it in your mind?) or manipulating deliberately formed images of simple objects (e.g. imagining a green apple and turning it red). They were then asked to note any images in relation to their psychotic symptoms as part of homework and were interviewed using the above format at the next session.

Behavioural components

Safety behaviours

It is often extremely important to assess safety-seeking behaviours that patients use to prevent a feared outcome from occurring. Once identified, such behaviours can be manipulated to test hypotheses and facilitate disconfirmation of beliefs or interpretations of intrusions. Any impact that such behaviours may have on the frequency of intrusions is also important to assess. Such factors can be identified using questions such as:

- "When you thought that this was happening/going to happen, what did you do to prevent it?"
- "If you had not done this, what would have happened?"
- "Is there anything you do to control your symptom?"
- "Do you do anything to help you cope or to hide the difficulty?"

As implied in the model in Chapter 3, it is important to assess whether safety behaviours are functional (i.e. how likely the feared outcome is). It is also useful to assess people's strategies for controlling unwanted thoughts (which can be cognitive or behavioural); this can be done by verbal enquiry or using the thought control questionnaire (Wells & Davies, 1994).

Avoidance

This can be conceptualised as an extreme form of safety-seeking behaviour and assessed using similar questions such as:

- "Is there anything that you avoid doing because of this problem?"

- "Do you ever try to escape from this situation?"
- "Does this difficulty stop you from going anywhere?"

Affective components

Emotional responses should be assessed and rated for intensity in relation to individual situations, idiosyncratic thoughts and behaviours. It is also important to assess when the emotion is detected in relation to other components, as it may act as a cue or trigger. When eliciting and rating emotions it is important to use the patient's own terminology and to check that there is a shared understanding of specific words (for instance, a patient may use "mad" for angry or "bad" for sad, while another may use the same terms to refer to paranoia and guilt respectively).

Physiological components

Physical responses to individual situations, idiosyncratic thoughts, emotions and behaviours should also be assessed (again, the temporal occurrence should be noted as physical sensations can be present at any point in a cycle). Particularly common sensations are the anxiety sensations that are often implicated in panic attacks (such as palpitations, dizziness, blurred vision, tension, breathlessness, sweating, trembling or shaking, butterflies in the stomach and difficulty in swallowing). It is also useful to assess whether such sensations are used as evidence for beliefs or criteria for the initiation or termination of certain processes (e.g. allocation of attention, stereotyped behaviours, etc.). Such physiological factors can be assessed using questions such as:

- "Did you notice any physical changes in response to that?"
- "When in that situation, what was happening to your body?"
- "When you were thinking that, how did you feel physically?"
- "Was there a physical feeling that made you believe that this was really happening?"

Triggers and mediators

The above components can all act as triggers for certain thought–feeling–behaviour cycles. In addition, specific events, circumstances, situations, people or substances can be found to reliably induce certain symptoms or experiences. Such factors can also ameliorate or exacerbate symptoms; this can be assessed using questions such as:

- "Have you noticed anything that makes it better (or worse)? If so, what do you make of that?"

- "Is there any particular place or time that such things happen more often?"
- "Is it worse when you are on your own or with people?"

Longitudinal assessment

In addition to the here and now focus of cognitive therapy, it is important to have a historical context in which to base any analysis of current difficulties. In particular it can be useful to gain information regarding a patient's early life experiences and the beliefs that they have developed as a result of these.

Early experience

The role of early experience in the development of patient's problems is central to Beck's cognitive model. This is particularly the case for psychotic patients, as has been discussed in Chapter 3. It is important to gather information regarding a patient's personal and social history, focusing on areas such as family life, school experiences with peers and teachers, friendships and sexual relationships. As has been argued in Chapter 3, the cultural acceptability of interpretations of events seems to be crucial in the labelling of a symptom as psychotic. Therefore, assessing a person's cultural background, paying close attention to religious influences and experiences, factors that the patient feels makes (or made) him or her different from other people and eccentric, and occult influences (such as those cited in DSM-IV in relation to schizotypal personality disorder) is vital. Common themes that are regularly found in clinical practice (and which are supported in the research literature: see Mueser et al., 1998) are unwanted sexual experience, being bullied at work or school and physical assault. It may well be worth asking about such experiences directly, or possibly indirectly via the presentation of normalising information, for example telling people that such experiences are commonly found in people who hear voices or have unusual beliefs, with a summary of the relevant percentages from studies (see the appendix for an example), and then to ask if any of these have happened in the patient's life. Read (1997) recommends specifically enquiring about physical and sexual abuse in a sensitive manner; this can be done by asking general questions, for example about happiest and worst memories from childhood. If people do not disclose adverse experiences in response to general questions, it is worth asking more specific questions, for example about how discipline was enforced at home and school, and finally asking about whether they have had any sexual experiences about which they have felt uncomfortable (rather than unwanted, as this can often be an ambiguous issue for people). The most important consideration is in how to *respond* if adverse experiences are disclosed; it is important to ensure that the person feels listened to, safe and that he or she is not being judged. It is important to check that the person has some coping strategies and social support, and it is worth sharing the possibility that symptoms such as critical voices may get worse in the short term as a result of disclosure.

Core beliefs and dysfunctional assumptions

In addition to an understanding of the maintenance of specific situations, some recognition of core beliefs and underlying assumptions related to the presenting problems is required for a full conceptualisation of a problem or set of related problems. As explained in Chapter 2, core beliefs are deeply held beliefs that usually take the form of absolute statements about the self, other people or the world (for example "I am bad", "Other people cannot be trusted", and "The world is dangerous"). Dysfunctional assumptions are rules for living that often take the form of "If . . . then . . . " statements (for example, "If I am not liked by everyone then I am unlovable" or "I must be in control at all times"). These beliefs are usually formed as the result of early experiences, and many assumptions are like family rules. They can be elicited in a variety of ways. Ways of identifying them include examining direct statements made by patients, asking how certain experiences affected them and what it made them believe about themselves, others or the future, and the downward arrow technique. The latter is based on the fact that negative automatic thoughts are often reflections of these underlying assumptions and core beliefs. Thus, the downward arrow technique uses negative automatic thoughts to try to work backwards to elicit the beliefs, as illustrated in the following excerpt:

Therapist: What upset you yesterday?
Patient: That the white van was parked outside again.
Therapist: And what did that mean to you?
Patient: That they were watching me.
Therapist: And what was so bad about that?
Patient: It meant that the conspiracy is still happening, and I'm under surveillance.
Therapist: And if that is true, what is the worst thing about it?
Patient: That they know all about me.
Therapist: And what does that mean to you?
Patient: That they know how bad I am.
Therapist: And if that is true, what is the worst thing about that?
Patient: That I will never have any friends.
Therapist: And what does that say about you?
Patient: That I am unlovable.

In addition, there are several questionnaires that can be used to assess core beliefs and assumptions including the Schema Questionnaire (Young & Brown, 1994), the Personal Style Inventory (Robins, Ladd, Welkowitz, Blaney, Diaz, & Kutcher, 1994), the Dysfunctional Attitudes Scale (DAS: Weissman & Beck, 1978) and the Meta-Cognitions Questionnaire (Cartwright-Hatton & Wells, 1997). The latter examines assumptions about thoughts and thinking. A more detailed discussion of core beliefs and dysfunctional assumptions is given in Chapter 11.

As pointed out in Chapter 3, it is important to assess whether a belief is currently functional, or has been in the past. This can be done using two columns to consider the advantages and disadvantages of a belief in conjunction with a discussion about why a belief developed, where it came from or whether it has ever been useful.

Related concerns

Assessing co-morbid difficulties in psychotic patients relies on the same methods of assessment that would be used if the problems were occurring on their own. Thus, if a psychotic patient complains of panic attacks and prioritises this on their problem list, then the use of panic diaries, the Agoraphobic Cognitions Questionnaire (Chambless, Caputo, Bright, & Gallagher, 1984) and symptom induction would all be indicated. Common problems that occur co-morbidly in psychotic patients include substance and alcohol abuse, post-traumatic stress, depression and social anxiety. Therefore, assessment should at a minimum include brief questioning about such difficulties. A more in-depth assessment using a combination of cognitive behavioural interviewing, standardised questionnaires and idiosyncratic ratings can be carried out if indicated.

A particularly important issue to assess is suicide risk. This is because patients with a diagnosis of schizophrenia are known to be at higher risk of suicide than the majority of psychiatric patients. This risk can be assessed using verbal questioning about suicidal ideation and intent, whether a method and timescale have been decided upon, any history of suicide attempts and some consideration of the advantages and disadvantages of dying (including eliciting deterrents such as the effect it may have on family members or religious beliefs). Questionnaires such as the Beck Depression Inventory (especially items 2 and 9) and the Beck Hopelessness Scale are useful.

Another important are to assess is antipsychotic medication and its side-effects. The types of drugs and the dosages should be recorded, and the patient should be asked about any side-effects. Standardised questionnaire measures such as the Liverpool University Neuroleptic Side Effects Rating Scale (Day, Wood, Dewey, & Bentall, 1995) can be useful in determining the frequency of side-effects and whether or not patients attribute them to their medication. Cognitive deficits in memory and attention may also be assessed (these may or may not be related to medication). These can be important to know about from the start, as severe deficits will have implications for how therapy is conducted (for instance a slower pace, shorter sessions, visual rather than verbal presentation of information). They can be assessed using informal observation in sessions, discussion with the patient, carers and staff or using formal neuropsychological tests. However, the most important consideration in relation to such deficits is how to overcome them, and a more naturalistic, idiosyncratic approach may be preferable.

Previous experiences of therapy and expectations regarding what will happen in therapy (for example assumptions about who will do the hard work and what the likely degree and rate of change will be) should all be identified in order to correct any misconceptions. Motivation to change should also be assessed in order to make decisions about the timing of review sessions, the nature of homework tasks, the amount of time that will be required engaging the patient and to make some predictions about the likelihood of success which may affect the setting of goals.

A summary of the elements required by a comprehensive cognitive behavioural assessment is presented in Table 4.1.

Other sources of information

There are several methods of gathering information for assessment and monitoring purposes in addition to the verbal cognitive behavioural interview. These include self-monitoring measures, self-report questionnaires, clinician-administered structured or semi-structured interviews and rating scales, and behavioural tests and observation.

Self-monitoring, self-report measures and structured interview tools

There are many standardised self-report questionnaires and clinician-administered interviews and rating scales that have been designed for use with psychotic patients. There is also an abundance of such measures that have been designed for other target populations but which are extremely useful for assessing co-morbid problems in psychotic patients.

Several self-report measures are particularly useful and should be administered regularly; these include the Beck Depression Inventory (Beck, Ward, Mendelson, Mock, & Erbaugh, 1961), the Beck Hopelessness Scale (Beck, Steer, Kovacs, & Garrison, 1985b), which may be especially useful when there is thought to be a risk of suicide risk, and a measure of anxiety such as the State-Trait Anxiety Inventory (Speilberger, Gorusch, Lushene, Vagg, & Jacobs, 1983). Another important area to assess is trauma (both PTSD symptoms and traumatic life experiences), as PTSD is often unrecognised in people with psychosis. Several measures of PTSD symptomatology have been extensively used with people with psychosis, including the Impact of Events Scale (Horowitz, Wilner, & Alvarez, 1979) and the Post-traumatic Symptoms Scale (Foa, Ehlers, Clark, Tolin, & Orsillo, 1999). Mueser and colleagues have specifically developed a revision of the Trauma History Interview to examine traumatic life events in childhood and adulthood, which includes assessment of experiences of hospitalisation and psychiatric services (Mueser et al., 1998). This is important, as there is evidence showing that people can develop PTSD in response to their psychotic symptoms and psychiatric admissions (e.g. McGorry et al., 1991; Morrison & Frame, 2001).

For psychotic symptoms, the Psychotic Symptoms Rating Scales (PSYRATS: Haddock, McCarron, Tarrier, & Faragher, 1999) are very useful tools, both for

Table 4.1 Elements of a comprehensive assessment

Aims
Inform formulation
Problems and goals
Educational, socialisation, intervention

General
Why are you here?
Expectations or worries regarding therapy
Confidentiality
Therapist gender preference
Explanatory models
Potential for rapport
Risk and mood
Motivation for change
Other agencies
Medication

Life history
Family, friends, school, childhood, occupation
Trusting relationship/someone to confide in
Sexual/romantic relationships
Social support
Are they content/where are they in life?
Traumatic events in childhood and adulthood

Problem history
Onset
Triggers
Mediators
Time course

Current problems
Frequency, intensity, emotional distress, consequences, preoccupation, belief
Cognitive, behavioural, emotional, physical, social/environmental factors

Cognitive
Beliefs about self, world, others and future
Underlying assumptions/rules for living
Content of beliefs – recurring themes/intrusions
Worries, negative thoughts, intrusive thoughts, voices
Metacognitive beliefs: positive and negative beliefs about thoughts and symptoms
Survival strategies
Thought control strategies
Thinking errors/biases
Allocation of attention
Memory

Behavioural
Self-medication
Avoidance/escape
Coping

Table 4.1 continued

Safety behaviours/neutralising
Compensatory strategies
Activity (or lack of)
Mastery and pleasure
Self-harm, impulsivity, risk taking, violence/aggression
Consequences

Emotion
Lability
What feelings are difficult?
Can they be labelled?
Blunting/absence of emotion
Hopelessness
Negativity
Guilt
Sadness
Enjoyment
Love/intimacy/loneliness
Fear/paranoia
Disgust
Anger/irritability
Frustration
Excitement/mania/hyperarousal
Isolation/alienated

Physical
Sleep
Side-effects
Appetite
Vim/energy
Substance use
Tiredness
Health
Body sensations
Sexual function
Weight loss/gain
Disability/sensory impairment
Physiological symptoms of anxiety
Drugs

Environment
Accommodation
Social networks: friends, carers, professionals
Vulnerabilities
Financial situation
Legal situation
Family relationships
Occupational/vocational stuff
Subcultural values
Religion

providing useful assessment information about hallucinations and delusions and for monitoring change in these symptoms. These scales assess dimensions of hallucinations and delusions, such as frequency, preoccupation, amount and severity of distress, impairment and conviction (for both); and location, loudness and control (for hallucinations). All items relate to the last week (although the scales can be adapted for other time-frames). They are easy to administer and are reliable and valid.

There are also several standardised structured psychiatric interviews that can be used to assess positive and negative symptoms. These often cover broad symptom areas, are relatively easy to administer and to train people in their use, and are reliable and valid. Examples include the Positive and Negative Syndrome Scale (PANSS: Kay & Opler, 1987; Opler, & Fiszbein, Kay, 1986) and the Brief Psychiatric Rating Scale (Ventura, Nuechterlein, Subotnik, Gutland and Gilbert, 2000). More detailed assessments suitable for people with diagnoses of schizophrenia include the Scale for the Assessment of Positive Symptoms (Andreason & Grove, 1986), the Scale for the Assessment of Negative Symptoms (Andreasen, 1989) and the Assessment of Thought, Language and Communication (Andreasen, 1979a, 1979b).

Several self-report measures can be used to assess psychotic experiences or beliefs in both patients and non-patients. These include the Beliefs about Voices Questionnaire (BAVQ: Chadwick & Birchwood, 1994), which assesses malevolent and benevolent beliefs about voices, and emotional and behavioural responses to voices (such as engagement and resistance). The Interpretation of Voices Inventory (Morrison et al., 2000) was developed to assess hypothetical interpretations of voices (so can be completed by people who are not currently hearing voices), and includes beliefs about loss of control as well as positive and negative beliefs about voices (this questionnaire is in the appendix). The Peters Delusions Inventory (PDI: Peters et al., 1999) measures the frequency, conviction, preoccupation and distress associated with a variety of unusual beliefs, and can be used with patients and non-patients. Other useful questionnaires examining predisposition to psychotic experiences include the Revised Launay-Slade Hallucination Scale (Morrison et al., 2002b), which examines vividness of imagery, visual halluci- nations and auditory hallucinations (this is in the appendix), and the Paranoia Scale (Fenigstein & Vanable, 1992). A particularly useful questionnaire is the Personal Beliefs about Illness Questionnaire (PBIQ: Birchwood et al., 1993), which examines the perceived consequences of psychosis for the person concerned; these include stigmatisation and seeing oneself as mentally ill.

Idiosyncratic measures designed with the patient can also be extremely valuable and can take the form of belief ratings (0–100 per cent), frequency counts or estimates of frequency, distress, intensity and other important dimensions using visual analogue scales or some other methods that the patient is comfortable with.

Behavioural tests and observational methods

Behavioural tests can be a very useful strategy for obtaining information about presenting problems. Such tests allow the therapist and patient to access information that may be unavailable from verbal questioning about a recent specific incident. Recreating such an incident often allows previously elusive thoughts, images, emotions or behaviours to be easily identified. For example, a patient who is paranoid may say that he or she felt uneasy yesterday when standing outside a shopping centre, but be unable to remember what was going through his or her mind. Taking the patient to the same place or somewhere similar may allow easy access to "hot" thoughts such as "Those people are reading my mind" and "They know that I am evil". Once such thoughts are identified, belief ratings can be taken and evidence in support of them elicited. Such thoughts may also be associated with safety behaviours that may be directly observable (e.g. putting on a woolly hat to try to prevent mind reading or to avoid eye contact) or that may be identified through questioning (e.g. thought control strategies).

Finally, it is important to remember that assessment is a continuous process that is ongoing throughout treatment. For instance, whether or not homework assignments are done may be a useful source of information (if it is not done the cause could be a fear of failure or the belief that writing something down may make it happen; if the homework is done extremely thoroughly this could be indicative of perfectionist tendencies or obsessional beliefs).

Chapter 5

Formulation of the case

Is formulation important?

Formulation is as intrinsically joined and necessary to therapy as fuel is to a motor vehicle. Formulation of psychological problems at both the maintenance level (what keeps a problem going once started) and the developmental or historical level (what may have caused the problem) are what has allowed successful development and application of cognitive therapy over the years. In essence, it must be stressed that the techniques and tools of cognitive therapy should be implemented only in the context of an understanding (on behalf of both the therapist and patient) of why the problem developed, how it is maintained, and why a particular intervention may be effective.

The cognitive formulation may be described as the therapist's compass and as such no clinician setting off with a patient on the voyage of therapy should be without it. Without our compass we have no idea of where to start, which direction to take, when to end and what to be on our guard for throughout the journey. As Goldfried (1995) wrote on the importance and role of formulation, "The assumption underlying the patient making links is that a clear and presumably more accurate formulation on the patient's part will serve to lower their emotional distress and promote more effective functioning" (p. 222). In 1976, Beck wrote that a specific formulation for each case is crucial to provide a framework for understanding the patient's maladaptive behaviour and modifying dysfunctional attitudes. Furthermore, formulations in clinical work guide the clinicians' understanding of the patients' difficulties and distress, help the patient to form an alternative understanding of their problems and guide the choice of intervention strategies.

It is generally recognised that patients who leave therapy feeling better, with high regard for their therapist but no idea of why they are better or what occurred, are not a treatment success. Over the years, cognitive therapy has been shown to be helpful with a wide range of patients with different disorders and these effects have been shown to be retained at follow-up. Thus, cognitive therapy has been shown to be effective not only in remitting psychopathology, but also in preventing relapse. What has this to do with formulation? Without a model for understanding our difficulties, or how they became entrenched or maintained, how can we begin to prevent them in the future? Also, how can we be motivated to engage in a therapeutic activity (both in and out of sessions) if we have little idea of how this relates to our difficulties and their maintenance?

What is a formulation and why should we do it?

In her book, *Cognitive therapy in practice: A case formulation approach*, Persons (1989) describes a case formulation as "a hypothesis about the nature of the psychological difficulties underlying the problems on the patient's problem list". She outlines two levels at which a model should conceptualise problems as occurring. First, there is the level of overt or real life difficulties. These are difficulties such as depression, paranoid beliefs, voices, distress about voices on behalf of the patient, or distressing beliefs such as ideas of reference or imagined physical deformation (e.g. a patient who believes her ears to be so large that people point and whisper at all times). Second, there is the level of underlying psychological mechanisms that are proposed to cause the overt difficulties.

For example, Claire (aged 33 years) had been given a diagnosis of schizophrenia at the age of 17. She would become highly distressed on hearing any sound and would think "there are bad men on the roof/outside who are going to attack me" *or* "the neighbours are talking about me and saying how bad I am". This would lead Claire to become highly anxious, withdraw to her room and check outside for intruders. This is the level of overt or life difficulties, and early models or formulations given to Claire spoke only at this level to give alternative explanations for her current distress. Initially, models shared with Claire talked simply about how interpretations of events such as a sound outside at night or a look from a neighbour can affect our mood and be affected by mood.

Persons (1989) outlines what she believes are nine of the most important roles of the case formulation. These roles are as applicable to patients with psychotic problems and to those classically treated with cognitive therapy. Their utility in working with this patient group is outlined here.

Understanding the relationships between problems

This can help both therapists and patients reduce what can appear to them a huge list of problems that appear insurmountable – the reduction by highlighting interrelationships can allow this to feel more manageable to the patient. The patient may come into therapy feeling that he or she has a whole array of difficulties which may appear a random collection of unrelated problems: voices, concerns about other people conspiring against them, fear of leaving the house, boredom, lack of social contacts, anxiety, low mood and tiredness. Without a formulation it may seem difficult to work out where to begin. However, the formulation will highlight the relationship between each of the difficulties and allow both patient and clinician to find that problem which must be tackled to allow others to be addressed.

For example, Helen was a 61-year-old woman who had an eighteen-year history of beliefs that she had formed a "special bond" with men whom she met by chance. At the time of referral, she believed herself to be in love with a man called Richard, who she had spoken to for the first time on the telephone five years previously, while attempting to contact the man who was the focus of her last attentions. She believed that Richard was also in love with her and wanted to be with her. She believed this despite his refusal to talk to her, his going ex-directory, asking family members to ask her to refrain from calling and not attending meetings that she informed him of by letter.

Helen had previously held similar beliefs about two other men in the past and her harassment of these two men had led to police involvement which culminated in her being bound over and served with a restraining order by a court. She had neither met nor seen Richard, but believed that they were meant for each other. She believed his lack of contact was due to being unsure of her feelings for him and that if she continued to inform him of her true feeling that this could be resolved.

During the initial therapy session, Helen spoke about Richard constantly and asked the therapist to facilitate a meeting and sort out their relationship. The therapist discussed this further and spoke about reviewing the evidence that was available so far about her relationship with Richard to help her decide what to do. At this point, Helen became extremely tearful and anxious, exclaiming "What if I find out that he is married like he says?" and "What if it really is true when he says he doesn't want me?" The therapist therefore worked with Helen to examine the advantages and disadvantages of finding out more about Richard's feelings. Helen felt that, rather than discover Richard's feelings, she would prefer to look at her relationship with her live-in partner.

Formulation of Helen's anger and frustration with her partner and her behaviour towards him showed both therapist and patient that this was due to thoughts such as "Richard won't come and live with me because he knows that your health is bad and that you love me and would go to pieces without me". On using this cognitive formulation, the therapist and Helen agreed that looking at her current relationship would not be useful before they were able to spend some more time evaluating her relationship with Richard.

Choosing a treatment modality

A formulation may predict the way in which the intervention should be focused. Should the therapy involve significant others or should it be individually based? For example, Celia had been given a diagnosis of schizophrenia fifteen years previously in her mid-teens. She experienced a wide range of anomalous experiences, many of which led her to produce frightening explanations for them. However, on assessment, it occurred that much of her anxiety centred around her fears that once frightened, her anxiety would immediately lead her to become increasingly ill, culminating in her hospitalisation (this catastrophic fear of relapse is very common in people with psychosis, and is often the result of aversive contacts with mental health services).

This belief was maintained, in part, by her mother (who, it appeared, would meet DSM-IV diagnoses for both generalised anxiety disorder (GAD) and panic disorder), who would immediately distract Celia once she became anxious. Following initial sessions where Celia was socialised to the cognitive model of emotion and asked to record her thoughts when anxious, her homework was returned uncompleted because she reported that her mother had informed her that it was unhelpful for her to spend more time contemplating her concerns.

Following this information, this block to therapy was added to the formulation and used to help understand why Celia had not gathered any information to disconfirm any of her concerns. This new formulation was used to help patient and therapist decide that any therapy was likely to be more successful if both the rationale and treatment protocol were shared with all family members.

Choosing an intervention strategy

A formulation may help to predict ways to intervene. This can also allow the clinician and patient to understand difficulties that may emerge, and whether ambivalence about changing one behaviour constitutes a difficulty for the changing of another targeted behaviour. An obvious example of this is the relationship between voices and the patient's beliefs about their omnipotence and cause. Helping patients to ascertain whether it is their experience of the voices, concerns about their origins, or worries about the effect that the voices may have on their behaviour which causes distress can help patients understand the relationship between thoughts and emotions and decide which one should be examined first.

Choosing an intervention point

The formulation may point to a place where the intervention has to begin for treatment successes to occur. For example, if a patient wished to address his or her lack of social relationships as the first goal, but feared that leaving the house would lead him or her to be attacked, then the latter fear would have to be tackled before the patient was able to engage in any social situations.

Predicting behaviour and understanding and managing non-compliance

The formulation is used to help the therapist predict the patient's behaviour, and it is especially useful in predicting difficulties in the treatment process (e.g. difficulties in completing homework). For example, Janet was a 60-year-old woman with continuous auditory hallucinations and pervasive delusional beliefs. She believed that her voices were being beamed down from satellites in the sky as arranged by her old neighbours, the police, a solicitor she had had previous dealings with and her present neighbours. She believed this to be due to her being punished for a few items that she had stolen thirty years previously.

Janet's early life had been exceptionally difficult and she had frequently been told that she was stupid and it appeared that her husband was currently reinforcing this message. When asked what she should do for homework in relation to the items on the agenda for that session, she would become distressed, saying "I'm too stupid".

This core belief was included in the formulation and together the therapist and patient discussed how it might affect her engagement in therapy and her attempting of homework assignments. Therefore, this belief (and others such as "I deserve to be punished") had to be tackled before Janet could begin to look at different interpretations of her experiences.

Understanding and working on relationship difficulties

This may be a particularly important role in working with patients with psychotic experiences. It is not unusual for delusional beliefs to incorporate the psychiatric system (e.g. in a conspiracy theory). Additionally, many patients will have had aversive experiences at the hands of the mental health system over the years. It is likely that at some point, they may have been admitted to hospital against their will, been given a stigmatising label or told that non-compliance with a treatment regime would culminate in an involuntary admission. It is important to incorporate such information in a case formulation.

Making decisions about extra-therapy issues

For example, should the therapist become involved in supporting applications for rehousing or additional benefits? The formulation should be used to answer questions, such as "Are these difficulties caused by beliefs about self-efficacy rather than skills deficits?" If this is the case the clinician and patient should be aware of this and use therapy to help the patient accurately assess their self-efficacy. If the therapist simply attempted to solve the problem for the patient this would not be possible, and may lead to a further decline in beliefs regarding self-efficacy.

Redirecting an unsuccessful treatment

The failure of an intervention may suggest that the formulation is incorrect or incomplete. At this point, collaborative efforts must be taken to review the formulation and understand omissions or inaccuracies that have led to the incorrect application of therapeutic strategies.

Perhaps it is when working with individuals with psychosis that the importance of the formulation can be emphasised most. The patient may well be fearful, apprehensive, have little understanding of why a therapist may be able to help with problems that may appear (to them) so external to the field of mental health, and have little idea of the likely benefits of struggling with psychological techniques. A case formulation can be vital in addressing each of these issues.

The use of formulation in working with individuals with psychosis

Normalisation: an alternative to a bad choice

When working with individuals with psychosis, the formulation will have an extremely important role in the normalisation of psychotic experiences. Most patients will be faced with one of two options. Consider patients who believe that their voices are the result of persecution by "new people about to be born". They are likely to be faced with the choice between believing that they are genuinely being persecuted, or that they have a severe mental illness known as schizophrenia. The latter explanation may have a negative effect on their self-esteem (and may be more distressing than the former) and might be fairly difficult to believe with no mediating explanation of how this "illness" or "brain disease" leads them to hear voices which appear to know so much about them, their lives and their internal mental processes. Recent psychological studies have led us to believe that experiences such as hearing voices are, in fact, on a continuum of normal experience and much more common than previously thought (see Chapter 3). If some of this information can be imparted to our patients as part of our formulation, not only does it present an alternative to the patients' delusional beliefs, but it also presents a realistic one, backed by research evidence and one which allows the maintenance of self-esteem.

A psychological formulation at both the maintenance level (including cognitive models of hallucinations and delusions) and at the historical level (including an understanding of how past events can affect beliefs and assumptions so that a critical incident may make these active, and coupled with an understanding of how some people might misattribute heard thoughts to an external source), can help the patients to hold another more helpful and perhaps plausible explanation of their experiences. Following this, the clinician and patient may begin to explore the evidence for each of the remaining hypotheses.

Examining and explaining the "why me?" question

Because of the stigma that is often associated with a diagnosis of schizophrenia, it is important to give patients an alternative explanation for the development of their difficulties. Models of psychosis and of the development of psychosis can help to provide alternative models of understanding difficult symptoms, which may be more acceptable to patients.

Prevention of relapse

A formulation and alternative understanding of development and maintenance of difficulties should help patients identify their vulnerabilities and the factors that are maintaining their symptomatology. Once identified, the formulation should help patients identify those circumstances that may cause difficulties in the future and to identify and assess anomalous experiences and cognitions which might otherwise lead to the exacerbation of their psychotic experiences.

Engagement

As mentioned earlier, a shared formulation allows both patient and clinician to engage in the collaborative evaluation of an alternative hypothesis or explanation for symptomatology. This shared model and its shared exploration helps the engagement process since clinician and patient are both involved in the shared search for information and an understanding of the patient's difficulties, rather than in an expert and patient model.

How to conceptualise a patient's difficulties

It is important to recognise that the development and the use of the case formulation cannot be viewed as discrete processes, but rather is a working hypothesis. Both the development and the use of the formulation should be considered to be ongoing and modifiable throughout the therapy. The development of a case formulation begins on meeting the patient, although the referral letter, discussions with other professionals in the team, ward staff and perhaps family members, and knowledge of the condition's associated psychopathology may guide the assessment. Therefore, the therapist should ensure that the assessment is thorough and continuous throughout treatment.

In short, a case formulation involves information regarding

- the patient's current problems
- development of hypotheses regarding underlying mechanisms
- the relationships of these mechanisms to their current problems
- the precipitants of the current problems
- the maintenance of the current problems
- the origins of the central problems
- predicted obstacles to treatment
- underlying mechanisms and maintenance cycles regarding other current problems.

Importance of collaboration

One of the most important factors in the delivery of cognitive therapy is the principle of collaboration. The idea is that the clinician and the patient work as a team in identifying possible hypotheses for understanding difficulties and work to evaluate the extent to which each of these can explain what is going on. If patients have been within the mental health system for a number of years, hearing voices and having delusional explanations for these voices, they may have repeatedly been given an alternative (medical) explanation for these problems. They will have been given a diagnosis of schizophrenia, and been told that this is the cause of their voices and that neuroleptic medication should alleviate these. For their distress, disability and delusional beliefs to have continued, it appears likely that this explanation has had little impact on their perception of their problems. Clinical models of psychopathology may seem very clever to us, but unless models appear relevant to our patients, they will not be prepared to engage in an evidence search and this will not change their current thinking and distress levels.

Different levels of formulation

Stress-vulnerability

The stress-vulnerability model (Zubin & Spring, 1977) states that individuals have different levels of vulnerability or predisposition to certain symptoms, difficulties or illnesses (this may be biological or genetic in origin, or as a result of early life difficulties and psychological factors). This interacts with the level of stress that the individual comes into contact with. Thus, an individual with a high level of vulnerability may need only a small amount of stress in daily life to tip them over the edge from being asymptomatic to being symptomatic. Conversely, a patient with a low vulnerability may need to encounter much larger stressors prior to a psychotic episode. See Figure 5.1 for a diagrammatic representation of this model.

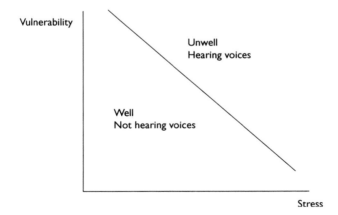

Figure 5.1 The stress-vulnerability model

Cognitive models of understanding emotional reactions

A simple model of understanding distress is often the first model presented to patients. This model explains how internal events (intrusive thoughts, anomalous experiences, bodily sensations, thoughts, memories, etc.) and external events (things said by other people, noises, smells, things said on television, letters arriving by post, things "seen" or "heard" by patients and not experienced by others in the environment, interactions with others) are perceived in a certain way by the patient. It is this interpretation of the event and the meaning attached to it that leads to distress, rather than the event itself. See Figure 5.2 for diagrammatic representations of this kind of model.

Cognitive models of the development and maintenance of psychotic symptoms

Cognitive models of specific psychotic symptoms, such as the model of voices outlined in Chapter 3, can be useful in formulating the distress associated with such difficulties. See Figure 5.3 for an example of a case formulation based on this model. Bill, 37, heard third-person voices that told him he was mad and that he would have to go to psychiatric hospital, and they also discussed him never getting a girlfriend and told him he would get into fights. He believed that the voices were a higher power communicating with him, and that they would make him

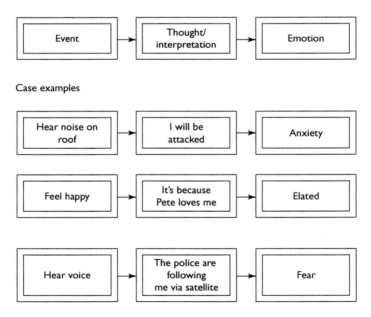

Figure 5.2 A cognitive model of maintenance of emotional distress

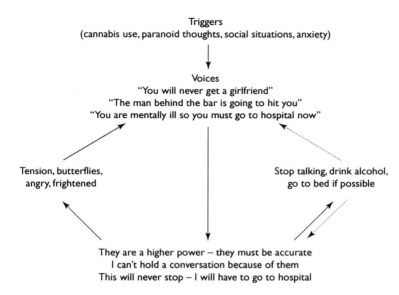

Triggers
(cannabis use, paranoid thoughts, social situations, anxiety)

Voices
"You will never get a girlfriend"
"The man behind the bar is going to hit you"
"You are mentally ill so you must go to hospital now"

Tension, butterflies,
angry, frightened

Stop talking, drink alcohol,
go to bed if possible

They are a higher power – they must be accurate
I can't hold a conversation because of them
This will never stop – I will have to go to hospital

Figure 5.3 A formulation of the maintenance of voices

end up in hospital and also make him appear foolish in social situations. He therefore felt upset and tried to avoid these feared outcomes by adopting safety behaviours such as drinking alcohol or spending long periods in bed.

Developmental formulations

It can also be useful to incorporate in the formulation the development of key beliefs and assumptions, and the early experiences that led to this. This can be done using idiosyncratic formulations derived from the specific model of psychosis outlined in Chapter 3. See Figure 5.4 for an example of this kind of formulation in relation to Doug (35 years of age), who was very concerned about being attacked when he left his house, and experienced highly vivid images of being assaulted. He was hypervigilant for threat, which seemed to be related to his experiences of prison, where he believed paranoia to be a useful survival strategy.

Alternatively, the generic Beckian cognitive model of emotional disorders can be used to incorporate much of the same kind of information. For example, Steve (aged 25) was referred to the service by his community psychiatric nurse (CPN) and his consultant psychiatrist. He had a huge array of delusional beliefs and had been hospitalised on many occasions. He believed himself to be a variety of pop stars, footballers, actors and celebrities, and spoke about how numerous actresses had lost their virginity to him. When any new books were published, Steve believed that either he had written them or they were in fact a biography based on his life.

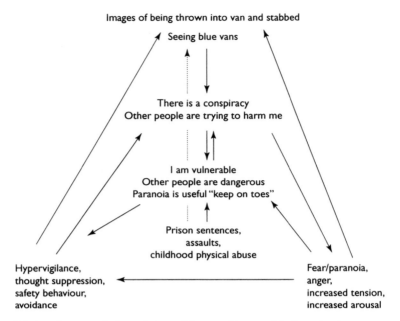

Figure 5.4 An idiosyncratic formulation of the cognitive model of psychosis

Steve had not been free of delusions since his first contact with services fifteen years previously, although at times he was less bothered by them. During periods of hospitalisation, this was often preceded by his concern that the record companies owed him money for royalties or that his mother and stepfather had stolen millions of his money. At these times, he would become aggressive to his parents and would take compact discs from record stores in lieu of royalties and would become quite distressed if this were questioned. He held these beliefs with total conviction and was at first unwilling to look at the evidence pertaining to them.

Due to the nature of Steve's difficulties, and the feeling that his grandiose delusions were in some way protective of his self-esteem, we decided to look at his early experiences and the development of his ideas. His recall of his early life had become peppered with grandiose delusions although much of the memory of his history appeared relatively intact. He described his father as a heavy drinker who became violent at times. When Steve was 9 years old, following a period with "lots of drinking and lots of arguments", his parents split up and he moved away with his mother and the man that she had been seeing. He describes this as an unhappy time in his life, saying he felt cut off and left out. He said that his mother and her boyfriend were very strict and that no one talked to him. At the same time he changed school, and while describing being the most popular person in the school, playing professional basketball, filming movies on the premises and being the "hardest" person in the school whom kids would come from miles around to try and beat, he also acknowledged that he was bullied at this point. He described feeling picked on by the teachers and always getting worse grades than he thought he deserved.

In his late teens Steve began taking acid, ecstasy, hallucinogenic mushrooms and amphetamines and would steal money from his mother to finance his substance use. Things came to a head following his school examinations when he was the only one of his peer group to get bad grades. He describes breaking down at this point and being unable to understand why his grades were so bad. He began to spend long hours trying to work it out, pondering whether it was a consequence of anti-Irish sentiment (his surname is Irish) or of jealousy for his other achievements. He began to spend hours sitting alone and went on "a search for god". See Figure 5.5 for the formulation that was developed on the basis of this information.

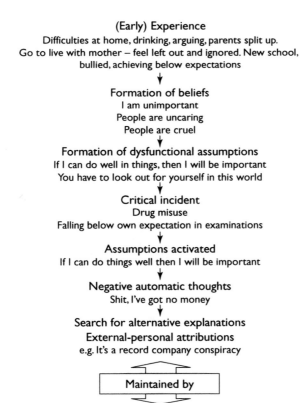

Figure 5.5 A Beckian historical formulation

The formulation assumes that, when Steve's dysfunctional assumptions were highlighted and the conditions necessary to satisfy them were not met, that the threat to his self-esteem was so great that the external-personal attributional style he had developed became accentuated and was utilised in an attempt to protect his self-esteem (as Bentall's work suggests).

When to use each type of formulation

Presenting developmental or maintenance formulations

As mentioned earlier, the cognitive formulation is a compass to guide both the therapist and patient through the maze of therapy. It is a guide rather than a rule and should change throughout the course of therapy as both parties discover more about the maintenance and cause of the patient's difficulties.

One of the questions most frequently asked by novice cognitive therapists is what formulation to use at what stage in therapy. Should they find out all about their patient's early life and form a historical formulation, should they assume a stress-vulnerability model, should they begin to explore basic links between cognition and affect or behaviour, or should they present a complex cognitive formulation of hallucinations of delusions? There is no simple answer to this problem, because the formulation should be related to the question that needs to be answered or to the information that needs to be relayed to the patient at the given point in therapy. Deciding which approach to take will depend on many factors, some of which will be unique to the patient.

The formulation used at any point may depend on the goals of the patient: what is it that the patient wants to achieve? If the patient's goal is to feel less upset in the evening when their voices are at the worst, then it may be useful to present an alternative psychological formulation of voices. However, should the first goal be to be less upset when rowing with a friend, it may be useful to help the patient understand basic links between cognition and affect in order to identify factors that mediate in the emotional state following such events. Another factor that should be taken into account is the patient's need for information. The therapist should consider whether it is important to provide normalisation about psychotic experiences at each point in treatment, and also which issues seem most important to the patient at that particular time. If the patient appears overwhelmed by the question of why his or her difficulties have arisen ("Why me?"), a developmental formulation may be most helpful.

Decisions about formulation should also be informed by the stage of treatment that the patient has reached. What has been achieved so far? What has or has not been helpful? How has the patient dealt with earlier formulations? How does the patient now understand his or her difficulties?

For example, Mary (aged 34 years) had a long history of persecutory delusions. She was virtually housebound (unless accompanied by her father for hospital visits) and in a constant state of arousal due to her fears that others were "telling lies about me to frame me". Previous formulations had looked at her interpretations of ambiguous stimuli and had tried to demonstrate how information-processing biases might render these inaccurate. Treatments based on this approach (e.g. thought records and behavioural experiments) had been unsuccessful. Therefore, the therapist and patient devised a developmental formulation looking at how her beliefs about her own vulnerability and the cruelty of others may have been the result of the bullying and rape she suffered during her school years. This formulation was developed to understand why Mary would interpret any ambiguous looks from other people as sinister and threatening. This level of formulation allowed Mary to develop an alternative model of why she felt persecuted in certain situations. While she had previously been unable to review the evidence for her persecutory delusions, she was now able to question herself ("Is it possible that instead of them telling lies about me earlier today, I think like this because of what happened to me when I was younger?").

The level of formulation shared with the patient may also be affected by current cognitive deficits or limitations, the level of understanding of the patient, or by factors such as medication effects and side-effects. It may also be important to consider the patient's own formulation of his or her difficulties and whether they sit well with the different formulations the therapist may offer.

Again, it is important to stress that there is no definite answer with respect to what formulation to use at any particular time. However, an idea of a usual sequence of formulations is outlined later in the chapter. Most important is always to be guided by the patient and always remember to ask his or her opinion about the utility, timing and appropriateness of any formulation given.

Other difficulties

Many patients with psychosis have extremely high levels of arousal and may be very distracted during sessions because of auditory, visual, tactile or olfactory hallucinations. The therapist may also be incorporated into the patient's delusional system, thus reducing his or her capacity for attention to information and engagement in the session. Coupled with these difficulties, they may be on high levels of neuroleptic medication, tranquillisers and anticholinergic drugs (used to control neuroleptic side-effects, but unfortunately having side-effects of their own, including detrimental effects on memory).

Socialising the patient to the formulation

The formulation should be developed collaboratively with the patient and presented as one of many possible hypotheses for understanding the problem in question. The patient and therapist should then enter a stage of working to evaluate whether it is a helpful and valid explanation of the problem. The formulation can be placed alongside any number of others, which the patient considered might be plausible options.

Typical progression of formulations

Often the process may look similar to that drawn out here.

1   *Normalisation information.* This involves presenting patients with information about their experiences and how they lie on the continuum with normal experience.
2   *Models to help patients understand current feelings of distress:*

   • noticing anomalous experiences or events in their environment
   • linking these to the interpretation made by the patient about these
   • linking this to the affective state experienced by the patient and the behaviour in which he or she later performs
   • linking problematic behaviour to the recurrence of events or the maintenance of interpretations
   • understanding some information-processing biases that are present or can occur in people with psychotic or emotional difficulties, e.g. thinking errors, changes in memory recall, changes in selective attention and the biased interpretation of ambiguous material
   • understanding how these can affect thinking
   • learning that these processes may lead to non-evidence based or inaccurate thoughts
   • understanding how this can lead to further information-processing changes that maintain beliefs.

3   *Models of particular symptomatology that patients place on their problem and goal list* (e.g. cognitive models of delusions or hallucinations). For example, Claire (mentioned earlier) had been ill since she was 17 and had numerous "strange" ideas and experiences. She had many auditory and visual hallucinations involving teddy bears running towards her and would see large men in cars ready to attack her. During early sessions with Claire, one of the difficulties which appeared to most distress her was her fear that she was either 1 year old or 100 years old (this occurred about three or four times a day). At these times she believed that, if she looked in the mirror, she would see herself aged accordingly. On questioning, it appeared that this thought occurred only when aeroplanes were flying above her. Claire and her therapist began to examine this experience and discovered that when planes were overhead Claire would think about life and death and her own beliefs about her own vulnerability. This would cause Claire to feel anxious and the physiological consequences of this included muscle tightness in the facial area. She would then interpret this experience as evidence that she was 1 or 100 years old. Because she believed this so strongly she would rarely go near glass or mirrors. If she did happen to glance in a mirror for a micro-second, her strong expectations would lead her to imagine a baby's or an elderly woman's face.

4   *Other maintenance formulations.* The therapist might consider whether the patient has Axis I problems additional to psychotic symptomatology (e.g. panic disorder or social phobia)? Such difficulties may present problems in themselves and may also tie in and exacerbate the patient's psychotic experiences.

5   *Problem development: stress-vulnerability models.* This may involve helping patients to understand why their difficulties developed when they did. The presentation of specific hypotheses about the interaction between stressors and personal vulnerability factors may begin to allow patients to understand why their difficulties developed at a particular point in their life.

6   *Historical formulations for understanding problem development and vulnerability.* Finally, the therapist and patient can draft a historical understanding of the development of their difficulties. The patient's early experiences are elicited to help the patient and therapist discover the core beliefs and underlying assumptions set down by critical events. This may further facilitate an understanding of how particular kinds of incidents can trigger dysfunctional assumptions and hence lead to the generation of negative automatic thoughts. Historical formulations often come towards the end of therapy in order to aid relapse prevention. However, they can be used much earlier in therapy if the patient asks "Why me?", if the therapy becomes stuck, or if the patient hands the therapist relevant information on a plate.

For example, Mary (mentioned earlier) had an array of pervasive persecutory delusions, which caused her much fear and prevented her from leaving her house. The movement of anyone past her flat, people on the radio or TV or newspaper articles, would cause her to become upset. Work focused on this symptom proved unsuccessful but the development of a historical formulation (incorporating her experiences of being raped and bullied) allowed Mary to adopt an alternative explanation and reduce the distress caused by her delusional beliefs.

The development of a case formulation in cognitive therapy

The development of a case formulation is done using both direct and indirect sources of information. Indirect information consists of knowledge about the nature of the disorder(s) and its maintaining factors, cultural factors and external events in the patient's environment. Direct sources of information are those elicited from the patient or others present at interview, and include automatic thoughts and feelings and non-verbal behaviour, both in and out of the therapeutic interview, and behaviours elsewhere that are described by the patient.

The therapist uses a combination of direct and indirect information to decide on and personalise the formulation, which should be shared with the patient. When dealing with patients with psychosis, care must be taken to suggest that the formulation is one possible hypothesis that can be checked out alongside others.

It must be remembered that the formulation is used as a guide for therapy and not a prescriptive rule. As such, the formulation must make sense to both the therapist and the patient so that both can be following the same path of treatment. Thus, therapists must always remember to ask their patients how the formulation fits with their experiences and to utilise their feedback to modify the formulation if required.

Part II

Process of therapy and change strategies

Chapter 6

The principles and structure of therapy

This chapter considers the principles and structure of cognitive therapy for psychosis, both in relation to individual treatment sessions and the overall sequence of therapy. Structure in treatment is an essential characteristic of cognitive therapy regardless of diagnosis. Structure within individual sessions helps both patient and therapist to focus on a specific topic and the related discrete targets. It enhances collaboration and fosters shared responsibility for session content, setting the scene for shared responsibility for activity both in sessions and between sessions. Longitudinal structure is important when summarising treatment both during the active phase and when addressing relapse management. Demonstrating and sharing a structured logical process in therapy helps the patient make sense of therapy, both during and after the event. The patient needs to know what has been covered and why, and what is to come during active treatment. Planning relapse prevention or management focuses on the gains the patient has made, how they were made, what skills were acquired, and how they will be put into practice in the future.

Patients with psychotic symptoms benefit from structure but may take a while to be able to operate effectively within it. Collaboratively ensuring that the structure is adhered to is a positive, if novel, experience for most people; rigid adherence enforced by the therapist, however, is potentially negative and will have a significant effect on collaboration and the therapeutic relationship. Structure has to be balanced and manipulated to meet the patient's needs, rather than slavishly followed. While cognitive therapy sessions are usually about an hour long and generally occur at weekly intervals, some patients who experience psychotic symptoms may only be able to tolerate shorter or less frequent sessions.

The following section will help practitioners identify what should be done during a therapy session, why it should be done and how it might be done with people who experience psychotic symptoms.

The principles of cognitive therapy

Inherent within the practice of cognitive therapy are the main principles or features of this therapy, which should enable the practitioner to maximise their treatment efficacy and adherence to the model. Primarily, *cognitive therapy is based on the cognitive model of emotional disorders* and is thus theory and model driven rather than a collection of techniques. Additionally, as Judy Beck (1995) points out, this should be based on an ever-evolving formulation which is constantly refined throughout therapy as additional data are obtained. Both the model and individual conceptualisations are explicitly shared with the patient throughout therapy.

Second, *cognitive therapy is educational and collaborative*. This means that the patient and the therapist agree on targets and then set out ways in which these can be achieved. Early on in therapy the therapist may need to be more didactic in the presentation of information and take a stronger role in the setting of the sessions agenda, but this should become a more evenly split task throughout therapy. Collaboration is especially important when working with psychotic patients for reasons that are discussed later in this book.

Third, *cognitive therapy aims to be time limited*, and while this is mainly between ten and twenty sessions, the important feature is the explicit time limitation that is given to the patient, with reviews being used to collaboratively decide on the need for further intervention. Within this time-limited format, explicit and realistic targets or goals are collaboratively set which are assessed by both parties to be appropriate for the decided contract.

Fourth, *cognitive therapists primarily use the Socratic method (guided discovery)*. That is to say, instead of providing answers to the patients' questions or problematic negative automatic thoughts, the therapist asks questions which help the patients to provide their own answers. By utilising this therapeutic strategy, the patients will have an understanding of the process of therapy, rather than purely the results, and can, therefore, be active participants in their own recovery and relapse prevention.

In her keynote address at the European Congress of Behavioural and Cognitive Therapies in 1993, Christine Padesky outlined her view of the importance of using a Socratic dialogue style. She expressed the opinion that if we lose the collaborative empiricism of cognitive therapy, we lose its long-term benefits. She argued that the goal of cognitive therapy is not simply to make our clients think differently or feel better today, but rather to teach our clients a process of evaluating their goals, thoughts, behaviours and moods so that they can learn methods for improving their lives for many years to come. She postulates that this is achieved largely through true Socratic questioning for which she offers a definition:

> Socratic questioning involves asking the client questions which (1) the client has the knowledge to answer, (2) draw the client's attention to information which is relevant to the issue being discussed but which may be outside to the client's current focus, (3) generally move from the concrete to the more abstract so that (4) the client can, in the end, apply the new information to either re-evaluate a previous conclusion or construct a new idea.
>
> (Padesky, 1993b)

The fifth feature of cognitive therapy is that *a sound therapeutic relationship is a necessary condition of good cognitive therapy*. A patient must be able to feel that she or he is able to trust the therapist and will be taken seriously by the therapist. While this may be uncomplicated for some patients referred with Axis I problems, engaging people with psychosis in a therapeutic relationship may be more problematic and can be a suitable focus for initial treatment. The need for a sound therapeutic relationship can be illustrated by the following analogy. If you are stuck, fearful and shaking, halfway up a cliff and perched on a small ledge, a rescuer would need to possess both of the following attributes to help you return to solid ground: first, the necessary skills and tools to help you climb up or down the rock face, and second, the ability to induce trust in him or her so that you will be able to utilise these techniques in your ascent or descent. Either of these skills existing in isolation would not allow clients to develop the necessary confidence needed to disrupt their current status quo. The therapeutic relationship with people with psychosis is examined in more detail in Chapter 7.

Finally, *cognitive therapy is structured and problem orientated*. Each session starts with an agenda that is decided on by both the therapist and the patient and specifies which problems will be tackled within the session and any educational information that needs to be taught. The therapist will help the patient to identify the obstacles that hinder him or her in problem solving. These can be skill deficits or dysfunctional ideas that impede the use of previously acquired skills. Alongside this, *homework* is always agreed at the end of the session and should involve a task that is relevant to the present goal and decided on in collaboration. The homework should not only be relevant for the patient's progress in therapy, but also enable them to understand the process of therapy and determine future directions for implementing their learned therapeutic techniques. Structure in therapy sessions is particularly important when working with people with thought disorder.

Although these basic principles apply to the practice of cognitive therapy with all patients, therapy does vary considerably according to a number of factors. These include the difficulties of the individual, his or her goals, the ability to form a strong therapeutic relationship, motivation to change and previous experiences in therapy. The emphasis in treatment depends on the particular problems that the patient presents with.

Judy Beck (1995) outlines the three stages which she feels constitute the development of expertise as a cognitive therapist. In stage one therapists learn to structure the sessions, to use basic techniques and to learn the basic skills of conceptualising a case in cognitive terms based on information gleaned during the session. In stage two "therapists begin integrating their conceptualisation with their knowledge of techniques", strengthening their ability to understand the flow of therapy and to identify critical goals of therapy. Alongside this, they expand their repertoire of techniques and become "more proficient in selecting, timing and implementing appropriate techniques". Finally, at stage three, therapists automatically integrate new data into the conceptualisation. They are able to "refine their ability to make hypotheses to confirm their view of the patient and his or her difficulties" and are able to vary the structure and techniques of basic cognitive therapy as appropriate, particularly for difficult cases.

The structure of individual treatment sessions

A format for structuring individual treatment sessions, developed by Blackburn and Davidson (1995), identifies six sections of an effective session structure for cognitive therapy:

- reviewing the patient's state
- setting the agenda
- reviewing homework
- identifying session targets
- agreeing homework
- eliciting feedback.

Reviewing the patient's state

Review of the patient's state should include the current state and the time between sessions and is usually generated by asking the patient how things have been since the last session. It is vital not to allow this part of the session to develop into an elongated description, by the patient, of the past week; this section is for the therapist to gain some idea of what has happened that is significant for the person, and should be done in a very short time. Too much time spent on this reduces the time available for other sections and once this pattern is established in sessions it can be difficult to change. One way to limit this is to recognise quickly what has meaning for the person, and say, "It sounds like this was/is really important for you, is it something we should make time for and discuss today?" Patients then feel they are being listened to and understood, and the opportunity for exploration is assured. If patients report their state to be "Well, just the same", then the therapist will need to use more specific questioning to elicit experiences that might generate material that has meaning for therapy. A starting point could be to find out what the person has been doing and looking for any clues that might indicate significance (i.e. things such as an affect shift and other non-verbal changes). Asking about what the person has enjoyed that week or done differently may be helpful. If it is not possible to elicit any material from these enquiries it is worth going back to material from the previous session that the patient indicated was a problem and checking out what has been happening in that area. A structured approach to the review of the last week, making ratings of dimensions of target problems identified on the problem list can be useful (e.g. frequency and duration of voices or going out; conviction in a certain belief, intensity of affect). Using material from the patient's current and recent experiences makes the agenda more relevant for the patient and enhances collaboration; homework will be agreed from session targets and adherence will be influenced by relevance of subject. When checking out the current situation it is often useful to check whether there has been any change in medication, especially if the person presents differently. If someone appears tired, agitated, or restless, this will have a significant effect on the session and will need addressing at the start (it may need to be an agenda item in itself).

Setting the agenda

Setting the agenda is crucial if structure is to be introduced and adhered to. It must be set collaboratively and the items must have meaning for the patient and the therapy. Asking patients what they think should be included in the agenda does not mean the patient sets the agenda but that all the items are negotiated by patient and therapist. If the therapist suggests an item, a brief rationale for its inclusion should be given (this helps in negotiation to decide if it should be on the agenda, if it is what priority it should be given, and how much time it should be given). Some patients may find it difficult to tolerate an hour of therapy without breaks and the therapist should agree with the patient on whether breaks should be included, how long they should be and when they should occur. Including breaks can reduce anxiety, enhance concentration and make it more likely that the patient will attend further sessions. Recognition by the therapist that therapy may be a difficult undertaking for the person also strengthens the therapeutic alliance.

One common problem when setting agendas is the temptation to put too much on them. Less is more in this case (and particularly so for psychotic patients). Too many items will either lead to running out of time or moving too quickly through them and not dealing effectively with items. Themes and concepts need to be tackled slowly and may need to be repeated many times. Feedback from patients to check out their understanding is a regular feature; this does not mean getting a yes or no answer, but rather entails patients outlining their understanding of an issue, which frequently takes time. The reality is that in a one-hour session, after the five other sections are covered, there is likely to be only a maximum of thirty minutes for session targets.

The cognitive model, and the idiosyncratic case formulation, will inform what items the therapist will want to negotiate for the agenda. However, this will obviously be influenced by changes in the patient's state and experiences. When working with patients who experience psychotic symptoms, it is important, in the early sessions, to recognise the effects of medication, thought disorder, cognitive and memory deficits, and negative symptoms. These factors should then be put on the agenda, and discussed as possible influences for both the patient and the therapist to be aware of in therapy.

Once the agenda items have been agreed the order needs to be negotiated and prioritised. Homework review almost always comes first and agreeing future homework is the penultimate section. Reviewing homework will generate information to be used in session targets and agreed homework will relate to issues covered in the session. The items in between may follow a natural course and it would be sensible to utilise that and make the move from one item to another logical and related. Again, negotiation is the key; encourage the patient to experience having shared control and responsibility for activity in therapy. Deciding the time to be allocated to them and who will be the timekeeper must follow decisions regarding the items and the order. This may not need to be rigidly adhered to; if something important emerges and needs to be dealt with immediately then extra time should be negotiated.

All these points make the session efficient without making it seem too formal. At first it may feel odd for the therapist to conduct a session this way, but the benefits of structure quickly become apparent and, just as the therapist becomes comfortable with it, so does the patient. Indeed, many patients report feeling secure in the knowledge that an agenda will be set, since it adds predictability to the sessions and ensures that they have a forum to ensure that their concerns are identified early and will be listened to.

Reviewing homework

Homework review must be done thoroughly and there are key facts to be established: how much of the homework was done? Not all patients will do all of the homework all of the time. When it has been completed then appropriate positive feedback should be given, but a word of caution: if it was easily done it may not be significant in terms of achievement or accuracy. If the patient has done none of the homework, then ask what stopped him or her in a way that suggests you are seeking to learn from that information rather than it appearing to be a demand for an explanation. If it is at all amenable, homework that has not been completed can be done in the session, which emphasises its importance. For example, if homework was to fill in a record about thoughts, emotions and behaviours, this could be done retrospectively within the session.

What was easy and what was difficult? This information will inform choices of future homework and help identify possible obstacles, both internal and external to the patient. What did the person do to overcome any difficulties? This will help establish patients' repertoire of strategies, how much effort they are prepared to put into homework tasks, and how they generally view and cope with their problems. All this information will inform the discussion aimed at generating the next homework task and enhancing adherence. Has anything changed as a result of doing the homework? This allows a check of the significance of the task. If nothing has changed, then it is worth the therapist considering whether or not the homework was useful.

How will the information relating to homework be incorporated into the session targets? The agreed homework should be related to the previous session's targets and will have a clear link with those of the current session. Both positive and negative experiences of homework should be explored within the session, with reference to the formulation. There may, however, be occasions when homework generates something unexpected that cannot be ignored (e.g. suicidal ideation), and this will have to be placed on the agenda as a matter of urgency.

Identifying session targets

Session targets are directly related to the agenda items and occupy the bulk of the session. Within each area thoughts are identified and evaluated and alternatives are generated and discussed; the relationship of these thoughts to feelings and behaviour are then examined. The possibility of introducing change is explored, along with strategies for how this might be achieved. This sets the scene for the agreement of homework tasks.

Agreeing homework

Homework is collaboratively agreed upon and clearly relates to a problem area identified in the session target(s). Homework can be used to collect information or to test hypotheses in the form of behavioural experiments. There are a number of factors that can influence homework completion and should be addressed in this section of the session. The homework should be achievable and meaningful for the person both in how it relates to his or her problems and the expected gains for effort made. The actual task should be defined in detail with examples given in the session and written examples given to the patient alongside recording sheets. When using recording sheets endeavour to include clear, typed instructions on the form, as handwritten forms are more easily ignored, dismissed or forgotten by the patient. Give the patient enough copies to collect an amount of information which will be useful; if you give only one page, that is likely what will be returned. Giving the patient a folder to keep all the paperwork that will be amassed during therapy makes it less likely that homework will be lost, put off or disregarded. The rationale for attempting the homework should be fully agreed on and understood by the patient and, where possible, written down by the patient. Understanding must be established before beginning to look at obstacles and the gains for completing the work made explicit. Possible difficulties should be generated, and tasks may be revised after taking these into account if it is unlikely that they can be surmounted. Where possible, the patient should be encouraged to use problem solving to identify possible solutions with prompts from the therapist. If the patient cannot identify any homework, the therapist may have to suggest some and it could be useful to ask the patient what percentage of the homework he or she thinks will be achieved; if less than 100 per cent is the answer, then the reason for the shortfall can be discussed. Encourage the patient to be honest about difficulties; for instance, acknowledging that medication can make a person feel tired or apathetic, and may cause memory problems or interfere with thought processes, can make it easier to admit to a problem without fearing criticism for being lazy. Further discussion of the integration of homework in therapy can be found in Chapter 14.

Eliciting feedback

Feedback is elicited throughout the session when dealing with specific issues but must also take place at the end of the session in order to establish overall reactions to the session and the process of therapy. Feedback is also given as well as elicited. The therapist should use the agenda items to cue specific feedback and give a capsule summary of the whole session, or ask the patient to provide one.

Asking how patients feel about the session creates an opportunity for them to voice fears, concerns or misunderstandings, which if not dealt with promptly may add to the existing problems. Giving them the opportunity to ask questions about anything they are not sure of and asking what they found helpful or unhelpful is particularly important in identifying and dealing with possible psychotic misinterpretations (such as "When you scratched your head, I knew it was a signal for someone to follow me home"). If an important issue is raised at the end of the session it could be agreed to make it an agenda item for the next session. If it is not appropriate, and the issue could have an immediate negative effect on therapy (e.g. a risk that the patient may disengage from therapy, as in the example above), then it must be dealt with at that point.

Record keeping

Record keeping in therapy is often the domain of the therapist, but this does not fit well with the collaborative nature of the work and the partnership that cognitive therapy purports to foster. Patients should be encouraged to take their own notes in sessions or to contribute to the case notes, which can then be photocopied; this is particularly useful for patients who dislike sessions being audio taped or taking tapes home to listen to. Such notes are used for recording homework tasks and rationales, and keeping self-generated material safe. When therapy is drawing to a close and relapse work is the focus, then the person will have all the information to hand to identify vulnerabilities, triggers, options, and strategies to inform relapse prevention/management programmes. When therapy has ended the person has an accessible reminder of what worked when and why, and it can be a prompt for putting strategies into operation. Some patients also state that they find they have to get more emotionally involved with the work in-session if they do the writing (particularly for tasks such as considering evidence for and against or generating alternative explanations). Therefore, patients writing the notes can prove an extremely useful tool in accessing implicational meaning, or transferring knowledge from the head to the heart. An example of a completed patient record of a therapy session is shown in Figure 6.1; a blank form can be found in the appendix.

THERAPY SESSION RECORD

Name ....   Date ....

Therapist ....

Areas discussed

Cannabis

Not going out

Conclusions

Cannabis might be making my voices worse

Staying in makes me depressed

Work to be complete before next session

1 Keep a daily record of cannabis use and voices

2 Stick to activity plan we made

Reason(s) for doing it

1 I'll find out if cannabis and voices are connected – if they are I can make
  decisions about using it, and I'll understand why voices get worse at times.

2 I know that when I do more I feel better, keeping to the plan will get
  me to do something every day and my mood will improve. Getting out the
  house cheers me up.

Next session

Date ....   Time ....   Place ....

Figure 6.1 Example of completed patient record of therapy session

Overall process of therapy

Each individual patient will experience the process of therapy differently. Sessions
will vary in length, frequency and number, and the stages within the process may
not be completed in the same order, or indeed may not all be included. It is
recommended that the stages identified be followed as closely as possible, but
not to the detriment of progress within therapy. Rigid adherence is not required,
but a recognition that, overall, therapy must have structure to shape and guide the
process is.

Engagement

Engagement starts before face-to-face contact takes place; the layout and the tone of the appointment letter is the patient's first impression of the therapist, just as the referral letter creates an impression for the therapist, and most therapists would agree on how powerful that first letter is. A brief explanation of the purpose of the first appointment, what the patient may be asked to do and how long the session will last may help to reduce anxieties about the session and introduces the concept of sharing information.

The first session will focus on engaging the person and developing a rapport that will allow therapy to progress. People who have had previous experiences of mental health services may hold attitudes about therapy or mental health workers that will have an effect on establishing rapport. The therapist must be explicit about those issues that are not negotiable, such as confidentiality, communication with involved workers, and the protection of the patient and other people. Patients often believe that the therapist may have direct or indirect power to compulsorily admit them to hospital, and this can make them understandably cautious about describing thoughts, emotions or behaviours in case they are interpreted as signs of impending relapse. Similarly, patients may believe that the therapist can prescribe or alter dosages of medication, and may be reluctant to disclose information that they believe will increase the likelihood of this. Spelling out the limits of the therapist's power and what the patient can expect from the therapist fosters the growth of a therapeutic relationship based on honesty and trust. This cannot be achieved quickly and the patient may take time to test the therapist on these factors; the patient may even be encouraged to devise a behavioural experiment to do so.

Therapy cannot progress to the next stage until a reasonable rapport is established. The patient needs to know if the therapist can be believed, can be relied upon, understands the effect of the patient's experiences, and is committed to helping the patient to achieve his or her goals. Progressing without such rapport would be very difficult, since people would be unlikely to put effort into thinking and behaving in different ways and taking any associated risks. More detailed discussion regarding engagement can be found in Chapter 7.

Socialisation and normalisation

The next stage of therapy is socialising the patient to the model and normalising the patient's experiences. Decatastrophising symptoms by using research evidence related to isolation, sensory and sleep deprivation, and stress-vulnerability models helps the patient to begin to consider alternative explanations for experiences. Some patients may have a strongly held belief in a biological explanation and will have difficulties moving from an illness model for a number of reasons. An illness model implies innocence on the patient's part, and suggests something they are not responsible for developing and which is someone else's responsibility to treat.

The person may have a lot to lose by taking responsibility for the development of symptoms, and family and others may be less sympathetic or understanding if he or she is perceived as having control over them and not being a victim of them. If other professionals have supported this explanation, then it may be difficult for patients to consider an alternative from someone new to their treatment programme, and such mixed messages are unhelpful; patients being caught up in a disagreement between professionals are unlikely to improve their quality of life. Presentation of alternatives can easily be seen as confrontational and will serve only to entrench existing beliefs. The cognitive model outlined in Chapter 3 can be used to acknowledge the contribution of physiological or biological factors, incorporating these in the relevant sections of the model and formulation.

The next part of socialisation may be to introduce a generic cognitive framework, such as Padesky's (1996) five systems model of maintenance, which explains the relationship between thoughts, emotions, behaviours and physiology in a reaction to an event, and also emphasises the importance of the environment. Examples that do not reflect a mental health problem, but rather make use of everyday situations experienced by ordinary people can help to establish the concept of the model as an explanation for general human behaviour. The application of such a framework to their own distressing experiences can lead to increased insight, a reduction in feeling different in comparison to other people, and a sense of empowerment.

Formulation

Central to cognitive therapy is the concept of establishing a formulation of the patient's experiences, which is a tentative hypothesis of the development and maintenance of the patient's condition. The therapist helps the patient to identify early experiences that have shaped beliefs and dysfunctional assumptions and the antecedents of symptom emergence; this then leads to further exploration of symptom maintenance. The formulation is used primarily by the therapist to select appropriate treatment strategies and techniques in therapy but the initial benefit to the patient is the introduction of an alternative, normalising explanation of problem development and maintenance that incorporates past and present influences.

Problems

A problem list is established in the early sessions and will be incorporated into the introduction of the model and the formulation. It is usually only after an initial formulation is agreed that work on the identified problems begins in earnest. The first step is to identify problem areas in general and then define what the specific problems are in those areas. If the patient has a general problem in mixing with people it will be necessary to identify where it happens, who with, what the effect of the problem is, and other relevant dimensions.

When the problem list has been generated, decisions must be made as to the appropriate order in which they should be tackled. A hierarchy of easiest to most difficult is usually not the most appropriate way to do this. Rather, a plan should be developed that first tackles those problems which, when resolved, will have a beneficial effect on other problems. For example, a person who weighs 25 stones and experiences problems with mobility, feet, breathing and affording clothes, would gain greatest benefit from losing weight rather than first visiting a physiotherapist, chiropodist, doctor and outsize departments. This has to be balanced with deciding how successful individuals believe they will be in addressing a specific problem. However, they can do that only when goals have been identified. Prioritising problems can be a useful initial homework exercise.

Goals

Goals are problems that have been positively reframed. Problems are negative, exist in the past and present and are usually generalised. Goals are positive, based in the future and specific. Goals imply action, power and a sense of moving forward, rather than static helplessness, which a focus on problems may produce. Identifying goals is not as simple or easy as it may at first appear and begins with establishing general goals with the person that reflect the problem list. Before general goals can be broken down into smaller specific goals, a number of questions need to be answered and general goals reviewed. The golden rule in goal setting is to be SMART; goals should be

- Specific
- Measurable
- Achievable
- Realistic
- Time limited.

Addressing the following issues (the order is not important) will help the patient identify goals that meet these requirements. Is the goal realistic? The goal "never to feel angry" is unlikely to be achieved by anyone but "only getting angry in situations where it is appropriate, i.e. when most people would get angry" may be achievable. Is the goal significant? Will it bring meaningful change for the person in the areas identified in the problem list? Is the goal directed to change in the person or change in others? Individuals have direct control only over their own behaviour. Are the changes that will need to take place within the individual's control? People have a greater chance of achieving a goal the more elements of change are under his control. Loosing weight is easier than becoming prime minister. Can the goals be measured? How will they be measured? If they cannot be measured, then change cannot be verified. What will be a realistic time in which to achieve the goal? The goal of losing two stones in weight is specific, measurable, achievable and realistic, but doing it in two days is not. Goals should also be proximal; thus losing half a stone in a month is preferable to losing two stone in four months.

Identifying specific goals gives the blueprint for working towards the general goal. Working in terms of short, medium and long-term goals signposts progress in therapy, allows more opportunities for positive feedback, incorporates review points from which to renegotiate goals, and the opportunity to regularly review and identify strengths and weaknesses in the patient's application to making changes.

Interventions

Making the goals of therapy explicit and relating them to the formulation provide the ultimate structure of therapy. The destination for therapy is decided, the route tentatively arranged, but plans are made to take diversions, where indicated, and regular stops are planned to review progress and discuss the next leg of the journey.

Without goals cognitive therapy runs the risk of becoming Columbus therapy, referring to the man who set off and did not know where he was going, got there and did not know where he was, came back and did not know where he had been. Cognitive therapy is not just about travelling; there is a clear destination that is easily identified and the route remembered in case the journey has to be undertaken again. One important reason for identifying a destination is that you know when to stop travelling and the signposted stops on the way allow the picking up and dropping off of passengers. At some point in the journey, not always the destination, the therapist passenger is dropped off. This point will have been decided jointly in advance and marks the end of active therapy sessions.

Example of problems and goals

We will consider some examples of the shared problems and goals that have been generated in the first couple of sessions with patients. For example, Lucy generated the following problem list:

- worries about becoming a baby
- seeing myself as a baby in the mirror
- worries about intruders breaking in
- boredom
- nothing to do
- feeling sad.

This was rapidly translated into the following list of goals:

- to find out more about whether I am getting younger and younger and will become a baby

- to check out the images in the mirror
- to spend less time worrying about intruders breaking in
- to find a way of structuring my day
- having at least one person my age to talk to
- to feel better in myself.

Each of these preliminary goals was then "smartened up" (made more specific, measurable, achievable, realistic and time limited) in turn. For example, for the third goal, the reduction in worry was operationalised using an estimation of hours per day of worry and a rating of distress, both of which were set proximally in relation to the baseline. Hence, she aimed to move from worrying for about six hours each day to three hours each day, and from being 90 per cent distressed to 60 per cent distressed. These goals were identified, after the identification of a baseline, using questions like, "What is the smallest change in this difficulty that would still be meaningful in terms of an improvement in your quality of life?"

Fred generated the following problem list:

- invisible people touching me at night
- worries about harming Christ
- worries about whether I might harm other people in the future
- worries about social situations
- concern regarding medication.

This was again translated into a list of goals:

- to find out more about the invisible people touching me at night
- to reduce my belief that I harmed Christ when I was an inpatient at the hospital from 100 per cent to 80 per cent
- to evaluate my belief that I might be a risk to others, and hopefully reduce my belief from 80 per cent to 50 per cent
- to be less anxious some of the time in social situations (change from 70 per cent distress to 40 per cent) and to be able to go into a pub with my brother and father at least once a week
- to find out more about the tablets I take and to see if I can find one which makes me feel less blurry.

Trevor generated the following problem list:

- voices telling me that I am shit all the time
- voices talking at night stop me sleeping
- worries about the police doing this because of past offences
- feeling scared all the time
- unable to go out
- not getting on with my girlfriend.

These problems were translated into the following goals:

- to find out more about the voices and either (a) to reduce the frequency of the voices (from happening every hour to happening once every few hours) or (b) to stop the voices being so upsetting (change from 80 per cent distress to 50 per cent)
- to be able to sleep at night (change from an average of two hours' sleep to four hours' sleep)
- to evaluate my fears about the police being after me, and reduce the distress associated with this thought from 100 per cent to 75 per cent
- to be less scared (change from an average rating of 70 per cent fear to 40 per cent)
- to be able to go out of the flat sometimes (at least once every three days) and to go to the shop or to see my mum once per week
- to get on better with my girlfriend and to argue less (reduce number of arguments from six per week to three), maybe to go out on a date together once per week (e.g. to the pub or the bingo).

Ending therapy

Ending therapy can be as difficult for the therapist as for the patient. It is a goal in itself for therapy, and should be recognised as such by both parties, rather than left until both parties feel comfortable with it. If it is explicit and incorporated into the overall goal list, then it keeps both parties focused on the pace and direction of therapy. An initial number of therapy sessions should be negotiated fairly early in therapy, and, thereafter, regularly reviewed with reference to progress towards goal attainment. The end of therapy should be a consideration at each review point. The bottom line is that it ends when patients are either able to complete the rest of the journey on their own or when it has been decided to end the journey and travel no further. Helping patients recognise when the journey sometimes has to stop before the destination is reached need not be a negative experience for them. Identifying factors that impede travel at present and make it more sensible to postpone the journey than continue, while reflecting on how far the person has come, can be a positive outcome in itself.

How many sessions therapy involves, and over what time span, will depend on a number of factors: what length and frequency of sessions the patient can tolerate; the strength of the therapeutic alliance; the obstacles which may impede progress and whether effective strategies can be devised to overcome them; how many goals are set and the realistic time frame for achieving them. Booster sessions that are designed to evaluate and review the relapse prevention plan and response strategies employed will be dependent on similar factors. An overall view of the process of therapy is shown in Figure 6.2.

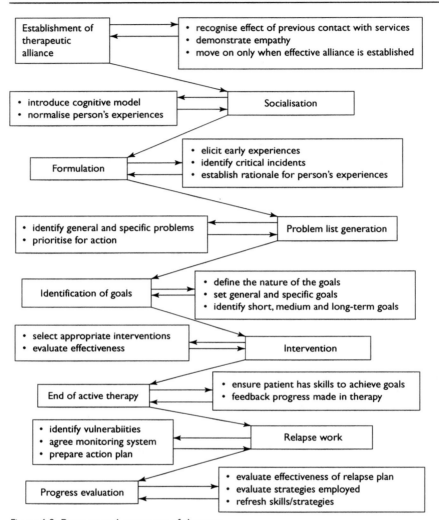

Figure 6.2 Process and structure of therapy

A case example

The overall structure and process of therapy is illustrated in relation to the case of Peter, a 42-year-old man born in England, of Irish parents, who has a distinct Irish surname but no discernible accent. During a period of intense Irish Republican Army (IRA) action in the area, he experienced harassment by work mates, who accused him of sympathising with the organisation and possibly collaborating in some actions. He lost his job when the company ran out of work and his wife left him and took their children. He began to drink heavily and experimented with illegal drugs, mainly cannabis and amphetamines. This led to him taking ecstasy for the first time, which resulted in him experiencing intense, distressing auditory hallucinations. These were in the form of male Irish voices, which threatened harm that would come to him for being a supporter of the IRA. As a consequence he isolated himself, left the house only when it was dark and was constantly watching other people for signs that they may harm him. He began to have more intrusive thoughts about harm, became increasingly anxious and his quality and quantity of sleep dramatically reduced. To cope with his symptoms he began to use cannabis, which in the short term had an anxiety reducing effect, but he used it heavily and as a result increased his level of paranoid thoughts which in turn increased other symptoms.

Engagement

Peter had agreed to consider cognitive therapy because he had been admitted to inpatient psychiatric services twice in the previous four years and wanted to avoid a further admission. Also he was worried that symptoms were beginning to worsen and he might be prescribed larger doses of medication that had side-effects that he disliked. Peter was initially guarded about disclosing information that might contribute to hospital admission and a good deal of attention was given to confidentiality, information sharing between professionals and collaboration between patient and therapist.

Socialisation and normalisation

Peter reluctantly took medication, but still experienced residual symptoms and wanted to explore approaches that would offer alternative strategies to dealing with his problems. Normalising his experiences reduced the guilt and anxiety he felt as a consequence of his psychotic experiences, and he found Padesky's (1996) five systems model particularly helpful.

Formulation

Sharing a cognitive behavioural formulation of symptom development and maintenance was a "revelation" for him. At this point his commitment to continue in therapy and undertake homework increased significantly.

Problems and goals

The agreed aim of therapy was to reduce the likelihood of hospital readmission. The goals were for Peter to identify and develop strategies for dealing with events/behaviours that cause or increase symptoms, and to develop ways of dealing with symptoms if they cannot be averted. Individual SMART goals were agreed for each problem. The main problems were psychotic experiences, isolation, cannabis use, prescribed medication and depression.

Interventions

Appropriate interventions for each goal were negotiated. For the depression and isolation, activity scheduling was employed along with thought records that included generation of alternative or balanced thoughts. Peter's cannabis use was explored by limiting use to four days out of seven and recording the difference in mood, paranoia, sleep and activity between the two periods. Prescribed medication was reviewed with the psychiatrist and a reduction, with regular symptom monitoring, was negotiated. Interventions for dealing with his psychotic experiences were developed as new information emerged from homework tasks. Peter learned that reducing cannabis use resulted in a significant reduction in paranoia and an increase in sleep and that raising his activity level and engaging in more pleasurable interests lifted his mood. He also found that spending more time with his family reduced his feelings of isolation and paranoia.

Ending therapy

Sessions were negotiated in two blocks of six, with reviews at mid-sessions, and were linked to goals and progress. Because the goals were identified early in therapy Peter was actively working towards them rather than intellectualising solutions. It was made clear that therapy would end when Peter had sufficient skill to attain his goals and not when he was "cured" or could make no further progress.

Main differences in delivery

It is clear that there are many similarities between cognitive therapy for psychosis and cognitive therapy for other disorders. However, there are several elements that become more important to emphasise when working with people with psychotic experiences. It is very important to ensure that regular feedback is obtained throughout the session. In particular, detailed feedback regarding the content of the session and the therapist's behaviour should be elicited at the end of the session using phrases such as "Has there been anything I have said or done that you would like to comment on or that has upset you in any way?" This can be used to check whether the therapist has become incorporated into the patient's delusional system, for example. Since psychotic patients have a tendency to misinterpret events in a culturally unacceptable way, it is vital to determine whether this has occurred within a session. For example, if a patient believes that the therapist clicking a pen, clearing his or her throat, or being interrupted by a knock on the door, is a sign of being involved in a conspiracy, then this is obviously important to find out and address. If it is not, then the patient may not turn up for subsequent appointments.

It is also important to make allowances for the memory and attention deficits that are found in people with psychosis. These deficits may be the result of antipsychotic medication, anticholinergic medication, preoccupation with ongoing positive symptoms, or biological factors. Because of these difficulties, the following elements of therapy can become all the more essential:

- setting homework, to generalise work done in sessions
- written copies of homework tasks and homework rationale
- session summary sheets
- shorter, more frequent sessions
- listening to the session tape as homework in order to improve memory for what has been covered
- session structure
- using the same structure to deal with problems in order to help instil the process of cognitive therapy (for example, always using an event – interpretation of event – feeling – behaviour cycle to examine distressing situations)
- shorter agenda
- therapeutic relationship and engagement to counteract suspiciousness.

However, as with all other aspects of therapy, these measures should be formulation driven and will not apply to all individuals with psychosis.

Ensuring therapist competency

It is advised that therapists record sessions using video or audio tape in order to monitor and improve the quality of their therapy. The use of taped material is essential for rating the quality of the therapy based on the essential components of cognitive therapy. The most widely employed measure is the Cognitive Therapy Scale devised by Young and Beck (1980), which is used by an independent rater to evaluate competence levels of the therapist, over thirteen items. Those components that have the greatest impact on in-session structure are the effective use of agenda setting, having realistic targets for agenda items, pacing and efficient use of time, eliciting feedback and reviewing previous homework.

Individual supervision in cognitive therapy should mirror the therapy itself. Padesky (1996) describes how the supervisor and supervisee work both within the individual session structure and across the process of supervision by setting agendas, agreeing a problem list, setting goals, devising strategies for change and identifying possible obstacles and designing strategies to deal with them. Homework is agreed, and feedback both elicited and given. Within this structure various supervision methods or modes may be employed to facilitate change depending on the supervisee's needs at any given point with any given case. Padesky (1996) also highlights the use of case discussion, video/audio or live supervision and role-play in both individual and group supervision sessions to help develop the next stage of competence for the supervisee.

Summary

Cognitive therapy with patients who are psychotic is similarly structured to cognitive therapy for other disorders, both in terms of overall process and individual session structure. It is also based on the same principles, which probably become more important when working with people with psychosis because of the nature of their difficulties and their previous experiences of mental health services.

Chapter 7

Difficulties in engagement and the therapeutic relationship

The therapeutic relationship that exists between the patient and therapist in cognitive therapy is acknowledged as a significant influence on the process of therapy (Beck et al., 1979, 1993), and the influence of the patient–therapist relationship on process and outcome is one of the oldest themes in psychotherapy research (Horvath & Symonds, 1991). A warm and trusting therapeutic relationship can have a significant impact on treatment process and outcome, but a less than satisfactory therapeutic alliance may have a significant negative effect (Burns & Auerbach, 1996). Therapeutic relationship and therapeutic alliance are distinct entities; the presence of a good therapeutic relationship is essential to positive therapy outcome, but only in that it enhances the effect of the therapeutic alliance (Bordin, 1974).

Rogers (1957) hypothesised that it is the therapist's ability to be empathic and demonstrate unconditional positive regard that is necessary for the patient's improvement; he went so far as to propose that as long as the therapist was able to offer a warm human relationship even the most recalcitrant psychotic patients could eventually be reached (Rogers, Gendlin, Kiesler, & Traux, 1967). Subsequent reviews, however, concluded that the therapist-only conditions merely provided a partial explanation of the complex relationship factors that influence therapy process and outcome (Gelso & Carter, 1985).

Much has been written on the subject of therapist factors or characteristics (Beck et al., 1979; Gomes-Schwartz, 1978; Orlinsky, Grawe, & Parks, 1994) in the therapeutic alliance, emphasising both technical skills and interpersonal factors. Warmth, accurate empathy and genuineness in the therapist affect both the therapist and patient's attitude and behaviour in therapy. Used carefully, they will enhance the effectiveness of the technical skills employed. Bordin (1974, p. 2) described the working alliance between patient and therapist as a "pantheoretic construct that substitutes the idea (that the relationship is therapeutic in itself) for the belief that working alliance makes it possible for the patient to accept and follow the treatment faithfully".

Bordin's (1974) concept of the alliance involves agreements and collaboration between the patient and therapist. He identified three interlocking components: bonds, which are the interpersonal attachments between the two parties; tasks, the agreement between parties on what needs to be done in therapy and why; and goals, the agreement on the short- and long-term expectations. In short, the therapeutic alliance is a facilitative mechanism that creates an atmosphere that enhances activity and is a therapeutic agent in its own right.

Although the alliance can be defined and measured in several ways (Horvath & Greenberg, 1986; Safran & Wallner, 1991; Suh, Strupp, & O'Malley, 1986), it basically reflects the individual qualities of the patient and therapist, and the interactions between them. The therapist cannot directly alter patient variables but can have an impact, indirectly, on the way he or she engages the patient and contribute to the relationship in terms of an empathic, affirming, collaborative and interactive style that incorporates the effective application of proven interventions (Orlinsky et al., 1994).

Current findings suggest that the quality of the therapeutic alliance in the initial stages of treatment, taking Bordin's three components into consideration, is predictive of a significant proportion of the final outcomes (Horvath & Symonds, 1991). These conclusions were drawn from a meta-analysis of studies that measured the therapeutic alliance in counselling and a range of psychotherapies with patients who presented with a wide range of problems. Although positive alliance development does not have to take place immediately it is obvious that if the patient does not engage early in therapy then optimism may turn to pessimism, activity in homework tasks may be reduced and disengagement may even occur. By the third to fifth session of therapy the quality of the alliance becomes increasingly reflective of the potential for future success (Strupp, 1989). Failure to develop a collaborative stance may also indicate that the patient has externalised the locus of change to the therapist or the environment; if this unrealistic expectation exists then a workable framework for therapy has not been established and positive outcome is highly unlikely (Horvath & Greenberg, 1994). The concept of the patient as his or her own therapist is central to the process of cognitive therapy and is established within the early sessions of therapy. Patients who become their own active therapist will be able to accept responsibility for change process issues and ultimately therapy outcome, and will be able to initiate and utilise therapy themselves in the future.

Engagement

Research indicates that the establishment of a good quality relationship and alliance between patient and therapist needs to take place in the initial stage of therapy to enhance the working alliance and increase the chances of a positive outcome. It may be hypothesised that people who experience psychotic symptoms will be more difficult to engage for a number of reasons, but there is little evidence to support this. Clinical experience would suggest that such people are not difficult to engage but may require that the therapist utilises rather different skills in this situation and that the pace of engagement needs to be sensitively managed.

Each patient presents with different experiences, problems, resources and expectations; it is this unique architecture which must be recognised and utilised in therapy by both parties. There are eleven key areas to focus on in the engagement and rapport-building process when employing cognitive therapy with a patient who experiences psychotic symptoms. These are

- the therapeutic relationship
- the therapeutic alliance
- normalising the patient's experience
- early establishment of a goal list
- sharing a cognitive model
- formulation and therapeutic alliance
- patient and therapist expectations of therapy
- influence of core beliefs and conditional assumptions
- maximising homework compliance
- patience
- supervision.

For each of the areas the rationale for attending to them will be discussed, the difficulties a therapist may anticipate or encounter identified, and strategies for either overcoming them or reducing the possible negative impact will be suggested.

The therapeutic relationship

Although we all think we know the characteristics of *empathy, unconditional acceptance, warmth and genuineness* when we believe we exhibit them, what are they and why are they important? Cognitive therapists propose that emotional responses are a product of a person's perceptions and evaluations of an event and not the event itself, and so therapist reaction to the patient is a reflection of the therapist's own perceptions and beliefs (Burns & Auerbach, 1996).

Empathy is related to and governed by communication skills; largely listening, feedback and self-expression skills. Listening skills can include what Burns and Auerbach (1996) have termed the "disarming technique", which is when the therapist finds truth in what the patient says, even if it seems illogical, distorted or unreasonable. How many people with a diagnosis of schizophrenia or psychosis-related problems will have experienced psychiatric services and been accused of being all three? An empathic set is characterised by the patient feeling accepted and understood, with the therapist being able to step into the patient's world and see it as they see it. Using the patient's own words can also acknowledge how he or she is feeling. Without being judgemental, the therapist can ask gently probing questions to further elicit thoughts and emotions.

It is important that the therapist avoids placing responsibility on the patient for what may appear to be negative situations. For example, telling the patient "You are confusing me with what you say happened" can sound critical and may imply that the patient is responsible for the therapist's problem – namely the inability to understand what is being related. A more empathic and caring statement would be "I'm not really clear about what you say happened, could you tell me a little more?"

Confrontation must be avoided at all costs; rather than helping the patient to consider the validity of the beliefs, there is a great chance that, in the longer term, there will an increase in the intensity with which beliefs are held (Milton, Patwak, & Hafner, 1978). In the short term, confrontation will interfere with the establishment of an empathic, non-judgemental relationship and may lead to patient disengagement and drop out.

Demonstrating warmth and genuineness is more difficult. Can genuineness be a skill? If you have to learn it and make yourself apply it, then how genuine is it? If the therapist gets it wrong and is perceived by the patient as being condescending, patronising or manipulative, then what will happen to the relationship and ultimately the alliance? The importance of warmth and genuineness should not be underestimated.

Measurement of the therapeutic relationship in cognitive therapy may involve measurement from the perspectives of the patient, the therapist or an objective source (Safran & Wallner, 1991). In a review of therapeutic empathy and outcome, Orlinsky et al. (1994) found that empathy was positively correlated with recovery and that patients are better judges than therapists of empathy in the therapeutic relationship. This suggests that the patient's assessment of the quality of the relationship is more likely to predict positive outcome than that of the therapist or observer.

The therapeutic alliance

The quality of the therapeutic relationship is a major influence on the quality of the therapeutic or working alliance. Like the therapeutic relationship, the alliance should be addressed and assessed during therapy because it is not static, but dynamic, and will be influenced by a range of process factors.

The California Psychotherapy Alliance Scale (CALPAS) devised by Gaston and Marmar (1994) purports to measure the alliance in psychotherapy. It consists of four sub-scales: patient working capacity; patient commitment; working strategy consensus; and therapist understanding and involvement. Some consideration of these scales may inform our thinking about the therapeutic alliance.

When measured from the patient's perspective, the Therapist Understanding and Involvement Scale (TUI) reflects components of the therapist's active involvement; the therapist's empathic understanding of the patient's difficulties, both within and without therapy; the therapist's understanding of the underlying reasons for these difficulties; and the therapist's commitment to help the patient overcome problems. Using the patient's assessment of the therapeutic alliance to identify weaknesses in the early engagement stages and address them will strengthen the alliance and enhance positive treatment outcomes.

Patient working capacity (PWC) reflects the patient's ability to work actively and purposefully in treatment. The patient needs to self-disclose important material and work with the therapist in a way that fosters the deepening of salient themes, and the resolution of problems. The degree to which a patient purposefully works in therapy usually derives from the interaction between the patient and therapist, as well as from the relevance of the material provided by the patient. Both parties can address patient resistance during therapy if the patient is capable of responding to the therapist's comments in an insightful manner. If this does not happen then the working alliance can be considered weak and in need of repair. It is important to look out for instances when a patient is overly attentive to the therapist's comments; this attitude may be more indicative of compliance, rather than reflecting collaborative working.

The patient's attitude towards therapy is reflected in the Patient Commitment scale (PC) and corresponds to an attachment, partly emotional and partly rational, to therapy and the therapist. Patient's scores on the subcomponents of this scale are significantly correlated to activity in therapy and outcome. The subcomponents are: confidence that efforts will lead to change; willingness to make sacrifices such as time and money; vision of therapy as an important experience; trust in therapy and therapist; participation despite painful moments; and commitment to complete therapy. Low scores in these items can indicate lack of commitment that may be resolved if identified early in therapy. Some patients will share their negative thoughts about therapy, and occasionally about the therapist, and these thoughts can become integrated into therapy. Patients who arrive late for therapy or cancel at short notice, prefer to "chat" rather than address problem areas, consistently forget to do homework, or forget what the homework was, may all be demonstrating a lack of commitment that, if unrecognised, could lead to drop out.

The patient and therapist need to agree on the therapeutic strategies to employ and goals to achieve in therapy for any therapeutic modality to be successful (Bordin, 1979). They must also share the same theory about how people can change. The Working Strategy Consensus scale (WSC) reflects the degree of agreement between patient and therapist on how people get help, how people change, and how therapy should proceed. It also examines the therapist's understanding of what the patient wants to get from therapy and to what degree the patient and therapist work together on the same salient themes and goals. Disagreement between patient and therapist about relevant goals may be the first point of confrontation in therapy. If a good working alliance is emerging, then it is possible for the therapist, albeit unwittingly, to decide on the goals of therapy (with the patient's best interests in mind) and to push the patient into agreeing to work towards them. People are not motivated to work towards a goal that is perceived as unattainable or unimportant in their present circumstances. It will eventually be obvious that change is not taking place, either because the patient will not complete homework satisfactorily, or if they do complete it, then there is no gain because the goal had little significance for the patient at the outset. The patient should be helped to identify goals that they consider achievable and worthwhile; once they have begun to work on these goals then the therapist can help them explore the validity of identifying further goals.

Normalising the patient's experience

It is common in psychiatric services for psychotic symptoms to be viewed as existing as distinct and different to normal experiences that may have a similar presentation. Kingdon and Turkington (1994) proposed that by not relating psychotic experiences to culturally or personally familiar experiences, it makes understanding such experiences difficult, both for professionals and patients. This unnatural classification of experiences could easily lead to the patient being labelled and stigmatised.

Strauss (1969) concluded that psychotic experiences should not be placed on a separate continuum but that they represent points on a single continuum of functioning, and a symptom-orientated as opposed to a syndrome-orientated approach is more useful when attempting to understand and explain psychotic experiences in individuals (Bentall, 1990b). This is more fully discussed in Chapter 1.

Patients come into therapy with a wide range of explanations for their experiences. These explanations have helped to make sense of the experiences and often will have reduced the distress that can arise from not knowing what is happening. This flawed insight is initially functional for the patient. However, the explanation itself may cause further problems (e.g. having to defend it to others or coping with the long-term effects of holding the belief). For example, if a patient believes that psychotic experiences are a result of alien activity, and that he or she has been singled out as the one human that they can communicate with, then this may well have a significant impact on social functioning (despite making the person feel special and important). Initial reactions by others are likely to be confrontational, followed by real concerns for the person's well-being, and pressure to seek medical or psychiatric help may follow. The patient may resist discussing the belief or even deny it while engaging in behaviours that are logical within the belief system that has evolved. Being available to receive communication could lead the patient to spend long spells alone, and this person may feel obliged to act on some of the information received without revealing the sources. Whatever the patient does, there will be an accompanying affective state that may appear strange or even bizarre to others who are not aware of the underlying beliefs. This can result in further problems for the patient in relationships and social functioning.

Considering alternative explanations with the patient begins with the use of guided discovery to explore a normalising rationale, rather than confronting the patient with what the therapist thinks is the true explanation. Turkington and Kingdon (1996) emphasise the establishment of a positive rapport with the patient before attempting to normalise their experiences. Some of the key points that they suggest the therapist should be aware of at this stage are:

- Using gentle peripheral questioning to begin to understand the patient's experience and recognise resulting affective responses in the patient.
- Accurately using the patient's own words consistently throughout therapy and not the introduction of the therapist's own language in summarising or discussing experiences.
- Avoiding working too hard at persuading the patient, through discussion or debate, that a normalising rationale is the true and only explanation for their experiences. The cognitive model is presented as an alternative explanation for consideration and exploration.
- Preparing patients in the early stages to come to terms with their "mis-interpretation" of phenomena (if that is an outcome of therapy) and the effect that the resulting experiences have had on their life.

Establishing the concept of a normalising rationale for a person's distressing or puzzling symptoms often begins with the introduction of a vulnerability-stress interaction model of symptoms. Zubin and Spring (1977) developed the concept of a vulnerability-stress predisposition which suggests that the more vulnerable a person is to the stress induced by challenging events, the less stress is required to precipitate a psychopathological episode. The next stage is usually to present research data, which demonstrates how symptoms such as hallucinations and delusions can be precipitated in most of the population, and link this into a vulnerability-stress model. The most widely used examples of stressors which can produce symptoms are studies which describe the consequences of sleep deprivation, sexual abuse, traumatic life events, hostage situations, solitary confinement and sensory deprivation. (See Turkington and Kingdon (1996) for specific data, or the more detailed discussion in Chapters 3 and 8; the appendix includes an example of information for patients.)

Early establishment of a goal list

An early component of therapy is the identification of a problem list, which is translated into the positive concept of a goal list. It is better to work on future positives than past negatives and establishing this list allows the therapist to demonstrate collaboration and reinforce the existing therapeutic relationship by showing an understanding of the patient's situation, validating his or her experiences and instilling hope in the future. If the patient and therapist can identify one goal to work on which will achieve a quick, successful result, and if the therapist and patient can ensure that this happens, then the patient will have been given a positive experience of therapy. The patient will know what it involves, what it feels like and what the benefits are, and hope and expectations of further success are likely to be increased.

Sharing a cognitive model

The basic point the therapist must emphasise is that thoughts are not reality. They are interpretations of reality, which influence our beliefs and emotions, and determine behaviour. Emotional responses and resulting behaviours are not inevitable consequences of antecedent events. If the therapist can draw on examples from his or her own, and others', experiences to demonstrate the model and subsequently use a non-distressing example from the patient, then the seeds of normalisation are sown. The model is proposed as a possible explanation for human idiosyncrasies, rather than a fact. The model is, after all, only a belief that the therapist holds (although one with considerable evidence to support it). A common example for describing the interactive relationships between thoughts, emotions, physiology and behaviour is shown in the following dialogue:

Therapist: Imagine you are in bed and it's two in the morning, you hear a loud noise and you think "it's the cat, got in through that open window and smashed some china", what emotions might you experience?

Patient: Well I might get annoyed with it or worry it had cut itself.

Therapist: And what would your behaviour be, based on your thoughts and emotions?

Patient: Oh I'd get up and see if it was OK, clean up.

Therapist: And what about your physical state, do you think there would be any difference?

Patient: Not really.

Therapist: Say you heard the same noise, again two in the morning, and you thought "it's my younger brother, been out drinking with his mates, I wonder if he's OK?" What might your emotions be then?

Patient: Well I'd be concerned for him, worry he might be ill or something.

Therapist: And what would you do?

Patient: I'd go downstairs and help him up to bed, see he was all right.

Therapist: Would there be an effect on your physical state?

Patient: I don't think so.

Therapist: OK, same noise, but what if your thoughts are "it's a burglar". What might your emotions be?

Patient: Terrified, probably angry with them, afraid of what might happen.

Therapist: What would you do?

Patient: Probably phone the police. I'm not sure if I'd go down and tackle them, I might be too afraid, probably push something against the bedroom door and stay there.

Therapist: Would there be any changes in your physical state?

Patient: I'll say, I'd think my heart would be nearly jumping out my chest, not able to get my breath, probably shaking a fair bit.

Therapist: What do you make of those three examples I gave you?

Patient: It looks like if you think differently you behave differently.

Therapist: Yes, and the way you think affects your emotions and physical state.

Formulation and therapeutic alliance

Chapter 5 gives a detailed account of the development and use of formulation in therapy, so this section will describe the impact that the formulation has on the alliance. As early as the first or second session the therapist should have a tentative formulation of the patient's experiences and problems within a cognitive model. This formulation is dynamic and flexible and represents the bigger picture. Working alliance is influenced by the degree to which both parties agree on the explanation for a patient's condition, the goals of therapy, and the way to achieve those goals. Sharing the formulation, in particular the maintenance cycle, will bring to light any areas where there is doubt about agreement early in therapy. Identification and resolution of any such areas will strengthen the alliance; if they are not addressed, then the therapist will not know whether the main problems for the patient are being tackled and whether real progress is being made. An accurate formulation shared within a good therapeutic relationship will enhance the likelihood of homework tasks being undertaken because they will be relevant, significant and achievable.

Belief is the key to progress. The therapist has to believe that the therapy can be effective and the patient has to believe that what the therapist suggests (the model) might be true. Therapists spend a lot of time persuading patients that "just because something is believable doesn't mean it's true". What they often forget to remind themselves is that "just because something is true doesn't mean that it's believable". Making the truth sound believable can be tricky. If the therapist is to be an effective persuasive communicator, then the following points should be considered:

- The therapist must be perceived as being knowledgeable.
- The therapist must be perceived as trustworthy in his or her motives.
- The message (in this case, the model) must be presented confidently.
- The lower the discrepancy between the held belief and the proposed alternative, the more receptive will be the patient's response.
- The more attractive (in terms of charm rather than looks) and likeable the therapist appears, the more effective his or her persuasion will be.

Patient and therapist expectations of therapy

"Therapists work hard, patients get better". This is a traditional set of expectations shared by those parties involved in psychotherapy and many parties who are merely observers. There is an alternative set which may be more realistic within a cognitive therapy framework: "Patients work hard, therapists get better". A good cognitive therapist is able to support patients to do the work they need to do in order to attain their goals. The more work that patients do, then the more material the therapist has to add to the formulation and the more effective the therapist becomes.

Patients who attend for therapy and expect to talk for an hour to someone who will come back to the next session with the answer to their problems (having worked it all out) may well be disappointed or even alarmed to find out that therapy will be somewhat different. It is in the first session that the therapist gets one of the very few opportunities in cognitive therapy to use a didactic approach. Once the therapist judges that he or she has a preliminary understanding of the patient's problems then the therapist can introduce the model of cognitive therapy and explain how therapy will proceed. Emphasis must be put on the collaborative nature of the therapeutic relationship, the patient as his or her own therapist, and the use of homework. In some instances, the use of a metaphor related to the patient's lifestyle can be used to establish an image of what therapy will look and feel like. If the patient is a car owner, then it may be useful to describe therapy in terms of an intervention used when the car starts to make previously unheard noises, behaves strangely, refuses to start or comes to a sudden halt. The patient (car owner) seeks help from the therapist (qualified mechanic) and between them they make an assessment of the problem. The therapist helps the patient to find out what is wrong and then works hard with the patient to put it right, while the therapist ensures that the patient gains the skills to undertake the repair alone if the car breaks down again. The therapist is not a splendidly liveried motoring organisation mechanic who single-handedly repairs the car using a glittering array of tools from an extensive stock while the patient sits in the car or is transported safely home by another part of the rescue service. There will be many similar metaphors that can be employed. For example, people who have an interest in losing weight will recognise that merely attending Weight Watchers doesn't reduce weight in itself (although it might if you lived three miles away and ran there and back); however, such an organisation can help to identify and measure the problem and to work with overweight people to develop strategies to help them reach an identified goal. It is important to find a metaphor that is relevant to the person.

One of the most influential factors in shaping patients' expectations of therapy will be their previous experience of psychiatric services. Experiences may have been positive or negative, helpful or unhelpful, worthwhile or futile, wanted or unwanted. The person who has had aversive experiences of using services may attend for therapy with a range of beliefs and expectations that could negatively impact on the therapeutic relationship. They may attend because a professional has recommended it and they are afraid to be seen as non-compliant, they may believe they have no choice, or they may simply be doing it to please someone. Alternatively, the person who has had aversive experiences of using services may completely refuse to attend therapy (information emphasising the empowering principles of cognitive therapy can be sent with appointments to try to avoid this).

Influence of core beliefs and conditional assumptions

It is anticipated in cognitive therapy that patients will engage in a collaborative relationship with the therapist within a few sessions. For patients who have had negative or aversive experiences in life, this can be extremely challenging. Patients' core beliefs and conditional assumptions that may interfere with the development of an effective relationship, or their willingness to be active in therapy, may not be recognised in the early stages. There is considerable benefit to be gained from tentative exploration of underlying schemas in the early sessions; both in helping to identify possible obstacles to progress and in deciding whether schema focused work should be a therapeutic goal. For example, patients who believe they are unworthy may have significant problems in personal achievement and may view the therapist's help as futile. Yet, if that underpins the conditional belief that "If I don't do what other people ask me then I will be rejected", then the patient may engage in homework but disallow success.

Maximising homework compliance

"Hands up all of you who have done the homework exactly as set. Now hands up all of you who did it on the exact days agreed. Now hands up all of you who can tell me why it was important to do the homework. And finally, hands up those of you who think it was all worthwhile." How many therapists could have held their hands up to all four? Yet, pity the poor patients who turn up to the next session not having done their homework, even though they agreed to do it.

What reasons do patients give for not doing homework? The same reasons as anybody else: "I forgot to do it", "I forgot what it was I had to do", "It was too difficult", "I couldn't understand what I was supposed to do, or there didn't seem to be much point". It is never possible, in therapy, to ensure that every patient does all the homework, exactly as agreed, on every occasion. It is possible to create the circumstances that will maximise the likelihood that homework compliance occurs.

There are six golden rules for maximising homework compliance:

1   *Decide work to be done jointly.* Patients, like therapists, are more likely to complete a task if they have had some part in deciding it. If the patient cannot generate any work then the therapist should suggest a possible range of options in broad terms and help the patient select and develop specific tasks from them.

2   *Clearly identify the rationale for doing the homework.* The patient needs to understand why the work is important to enhance completion. The relevance of the work is often forgotten outside the session, so it is important that the therapist checks the patient's understanding during the session and, ideally, ensures that the patient takes a written rationale for the work away from the

session. Clinical experience suggests that encouraging the patient to keep a self-written session record of the issues discussed, the homework decided, and the relevance of the work, increases the amount and quality of the work completed (see the appendix for such a session record).

3 *Check out obstacles.* Help the patient to identify and record what might get in the way of completing the work. Patients frequently report forgetting to do homework, or putting it off. Help them to work out why this might happen and what they, or others, can do to help them overcome the obstacles. If the list of obstacles seems overwhelming, then the work needs to be reconsidered.

4 *Make the homework meaningful but achievable.* The decision about what to do should be influenced by patients' beliefs about the relevance of the work and how achievable they perceive it to be. Do not make homework too easy; there should be a sense of achievement from completing homework, and in the early stages of therapy it will be easier to ensure success, but as therapy progresses more difficult tasks should be considered. Ask patients to rate how difficult a task would be on a scale of 0 to 10 to make it easier to agree on an appropriate task. Agree on more than one task being undertaken for homework, as this will increase the chances of success, but be careful not overwhelm patients with a multitude of tasks.

5 *Establish prompts.* Try to link work into prompts that occur naturally in patients' environments. Can they undertake a task at a set time everyday that follows a routine already established in their daily life, such as after a TV or radio programme? Can they put visual reminders up in their environment? Do they have a watch that can be used as an alarm to prompt them? Giving the patient a file to keep written information in can be an effective visual prompt, as long as they do not put it away out of sight. Grids for recording information with typed instructions are more likely to be completed than blank sheets or sheets that are handwritten. The more sheets the therapist gives the patient, then the more likely they are to be filled in, as some patients will complete only one sheet if that is all they are given. These may seem like minor points, but added together they can significantly influence completion of work, and without homework, progress is unlikely.

6 *Begin the use of homework from the first session.* Homework should be negotiated at each session in order to establish a pattern of active involvement in therapy and encourage the patient to become his or her own therapist and reduce dependence. Work done between sessions, in the early stages, will inform individual session targets and future goals and will give an indication of the patient's capacity to complete homework and highlight obstacles encountered. Typical tasks would involve reading appropriate material and simple recording of events and consequences.

Patience

Therapists who have worked primarily with patients who experience problems related to anxiety and depression may find work with patients who have psychotic symptoms progresses at a much slower pace. Many patients will be prescribed neuroleptic medication that can cause disruption to concentration, memory, volition and other factors that may affect involvement in therapy. It is essential to slow down the pace of therapy and move on only when the patient can demonstrate an understanding of the rationale for each stage. The therapist may need to summarise and feedback session content a number of times and draw on a range of examples to ensure that the patient retains an understanding of previous stages in therapy as progress is made. As mentioned earlier, the principles of cognitive therapy are probably more important to adhere to when working with people with psychosis than for many other client groups. Pointing out how much progress the patient has made, working out how gains were achieved and maintained, and giving appropriate positive feedback while acknowledging just how difficult some things in therapy have been for the person, will increase insight and should enhance motivation to continue in therapy.

It is tempting to point out the obvious to patients who are not drawing the "right" conclusions from well-placed interventions. Pointing out the obvious is being too directive. Helping the person to discover what is obvious to the therapist is the aim. Pointing out the obvious, even when couched in terms of "Is it possible that . . .?", is asking closed questions. In such cases, the therapist does a lot of talking and, at best, is uncertain that the patient means "yes". At worst, such a therapist *is* certain that the patient means "yes". Instead of "Ooh, look at those cows", you could try "Is there anything interesting in that field?"

Supervision

Clinical practice cannot be effectively developed without supervision. In cognitive therapy supervision parallels the therapy itself. Padesky (1996) suggests that a supervision problem list be established, goals be set, obstacles to goal attainment be identified, and strategies designed to overcome them be generated. Supervision may employ a range of methods such as role-play, observing clinical practice, and case discussion, and may be set in individual, pairs or group formats. The existing level of a therapist's competency will influence the focus of supervision (Padesky, 1996). Inexperienced therapists will need to master cognitive therapy methods, clinical processes and case conceptualisation skills. Intermediate therapists will focus on patient–therapist relationships. Advanced therapists will focus on all four but further develop their skills in therapy-focused supervision and supervision-focused supervision.

Supervision is mostly concerned with questions that need to be answered. The supervisor helps the therapist identify the type of problem, and can work through a structured checklist to identify where the problem lies and therefore the level at which supervision should begin.

Case examples

A couple of case examples will be used to illustrate some of the considerations outlined earlier and demonstrate the process of engagement.

Henry is a 42-year-old man who experienced persecutory auditory hallucinations and paranoid delusions. He was moderately depressed and complained of low energy levels and general apathy. He was not greatly distressed by his current symptoms but was anxious that they may worsen and result in a hospital admission, as had happened previously.

Henry was not convinced, before treatment began, that cognitive therapy would solve any of his problems or be of any great help because he had a biological explanation for his experiences, which meant he did not have to take responsibility for symptom management other than to keep taking the tablets. A cognitive model of symptom development and maintenance, using a normalising rationale, was discussed in the second session as a possible alternative to his biological model. Early experiences, precipitating factors and critical incidents were collaboratively identified and the first draft of a formulation was established. What Henry liked about the formulation was how he could see that, given what had happened in his past and what was happening at the time of the emergence of his psychosis, it was hardly surprising that he began to experience hallucinations and became paranoid. He described, at the end of therapy, what a profound effect the formulation had had for him, since he did not have to feel weak or guilty for his symptoms. He even confessed that he had to admit that there might be something in this therapy. He started to be more open about his thoughts, feelings and behaviours and started to collect related data as homework.

Although Henry appeared suitable for cognitive therapy, when measured by the Safran and Segal (1990) Suitability for Short-term Cognitive Therapy Rating Scale, his initial compliance with agreed homework was low. When discussed as an agenda item, it became obvious that he had not grasped the rationale behind the homework and when his mood influenced his motivation he "couldn't think of a good reason to tell himself he should do the homework". It was agreed that Henry should write down, in his own words, why it was important to do the homework and that the sheet should be clipped to the front of his file and left in a prominent place at home. The combination of a visible rationale and a visual prompt, which had been collaboratively negotiated within the context of a good therapeutic alliance, increased his homework activity.

As another example, David is a 36-year-old man who had a severe obsessive-compulsive disorder, experienced auditory hallucinations and paranoid delusions, and was depressed. He was diagnosed as suffering from a range of neurological disorders including narcolepsy, catalepsy and temporal lobe epilepsy. David considered himself to be severely disabled and experienced severe levels of distress at his situation.

A therapist might be forgiven for being overwhelmed by this presentation. Certainly the therapist in this case wondered where to begin and worried about where to go, but the biggest obstacle was perceived as not really trusting the patient. David was receiving a lot of financial benefits from the state, as were other members of his family, and he knew every allowance he was entitled to (and was in fact receiving it). In supervision, the therapist realised that her own conditional beliefs relating to fairness and disability were being activated, and this led to the perception that the patient may simply be attending therapy sessions in order to validate his condition. The therapist's prediction that David would not be motivated to change was also related to these conditional beliefs.

David destroyed this perception and prediction by session 3. He completed all the homework tasks and independently devised others he could do. His relief in finding someone who could give a non-biological explanation and treatment programme for his symptoms was repeated in every session. The quick reduction in his ritual behaviours reinforced his belief in the efficacy of cognitive therapy and he began to work harder at the homework. By session 6, he was almost free of the original psychotic symptoms, he no longer engaged in ritual behaviours and his temporal lobe seizures had reduced. As an example of how patient behaviour can influence therapist beliefs and commitment this is as good as you will get. The harder the patient worked, the stronger the alliance became, and the more the therapist found she trusted and liked the patient, and felt guilty about her first impressions.

Being open about reactions to patients, whether positive or negative, allows the therapist to explore the effect on the alliance. Negative reactions may lead to low expectations about patient commitment, whereas positive reactions may result in unrealistic goals being set and both patient and therapist becoming frustrated. It is important to recognise that how a patient makes a therapist feel can, and should, be addressed in a way that enhances the therapeutic relationship. For David, the therapist's change in her feelings led to him rating her more highly on involvement and commitment within the relationship.

Summary

A sound therapeutic relationship is a necessary condition for the effective delivery of cognitive therapy. A positive working alliance is required, and this is a multifactorial construct. There are several ways that a therapist can increase the likelihood of developing such an alliance, and there are several elements of cognitive therapy that can maximise the chances of building such a relationship.

Chapter 8

Cognitive techniques

Cognitive therapy for individuals with psychosis is based on cognitive models of understanding symptomatology and the aims of therapy are the reduction or alleviation of distressing symptomatology by cognitive change. Within the repertoire of cognitive therapy are a number of techniques that, when utilised according to a conceptualisation, should help achieve this aim. The therapeutic approach is guided by the specific problems and goals identified by the client. The formulation devised aims to help the client understand the cognitions and cognitive processes that underlie, maintain and exacerbate their difficulties. The therapeutic process will then involve the client and therapist being involved in a search to find out the role of such cognitions in the client's problems, and later evaluating their accuracy. If clients find their difficulties to be maintained by cognitions that are unsubstantiated by evidence, then substitution of more accurate thoughts and thought processes should help the clients to achieve their goals.

Beck (1976) defines a *cognition* as "either a thought or a visual image that you may not be aware of unless you focus your attention on it". He goes on to say that a cognition is an appraisal of events from any time perspective (past, present or future) and most often occurs in the form of automatic thoughts or images. These are thoughts, which tend to pop into one's mind spontaneously and, when negative in content, affect the mood in a negative direction.

Research has shown that the content of negative automatic thoughts that are implicated in psychological disorders is often not based in fact, and may be the result of biased information processing (see Chapter 2). Therefore, in order to improve mood and reduce distress, these should be elicited and evaluated during the course of therapy. This is just as true for psychotic patients. They will invariably have some negative automatic thoughts or images that overlap with other Axis I disorders (e.g. "I have failed my family" or "If I talk to anyone, they will laugh at me or ridicule me"). They will also have other thoughts that are more specific to individuals with psychosis (e.g. "The shop was out of bread because it was giving me a message to leave the area" or "If I leave my house, then the IRA will shoot me"). The triggers that may lead to an upsurge of negative automatic thoughts (NATs) may also be similar to those in other disorders, although they are often generated in response to auditory hallucinations. However, these thoughts, while different in content, have little difference in terms of their form, the feelings they can generate, their maintenance and the strategies that may be useful to deal with them. Therefore, although examples with psychotic patients will be given, the techniques used will be drawn and adapted from the field of affective disorders.

Eliciting negative automatic thoughts

Wells (1997) outlines ten ways of eliciting relevant NATs; these are illustrated using case examples from psychotic individuals.

Worst consequence scenario

The worst consequence scenario involves asking the patient "What's the worst that could happen if . . .?" For example, Paul (a 54-year-old man) would involve leaving the house at any point when he heard his voices. He was unaware of why he did this, but just felt anxious should anyone suggest this. When the therapist questioned him about what might be the worst thing that could possibly happen should he leave the house when the voices were active, he realised that his fear was that he might act on the suggestion of the voices and insult or hurt someone.

Recounting specific episodes

Recounting specific episodes involves discussing recent times when there was an increase in anxiety or anger or a decrease in mood. Questioning patients in detail about their internal events in the immediate lead up to this occurrence may help them identify the NATs playing a role in negative affect. Justin (a 27-year-old man) had been admitted with his first psychotic episode. He responded rapidly to medical treatment and was discharged from hospital but presented for treatment with symptoms of extreme anxiety. The following therapy excerpt illustrates this:

Therapist: What was your most recent experience of this very high anxiety?
Patient: Last night, an old friend from university rang and asked me to go to the pub with him and his girlfriend.
Therapist: When did you start feeling anxious?
Patient: I was all right until I got to the pub, I had one pint and then got really anxious on my way back from the loo?
Therapist: Can you tell me more about that?
Patient: I walked past a table of three lads who my friend had acknowledged on the way in, one of them said hi to me and the other two giggled.
Therapist: And how did that make you feel at the time.

Patient: Really, really bad, very anxious indeed.
Therapist: Try to imagine you are back there, feeling anxious, you've just walked past the three lads and seen their response, can you remember what was going through your mind at that time?
Patient: I think I was thinking that they knew I'd been in hospital, and might beat me up because they'd think I was a psycho.
Therapist: That must have been a frightening thought. How much did you believe that at the time?

Affect shifts

Affect shifts involve using changes in the patient's affect during the session, since such changes indicate the presence of negative automatic thoughts, memories or images being activated during the clinical session. This is often helpful for patients who have difficulties in identifying NATs in situations outside the therapy sessions. The following therapy excerpt illustrates this:

Therapist: You look quite anxious all of a sudden. Is that how you feel?
Patient: Yes.
Therapist: Do you mind me asking you about that?
Patient: No.
Therapist: Is there anything that ran through your mind directly before you started to feel like this?"
Patient: You crossed your legs.
Therapist: When I crossed my legs, what did that make you think?
Patient: I don't know.
Therapist: What did you think I meant by that?
Patient: I thought it meant you were bored of me and were telling me to go away with your body language.

Dysfunctional thoughts records (DTRs)

DTRs are forms for recording negative automatic thoughts and, later in therapy, for reviewing the evidence supporting and not supporting these thoughts in the search for a more accurate alternative explanation. See the appendix for a blank form for generating alternative explanations. These can be adapted to have helpful thoughts instead of evidence, or often when working with psychotic patients, it is useful to record the content of voices instead of automatic thoughts. It is also useful to view the voices as the situation and the interpretations of voices as the thoughts.

Exposure tasks

Exposure tasks can be useful for those patients who, while reporting high levels of negative affect outside the therapy situation, are unable to access the relevant NATs during sessions. This may be because access to salient NATs may be restricted when an individual's "fear mode" is inactive (Wells, 1997) and the person is unable to uncover such thoughts. Alternatively, once in session, if the affect is not recreated, the patient's belief in such thoughts may be so diminished that he or she has not got "gut level", or emotional belief in the power of the thoughts. Also, a patient may have become such a "successful" avoider that neither affect nor cognitions are readily available to his or her consciousness.

Exposure can, therefore, help to recreate the situation or induce strong emotions and help both therapist and patient to uncover the thoughts responsible for negative affect or unhelpful behaviours. Such exposure can take place either in reality or in imagination.

For example, Doreen (a 48-year-old woman) would leave the house only late in the evening, with her husband and only when necessary. On assessment, she was unaware of what was the reason for this other than it would cause her anxiety. The therapist and patient then decided that it would be useful to discover what caused her to become anxious in order to begin to allow her to leave the house (she wanted to increase her social contacts). It was decided that she would try to leave the house early one morning in order to understand what was causing her anxiety. During her next therapy session, she described how she had walked to the end of her path and saw two schoolboys. This had led her to think that the local children knew about her past psychiatric history and would throw stones at her. This identified a recurrent theme regarding stigmatisation and victimisation that proved to be present in many of her thoughts.

Audiovisual feedback

It may be useful to video record a client's session in order to view the tape together and try to work out what may have happened at certain times during the session, for example when the client becomes agitated. This is especially useful if clients are too agitated to discuss their affect shift during that session. Playing back the video when patients are calmer may help them to be able to understand the trigger and elicit the relevant NAT (for example, 'When you crossed your legs like that, I thought you were telling me you thought I was gay"). The use of audiovisual feedback can also be useful when examining negative symptoms such as flat affect (if it is employed as a safety behaviour) or for identifying themes in, or making sense of, thought disorder.

Role-plays

Role-plays are mainly of use with patients who have an element of social anxiety. Often paranoia can clearly emulate social phobia, or begins as severe social phobia, and for many paranoid patients their paranoid thoughts may well be triggered by social situations. Therefore a role-play may be an ideal safer environment in which to try and elicit such negative automatic thoughts or images. Role-playing in relation to voices is also a useful strategy. It can be useful to demonstrate helpful responses to voices (when the therapist adopts the patient role, and the patient adopts the role of the voice), with the roles reversing over time as the patient develops their ability to counteract the voices.

Manipulation of safety behaviours

Safety behaviours are behaviours used in order to prevent a feared catastrophe, and manipulating these can help to identify hot cognitions. For example, patients who believe that they are "going mad" or relapsing may focus on a stationary object and try to control their thoughts. Preventing these behaviours may make the catastrophic thoughts about relapse and associated memories more accessible.

Symptom induction

Symptom induction involves exposure to internal physical cues as a way to elicit thoughts. For example, Joanne (a 23-year-old woman) became highly anxious when her mother was around. In session she described how this anxiety would lead to a number of physiological sensations, which in turn would increase her anxiety. Therapist and patient attempted to recreate these sensations and then the patient was asked what she thought had caused them. The patient described that she thought the sensations she experienced were the result of her mother sending an electric charge through the walls in order to get her to leave home. It has been noted by Chadwick et al. (1996) that patients are frequently able to bring on their voices in a session. If patients have a problem inducing voices, asking them to imagine situations that usually elicit voices, or increasing their arousal, can often help to provoke voices. This kind of induction can help to access interpretations of voices and content of voices, and can be a useful behavioural experiment testing out beliefs about lack of control over voices.

Ask about imagery

As noted earlier, it is important to remember that cognitions can occur in the form of imagery as well as negative thoughts. It is important to ask the patient directly about these as patients may not realise their relevance or be aware of their existence. The semi-structured interview outlined in Chapter 4 is also useful in eliciting images. Patients may have images about the perceived source of their voices, images about their delusional beliefs or images of real events or memories from the past. For example, Geoff (a 21-year-old man) believed that he was being persecuted by a coven of witches, and had vivid images of being pushed into an oven by them (like in the fairy tale of Hansel and Gretel).

Other strategies to elicit thoughts specific to psychosis

Eliciting interpretations regarding auditory hallucinations

Asking patients specifically about their voices and their interpretations regarding the occurrence of these auditory hallucinations is an obvious place to start. This may be done using the following questions:

• When you heard the voice(s), what did you think had caused it?
• What worried you most about the voices?
• What were you worried would happen when the voices said . . .?
• What does hearing the voice mean to you (or say about you as a person)?

Interpretations of voices can also be identified using modified DTRs, using questionnaires such as the Interpretations of Voices Inventory (see appendix) or using downward arrows to access the personal meaning. Using the physical qualities of the voice can also provide helpful cues to identifying thoughts about voices (for example, is the voice male or female, what kind of accent does it have, does it remind the person of anyone they know or have known).

Asking about the content of the voices

As auditory hallucinations are generally accepted to be misattributed thoughts, cognitive techniques designed to elicit and evaluate the accuracy of NATs can also be used with voices with upsetting content. However, there are a number of methods that are particularly helpful in identifying the content of voices. Shadowing the voices onto a tape recording (repeating what they say) can be extremely useful. The tape can then be played in the session and the content discussed. Modified DTRs and diaries are also useful in identifying the content of voices, as can be prompting people for common themes, such as critical comments, or themes that would be suggested by the formulation (e.g. if people have the belief that they are bad, it is likely that the voices will tell them so).

The content of voices can also be evaluated in much the same way using any of the techniques described later in this chapter. For example, Stuart (a 34-year-old man) heard voices telling him that he was everybody's mother. He felt burdened by this and was unsure as to how he might live up to the demands of the job. Therefore, the therapist and patient rated his belief in what the voices had said and set about reviewing the evidence that supported this and the evidence that did not support this using the same techniques as with thoughts. The reattribution techniques will be described in more detail later in this chapter.

Verbal reattribution methods

Once cognitions have been identified, cognitive therapy aims to help patients to identify the role they play in the maintenance of their difficulties. Once patients have been socialised to this model, the therapist needs to help them to identify the accuracy of these cognitions. If such thoughts are found to be inaccurate, then the therapist and patient need to work together to use the evidence used to evaluate the accuracy of the thought to come up with a more accurate cognition, which should lead to a less negative affect. As Beck et al. (1979) note, "The therapist engages the patient in the reality testing of his ideas not to induce a spurious optimism by inducing him to think that 'things are really better than they are', but to encourage a more accurate description and analysis of the way things are". Many of the strategies outlined below are derived from the work of Beck and his colleagues.

The importance of Socratic questioning

It is important that Socratic questioning is used during reattribution and should be based on the principles of "guided discovery" rather than "changing minds" (Padesky, 1993b). Rather than pointing out to patients where the inaccuracies in their thinking lie, the therapist should help patients to review the evidence both supporting and not supporting their negative cognitions and use their "insider information" to come up with alternatives and to review the evidence. If the therapist attempts to "disprove" rather than discover, then information pertinent to the patient may well be lost or ignored. For example, what might help show a patient that the belief, "I've failed my parents", is inaccurate may well be very different from the criteria that the therapist would consider appropriate.

It is especially important with this client group, as they have often had numerous experiences of people telling them they are "wrong" or "mad" and invalidating their perspective on events. This will clearly do little to improve their quality of life. Often, the only (reasonable) reaction to attempts to disprove is "Ah, but . . .". It is worth noting that a useful exercise when training staff to consider this point is as follows. Ask them to work in pairs to "challenge" a strongly held personal belief (which could be "There is a God", "I am a mental health professional", "I am British", or "Manchester City (or even Bolton Wanderers) are the best football team in all the world"), and compare it when both persuasion and guided discovery are used. It can make for an uncomfortable few minutes.

Bearing in mind the importance of collaboration and guided discovery, several common verbal reattribution methods are now described.

Checking out the meaning of the thought

It is important to understand the idiosyncratic meaning of the cognitions to the patient. What do they mean when they say "the next door neighbour is after me".

Such vague statements can be difficult to challenge and evaluate; however, checking out the meaning to the patient will help specify this and allow both the patient and the therapist to understand the deeper level meaning. This has two possible benefits: first it may help the patient to understand what their fear or concern is really about, which may begin the process of reviewing its accuracy, and, second, it allows the development of a cognition which is more readily amenable to analysis.

Reviewing the evidence

Patients can be encouraged using Socratic dialogue to review both the evidence supporting and the evidence not supporting their troublesome thought. It is important that the therapist allows patients to review the evidence that supports their concerns prior to the evidence that does not support it (so that they feel listened to, and because it will be easier for them to generate). However, within this context it is first important to share with patients an analogy for reviewing evidence. What constitutes evidence? What facts can be used as evidence? Can gut belief or a sense of knowing be used as evidence?

Many therapists utilise their own metaphors or analogies for the process of reviewing evidence. A useful format for showing patients how the process should operate is the courtroom analogy, neutral friend analogy or scientist analogy; choose whichever is most appropriate for the individual patient. Thought records can be adapted to the specific needs of the patient or to take into account what is being evaluated (e.g. automatic thoughts, content of voices and interpretations of voices). For an example of a record form for reviewing evidence see Figure 8.1.

When examining the reasons for hearing voices, it can be particularly useful to generate a list of all possible explanations and rate the evidence for and against each (on an ongoing basis). It is important to include modulators as evidence (for example, if getting drunk stops the voices, is that more compatible with them being caused by telepathy from next door, God, or stress?). For an example of such a review of evidence, see Figure 8.2.

Balanced thoughts

Once the therapist and patient have reviewed the evidence and hopefully reduced the patient's conviction in the anxious, paranoid or depressive thought, it is useful to create an alternative thought based upon the evidence that has been generated. It is useful to do this alongside weakening belief in the negative automatic thought, as the generation of an alternative thought provides a new thought which the patient can try on for size, test out in practice and begin to gather evidence supporting this. For example, Kevin (a 22-year-old man) believes that a shopkeeper coughed as a signal for others to assault him, and left the shop in a hurry as a result. After reviewing the evidence (and considering why he, himself,

Interpretation	Evidence for	Evidence against
A higher power	• The voice can predict unlikely things happening • Imagery of higher power • Physical feeling – it feels very convincing	• It could be coincidence • A lot of what they predict does not occur
A sign of illness	• It can be associated with high mood • It can be triggered by paranoia	• It doesn't seem to happen at work • It is different to high mood
An unusual thought process	• It could be a stress response • It can be triggered by cannabis • What they talk about is similar to things I think about	• It feels real

Figure 8.1 Evidence for and against possible interpretations of voices

had coughed in the past), he decided that there were a number of possible alternative explanations that included the shopkeeper having a cold, or having an allergy, or being a smoker, or having a nervous cough. It was impossible to tell which was the accurate explanation, but he created a balanced thought that was, "The shopkeeper's cough meant that he had a cough".

Pie charts

The pie chart technique is useful when the therapist and patient need to work out how responsible all of a number of factors may be for events which have occurred. For example, Gary (a 33-year-old man) had a long history of psychotic symptoms and was often paranoid about many daily events (e.g. junk mail, wrong numbers, shops being closed, and passing comments from strangers when walking the dog). Previous work had enabled Gary to find evidence which did not support his paranoid thoughts, but he remained confused as to how plausible the alternatives he had generated were. Therefore, therapist and patient began to look at pie charts to help find the most likely explanation for the event he had witnessed, and to decrease his belief in his paranoid explanation. This is illustrated in Figures 8.3 and 8.4.

Event   Went to the chemist on the way to appointment. The chemist said "I'm getting a swing bin". She also sold Ribena.

Anxious or

paranoid

thought

When she said "I'm getting a swing bin" – she meant "You are rubbish – hang yourself". The bottles of Ribena were meant to be my blood and be a warning to me.

Belief at time – 75%

Anxiety at time – 75%

Evidence supporting the anxious or paranoid thought	Evidence *not* supporting the anxious or paranoid thought
1 She looked at me when she said it 2 They had bottles of Ribena on the counter 3 They began to tidy up when I went into the shop	1 It's ignorant not to look at someone you are serving: she might have been trying to be friendly 2 Staff tidy up the shop to keep it presentable or else people would go and shop elsewhere 3 Staff tidy up to look busy in case the boss comes in 4 The chemist could have been saying "I'm getting a swing bin" to the other woman in the shop, but looked at me because I just walked in 5 Most chemist shops sell Ribena: it is a popular product 6 Popular products are often put out on display

How much do you believe the anxious or paranoid thought now?____%

How anxious are you now?____%

Do you think this was a fact or just a thought?

Figure 8.2 Evidence for and against a paranoid interpretation

The generation of an alternative conceptualisation

Once clients have had some experience eliciting their thoughts, their therapist can use this to illustrate the role of cognitions in the maintenance of their difficulties and, subsequently, the role of changes in their affect and behaviour on their thinking. This alternative conceptualisation may help the patient to begin to challenge his or her belief that thoughts are 100 per cent factual, and may, in itself, begin to weaken conviction in the troublesome beliefs.

Event People ask me how my parents and my dog are.
They are always very polite.

Anxious or

paranoid

thought

> They are telling me that something is going
> to happen to them.

Belief at time – 50%

Anxiety at time – 50%

Are there any other factors which might explain the actual event?

Write these down, leaving your initial explanation as the last one.

1	They might just be being friendly	10%
2	Everyone in the neighbourhood knows our dog	10%
3	My mum and dad are popular in our area	20%
4	People know that I always walk the dog	20%
5	People often ask how elderly people are	10%
6	People who know I've been very ill probably don't know what to say to me	20%
7	They are telling me that something is going to happen to them	10%

For each explanation (starting from number 1), rate how

much (out of 100%) of what happened could be

explained by that factor.

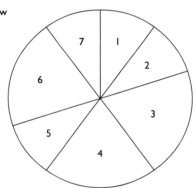

Figure 8.3 Considering alternative explanations for a personalised interpretation

Presentation of an alternative conceptualisation can help weaken belief in the patient's alternative hypothesis (the original, psychotic interpretation of events). For example, Chris (a 36-year-old man) had a long history of psychotic symptoms and had been admitted to hospital on a number of occasions. He was paranoid about almost all events during his day, thinking that others were constantly watching him, waiting for him to do something wrong or trying to frame him to cause him trouble with the authorities. He was unaware as to the reasons for this. Much previous work had been done in therapy to help Chris evaluate the accuracy of his thoughts but, while this was helpful, they appeared to be so widespread and frequent, the task appeared endless. Therefore, a developmental formulation

Event   Taxis, cyclists and people down my road, near my house.

Anxious or

paranoid

thought

> Handsel Trading want me to leave the city: they have sent taxis, hikers, cyclists and people with flowers down Stacy Road, near my house.

Belief at time – 85%

Anxiety at time – 85%

Are there any other factors which might explain the actual event?

Write these down, leaving your initial explanation as the last one.

1	Stacy Road is a main road	20%
2	Taxis are used by a lot of people	15%
3	It is the time of year for people to buy flowers	10%
4	I live near the country where hikers walk	15%
5	Stacy Road leads to the whole estate	20%
6	It's directed at me, to get at me	20%

For each explanation (starting from number 1), rate how much (out of 100%) of what happened could be explained by that factor.

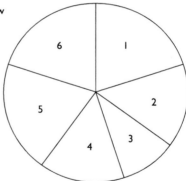

Figure 8.4 Considering alternative explanations for another personalised interpretation

was collaboratively constructed in order to help Chris develop an alternative explanation for his symptomatology. Chris described numerous years of bullying, victimisation and sexual assault, continuing between the ages of 11 and 21. A developmental formulation was developed to show Chris how these experiences may have led him to develop beliefs and rules about himself, the world and other people. It became apparent in this process that his beliefs about himself as weak and a victim and others as cruel and persecuting may render him susceptible to paranoid thinking. This was less upsetting than either believing that there was a conspiracy, or believing that he had schizophrenia and was mad.

Normalising information or provision of other education

When working with psychotic patients, it is possible that the event that may trigger off many of the individual's thoughts is an auditory hallucination. If patients hear voices, much of the distress and disability that are caused are the result of their interpretation of the voices. This often means that they are caught between a rock and a hard place, believing either, "I'm hearing the voice of the devil", or "I'm a schizophrenic and mad". Similarly, patients with delusional beliefs unrelated to voices are faced with a similar choice (for example, they are being persecuted or they are mad). Offering information pertaining to the frequency of auditory hallucinations or unusual beliefs, and their presence on a continuum with normal experience, can be an incredibly helpful thing to do. For example, simply working out with someone that if 5 per cent of the population hear voices, then in Britain alone, approximately 3 million people hear voices, can be a very empowering experience. This is especially so if they believed that they were the only person to have such an experience (or that the only other people were the people that they had seen on an acute psychiatric ward). As mentioned earlier, presentation of a psychological formulation can provide a third option that is less stigmatising and provides obvious ways of creating change.

The type of normalising information presented can include information about triggers, information about prevalence of experiences in the general population, information about intrusive thoughts, information about thought suppression and information about schizophrenia. It can be useful to discuss common triggers for psychotic experiences. These include trauma (such as sexual abuse, kidnap and combat), drug abuse, isolation and sensory deprivation, bereavement and sleep deprivation. Much of this information is covered in Chapter 3, but a more detailed account can be found in Kingdon and Turkington's (1994) book. Similarly, sharing information about the prevalence of voices (35–40 per cent of students have hallucinatory experiences, 5 per cent of the general population hear voices in terms of annual incidence, and 10–25 per cent have a lifetime incidence for hearing voices) can be important. The fact that voices are often unrelated to psychopathology is also an empowering fact for people to learn. The work of Verdoux et al. (1998) and Peters et al. (1999) also demonstrates that delusional ideas are common in the general population (with up to 70 per cent of people endorsing at least one idea that could be viewed as delusional in content). Garety and Hemsley (1994) and Kingdon and Turkington (1994) mention the polls that show British adults (Cox & Cowling, 1989) expressed belief in unscientific phenomena including thought transference between two people (over 50 per cent), the possibility of predicting something happening before it does (over 50 per cent) and ghosts (over 25 per cent), and American adults (Gallup & Newport, 1991) believe in ghosts (25 per cent) and believe they have had telepathic experiences (25 per cent).

If people have intrusive memories of previous psychotic episodes, it can be useful to share information regarding the prevalence of PTSD in response to psychotic symptoms or hospitalisation (approximately 40–50 per cent). If someone is concerned about having a diagnosis of schizophrenia, it can be empowering to share some of the information outlined in Chapter 1. For example, if the label of schizophrenia distresses them, people may be pleased to learn that there is little reliability or validity to the diagnosis, and that psychotic symptoms lie on a continuum with normal psychological functioning. Equally, they may find it reduces their distress to learn about the way other cultures view psychosis (for example, in some cultures, people who hear voices are viewed as a shaman). Provision of information about famous or successful people who hear voices or have had delusional beliefs can also be useful. Examples include William Blake, Joan of Arc, Philip K. Dick, Pythagoras, Gandhi, Zoe Wanamaker and Anthony Hopkins. Examples of standardised information about hearing voices that we give to patients can be found in the appendix. However, it is important to note that even the provision of educational interventions such as these should be formulation driven.

Encouraging an internally generated explanation for voices

It is often useful to encourage patients to consider whether their voices can be related to their own thoughts or internally generated. To facilitate this, it is helpful to provide information about the research (mentioned in Chapter 3) that shows that patients' voice boxes move when they hear voices and that talking to yourself in your mind (subvocalisation) can prevent voices. This should be presented in a neutral manner, and the patients should be encouraged to draw their own conclusions from this. Accompanying this, it is often useful to conduct behavioural experiments using subvocalisation (asking people to recite poetry or count backwards in their head and observe the effects on the voices). As described more fully in Chapter 9, it is important to have a firm prediction before the experiment and to frame it as a test of the person's belief about the voices. Analysis of voice content in relation to a person's thoughts and concerns, or the concerns of their peers, can also facilitate reattribution to an internal source. It is sometimes necessary to provide normalising information about intrusive thoughts (we sometimes give patients Rachman and De Silva's (1978) seminal paper on the subject) so that they can accept that having unwanted thoughts is a common experience. Identifying and challenging metacognitive beliefs (such as "all of my thoughts must be good" or "having a bad thought means you are a bad person") is sometimes necessary in order to facilitate reattribution. This can be done using the same methods outlined in this chapter (i.e. examining evidence, generating alternative explanations, etc.); for more details regarding challenging metacognitive beliefs, see Wells (1997, 2000).

Positive beliefs

The identification of positive beliefs about psychotic experiences is important. Voices are often positive (especially initially, with Romme's work demonstrating that they often emerge as a coping strategy for trauma or traumatic memories). They can provide comfort, companionship and advice for people. Paranoia can also be a positive experience for people (consider the number of people who deliberately induce paranoia by watching horror films or taking certain illicit drugs). Patients who are paranoid often report that it makes life more interesting and is like living on the edge, or that their paranoia has kept them alive and safe. Clearly, if someone were not distressed by their experiences then cognitive therapy would not seek to change them. However, it is often the case that people are ambivalent about such experiences, getting some benefits but also having some difficulties as a consequence. In such circumstances it can be useful to help people evaluate their positive beliefs (in terms of evidence for and against, advantages and disadvantages of holding such beliefs, and why the belief developed). It is also important to help people find other ways of getting the benefits or achieving the same function. For example, Harry (a 29-year-old man) heard voices that were sometimes critical and hostile, but sometimes were quite pleasant and offered advice and encouragement. He enjoyed the sense of companionship that the pleasant voices provided, and also derived some excitement from the hostile voices that told him he was going to be attacked, but also said that he was important. The therapist and Harry agreed to consider alternative ways of making him feel important and excited, and to look at ways of developing his social life. He was able to generate a number of options concerning each of these, and it was decided to try the following before attempting to change the voices: to attend a political party social club, which would make him feel more important and increase access to other people; to look for voluntary work (which would hopefully do both); and to join a five-a-side football league, which would provide excitement and companionship.

Working with imagery

Imagery, as mentioned earlier, is an important component of anxiety disorders and psychotic disorders alike (Morrison et al., 2002b). Hackmann (1997) recommends several ways of modifying imagery to make it less distressing, and these are applicable for patients with psychotic experiences. For example, Doug was very concerned about being attacked when he left his house. Whenever he went out, and often if he even thought about going out, he would experience highly vivid images of being assaulted. These images were always the same, and involved being bundled into the back of a transit van and then stabbed repeatedly. Interestingly, these images were similar to an event that he had witnessed on television, but also caused the same feelings as he had experienced when he had been mugged ten years previously (although he was not stabbed). Simply making this connection appeared to explain some of his distress, and he felt more in control of the experience as a result. A session was devoted to the collaborative discussion of ways of dealing with the images. He decided to experiment with three different strategies for removing the power of the image. These were to treat the image as a video (i.e. fast forward, rewind, freeze frame and eject it, and interrupt it with commercial breaks), to introduce a rescuer to the image (his friends would turn up and chase away the attackers) and to introduce humour to the image by incorporating his favourite cartoon character (Homer Simpson). He tried each of these in the session, and found the video method to be most successful in reducing his distress. This allowed him to feel sufficiently in control of the images to participate in behavioural experiments to evaluate whether or not he would be attacked if he went out.

It is also important to examine people's metacognitive beliefs about images. Some people believe that if you have an image of something, then it is likely to happen (this is thought–action fusion, which is commonly observed in obsessional patients). If someone believes that this is the case, it is important to help him or her evaluate the accuracy of such a belief. In the above example, if Doug had believed that having an image meant it was going to happen, he would have been extremely reluctant to go outside ever again, as it would mean he was definitely going to be stabbed. In such cases, it is often helpful to verbally evaluate the belief, but also to conduct behavioural experiments with less threatening images, which are easier to take risks with. Indeed, it can be useful to experiment with positive images, such as the patient (or therapist) winning the lottery, or Manchester City winning the premiership. The latter may be a bad example, as it is also important to ensure that the predicted outcome is extremely unlikely to occur naturally.

Imagery rescripting has historically been used mainly in the modification of core beliefs and will, therefore, also be addressed in Chapter 10.

Positive data logs

Positive data logs have mainly been used in the modification of core beliefs and therefore will be tackled in Chapter 10.

Historical review

Again, the technique of historical review has generally been used to challenge those beliefs or rules that have been held and become fixed over a long period of time. Therefore, this technique will be tackled in Chapter 10.

Questionnaires and surveys

Both questionnaires and surveys can be very useful when dealing with patients' misperceptions about the world or to gather evidence pertaining to their concerns.

This technique involves encouraging patients to gather answers to a set question by asking people around them. The advantage of this is that they can select the group whose answers will mean the most to them. The therapist can also conduct the survey, and sometimes patients prefer this option, as they may find the issue too personal to ask about or they may have a very limited social network. An example of this is given in Chapter 9 (as it is presented as a behavioural experiment).

Advantages and disadvantages

There are certain cognitions that are not amenable to checks on their accuracy. That is to say that standard verbal reattribution of looking at the evidence supporting and not supporting is not useful or feasible. Rather, the therapist needs to help the patient to look at the advantages or disadvantages of holding that belief, view or rule. For example, Helen strongly believed that Richard (whom she had never met) was in love with her. This had led her in the past to make numerous telephone calls to him and his family, turning up on his doorstep and attempting to get him to meet with her. This had resulted in a criminal conviction and an injunction being placed on her to keep away from Richard and his family. The therapist and Helen initially began to look at the evidence that supported and that did not support her belief that Richard was in love with her. However, as her belief in this fell, a marked affect shift was observed. On questioning, Helen replied that if Richard did not love her then life was not worth living. In light of this, the therapist and patient decided rather than looking at the accuracy of her belief that Richard loved her, it would be important to look at the advantages and disadvantages of holding this belief using the two-column technique (see Figure 8.5).

Following this the therapist and patient were able to decide that irrespective as to the accuracy of this belief there were a number of disadvantages to holding it. The therapy then tried to establish an alternative belief that was able to afford Helen the advantages of her belief without the disadvantages. She decided that "it is irrelevant whether Richard loves me, because my partner loves me and needs me and I love him", thus she was able to hold a belief which allowed her to discard her difficult belief and behaviours without the mood shift which appeared when the accuracy of this thought was questioned.

It is also useful to examine the advantages and disadvantages of a belief for both past and present. As mentioned earlier, it is common for a belief (such as paranoia regarding the actions or intentions of others) to have been very helpful in the past. However, if the person's situation has changed, this analysis of the pros and cons at the two time points can help people to evaluate whether the belief is no longer helpful, and whether it may now be safe to think about making a change.

Advantages	Disadvantages
Makes me feel special Keeps my belief in a soulmate Makes life feel special	Frustration when Richard and I do not meet Causes difficulties with present partner Peter Makes me cross with Peter for not being Richard – if Peter went would Richard come round – and I do love Peter very much Has got me into trouble with the police in the past My psychiatrist thinks this is a problem It upsets my daughter a lot I'm distraught when Richard tells me he is not in love with me Anger towards Richard's wife Unable to go away for the weekend as need to stay near house in case Richard decides to come and see me Would love to go away and stay with my daughter in the countryside

Figure 8.5 Considering advantages and disadvantages of a belief

Summary

A range of cognitive techniques and their application in working with individuals with psychotic symptoms have been described in this chapter. As mentioned earlier in the chapter, such techniques should be utilised only in conjunction with, and led by an individual conceptualisation as to the aetiology and maintenance of the clients' difficulties. Such techniques may be used alongside behavioural techniques, the provision of normalising information, and other schema-focused techniques.

Chapter 9

Behavioural techniques

Cognitive therapy for individuals with psychosis is based on cognitive models of understanding symptomatology. The aims of therapy are the reduction or alleviation of distress by cognitive change. Within this context, it is important to understand that the application of behavioural techniques shares this goal. In fact, Beck (1976) writes that "behavioural methods can be regarded as a series of small experiments designed to test the validity of the patient's hypotheses or ideas about him (or her) self"(p. 118) and in the same way about the world, future or other people. Within this process, even when the therapist and client may be utilising predominantly behavioural techniques, this will still be done within a cognitive framework.

Behavioural strategies offer the most powerful means of cognitive change in cognitive therapy (Chadwick & Lowe, 1990; Wells, 1997). Again, while some of the techniques used resemble those imported from other orientations, it is important to remember that these techniques are used to modify cognitions that are formulated as involved in problem maintenance.

Therefore, Wells (1997) points out that it is vital that procedures not originally based on a cognitive model are modified and finely tuned in order to produce optimal therapeutic effects. He continues by pointing out that behavioural techniques such as relaxation are commonly used in the treatment of anxiety disorders, but cautions the reader about the appropriateness of such techniques in treatments that aim to maximise belief change. Wells clarifies this further by pointing out that while relaxation, for example, is likely to modify particular types of belief, it may not modify belief in those thoughts most central to problem maintenance, e.g. "Anxiety is harmful and dangerous". Likewise, for other behavioural techniques within cognitive therapy, the importance of formulation-based application and modification is recommended.

Safety behaviours: special note before beginning any behavioural techniques

Wells (1997) points out: "Apart from automatic and reflexive anxiety responses highlighted in the schema model, behavioural reactions that are more volitional in nature are an important influence in the maintenance of dysfunction" (p. 6). Some of these volitional responses can be counterproductive because they maintain preoccupation with threat and prevent unambiguous disconfirmation of dysfunctional thoughts and assumptions (Salkovskis, 1991; Wells, 1997).

These safety behaviours play a significant role in the maintenance of anxiety and psychosis (see Chapter 3 for a detailed discussion). For example, people who are having a panic attack and who believe that their collapse is imminent are likely to engage in behaviour that they think will prevent the catastrophe. They may well engage in attempts to relax, modify their breathing or some similar exercise. Unfortunately such behaviours may unintentionally preserve the belief in the catastrophe, as it may be seen as the sign of another near miss rather than disconfirming that the worst would have happened. Similarly, if people believe that they are going to be attacked by their neighbours, they may leave the house only when they are sure that the neighbours are out and ensure that their doors and windows are locked at all times. Such behaviour will leave the person believing that they would have been attacked, but for these precautions. Wells (1997) summarises that it is likely that safety behaviours maintain anxiety (and hence distress) via a number of pathways:

1   By exacerbating bodily symptoms (which can be seen as evidence for feared catastrophes). An example of this is the patient who attempts to control his thoughts to prevent himself "going mad". However, such a strategy may have the paradoxical effect of increasing his preoccupation with thoughts and diminishing his appraisal of control. This is also relevant for psychotic patients, as many psychotic beliefs are culturally unacceptable interpretations of anxiety sensations.
2   The non-occurrence of feared outcomes can be attributed to the use of the safety behaviour rather than correctly attributed to the fact that the catastrophe will not occur.
3   Particular safety behaviours such as increased vigilance for threat may increase the person's exposure to danger-related information, strengthening negative beliefs. For example, James (a 19-year-old man) who believes that he is being spied on and persecuted, tunes in to all programmes, articles and conversations regarding espionage, phone tapping and persecution. These are then interpreted as evidence for the existence of a Big Brother type of organisation that is directed at him. Similarly, if you believe you are being followed by white vans, you are likely to notice them everywhere.
4   Safety behaviours may contaminate social situations and affect interactions in a manner consistent with negative appraisals. For example, Jill (a 26-year-old woman) believes that the neighbours are talking about her, so she elects to say very little about herself, avoids eye contact and rushes along the street to hide her shopping or personal possessions. While this behaviour is designed to protect her from gossip or to hide personal information from others, it may (paradoxically) have the effect of leading others to be more

interested in her behaviour, more vigilant as to her activities and more likely to discuss her behaviour with other people.

Therefore, it is important to identify safety behaviours in an exhaustive way, and to help people to consider experimenting with their safety behaviours by stopping them in a controlled way. The use of metaphors can help people to grasp the concept of safety behaviours and see the need to stop them to test out a belief. For example, we often use the metaphor of a person who is scared of vampires (assuming that the patient is not). If someone watched too much *Buffy the Vampire Slayer* and became convinced that vampires were planning to attack him at night, he may surround the bed with garlic, holy water and crucifixes. Describing this situation to a patient and asking them what the person would have to do to find out if he was really at risk will usually raise a smile and get them to see the need to stop the safety behaviour. If you then ask them to reflect on their own situation and see if there are any similarities, they can often see that their own safety behaviours may be preventing them from testing their own belief. More specific advice about designing and conducting behavioural experiments follows.

Specific behavioural techniques: use of exposure in cognitive therapy

Although exposure may need to be used to elicit negative automatic thoughts as part of the assessment process, should the individual's avoidance be so complete as to render these difficult to access, other uses of exposure tend to be utilised within the context of behavioural experiments.

Behavioural experiments

Wells (1997) suggests that behavioural experiments have three basic aims. These are socialisation, reattribution and modification of affect.

Socialisation

Behavioural experiments may be used to socialise patients in the cognitive model and demonstrate the principles represented in the formulation. Such experiments include trying not to think of something (e.g. a green giraffe) and watching the frequency of the occurrence of such a thought in consciousness. Such experiments may help socialise patients to models regarding intrusive thoughts, their normality and the role of thought suppression on their maintenance.

Reattribution and modification of affect

Behavioural experiments often represent reality testing procedures to offer a way of validating or changing patients' predictions based upon their beliefs. Behavioural experiments in this context may be seen as a series of tasks deliberately set up to test the validity of automatic thoughts or balanced thoughts following the use of a thought record. Once a thought or assumption has been identified and work has taken place to evaluate the accuracy of this cognition and the evidence behind this and the alternative view, the behavioural experiment can help the patient to test out each of the views. Experiments are extremely useful when an alternative thought devised following a thought record fits the data, but does not seem convincing to the client. Behavioural experiments may then be set up to directly test out this new belief. Alternatively, behavioural experiments may be set up to test out the accuracy of a thought or belief that may be problematic to the patient.

The use of activity scheduling (with mastery and pleasure) as a behavioural experiment

Often when a client first enters therapy, for those with multiple difficulties (such as auditory hallucinations, low mood, anxiety and paranoid thoughts regarding the voices), assessment may show that their general lives may have become highly impoverished. Their thoughts and speech may have become slowed down, along with concentration and attention (these may be viewed by services as negative symptoms). The therapist and patient might formulate the relationship that this has with other problems. The client's low mood can be exacerbated by his or her sense of failure and uselessness (which is often worsened by the stigma of schizophrenia) and attentional focus on the voices can make life appear wholly negative. This, in turn, can lower his or her mood, and increase anxiety and paranoia that, in turn, can lower motivation and maintain ever reducing levels of activity.

The therapist may ask clients how they feel they fill their day and whether their activity levels are high. The activity schedule can then be used to evaluate their cognitions such as "I do nothing" or "I have no time to do any more, my day is too full". The data collected from the use of the activity schedule can be used for a number of reasons:

* to identify the accuracy of thoughts and begin to introduce the possibility that their accuracy may not always be 100 per cent
* to identify the relationship between such thoughts and either behaviour or mood
* to use these results to collaboratively formulate how this may maintain difficulties.

Obtaining a baseline

At the first review, the client and therapist can look at the week's hourly activity ratings and use these to assess the accuracy of the client's thoughts. This information can then be linked to the emotion that the thought produced and other beliefs contingent upon it (e.g. "I do nothing, therefore I am useless", which may lead the client to feel depressed). As cognitive therapy does not promote positive thinking, but rather realistic thinking, we may find out one of two things: first, that the client is doing absolutely nothing. Although unlikely, the client and therapist could aim to identify the relationship of lowered behavioural activity rates to other problems. The therapist could then ask the client why he or she did not do anything, and use this to devise further behavioural experiments (see later). Second, that the client's prediction of what an activity record of the week would look like was incorrect. As described in more detail later, this allows us to challenge the idea of thoughts as facts and to begin to generate other thoughts regarding the utility of activity. These thoughts can be examined and used as the basis of helping the client begin to meet their goals.

Building on a baseline

The therapist may attempt to enquire as to the reasons for this level of inactivity – common responses are "Doing anything will only make the voices worse", "If I try anything, I'll only mess it up", "I won't enjoy it" or "I won't be able to do it". Already the therapist has an ideal opportunity to work collaboratively with the client to begin to evaluate a set of cognitions and their relationship to the problem or a facet of behaviour that could be seen as exacerbating the problem. For example:

Therapist: You say that you do nothing because it will only make you feel worse.
Patient: Yes.
Therapist: And what effect does that thought have on your behaviour, or in fact what effect would that thought have on anyone's behaviour.
Patient: Well, thinking it will only make me feel worse, makes it sensible for me to do nothing – so I stay on the sofa and watch TV.
Therapist: Are there any exceptions to that rule? Anything at all you do or could do that doesn't make you feel worse?
Patient: I don't think so.
Therapist: That sounds really difficult because we saw what an effect that had on your life and it sounds from earlier discussions we've had, like you're not that happy with the way things are.
Patient: Yes.
Therapist: Is it possible that there is anything you could have missed that doesn't make you feel worse. Is there any way that we could check out that *everything* makes you feel worse?
Patient: Only by doing it and seeing how much worse I feel.
Therapist: That sounds like a good idea. We might find out that some activities are worse than others. Any ideas more specifically about how we might collect the data . . .

The therapist could then, using the client's own ideas, add the idea of hourly activity recording (i.e. what the client was doing), alongside ratings of mastery (the sense of achievement that the client got from doing this activity) and pleasure (the sense of pleasure that the client got from doing this activity), both rated on a 0–100 scale. Additionally, ratings can be used to make the behavioural experiment more specific to the concerns of the client. If the client believes that leaving the house will make the voices worse, then the hourly rating can be changed to include a description of the activity coupled with 0–100 ratings of the frequency and distress caused by the voices.

The review of the data in the next session can be used to do a number of things:

- to directly challenge the cognition which appears to be maintaining the problem
- to use this information to understand how the more accurate information could be used to facilitate the client's goals
- to challenge metacognitive beliefs regarding the accuracy and factual basis of thoughts
- as an introduction to more information on the phenomenology and role of negative automatic thoughts
- as a basis for the understanding of why and how to challenge negative automatic thoughts.

The mastery and pleasure activity schedule can also be used to incorporate additional activities in order to gain further information regarding the accuracy of the initial NAT as well as alternative, balanced cognitions. There is a blank mastery and pleasure form with instructions in the appendix.

The following case will help illustrate the use of activity scheduling with psychotic patients. Danielle (a 31-year-old woman) was referred following a brief psychotic episode for which she was hospitalised. On assessment (after initial baseline), it was discovered that she had left the house on only about six occasions in the four weeks following her discharge from hospital, and she was reported to be showing negative symptoms. While at home, Danielle was not engaging in any of her studies or participating in any activity in the house. She was not getting dressed or helping her parents to prepare any food or with any chores around the house. At her first appointment, her Beck Depression Inventory (BDI) score was 38, indicating severe levels of depressive sympto-matology. On further questioning, it transpired that Danielle believed that engaging in activity was pointless because it would only make her feel more depressed. An additional concern was that leaving the house would make her so concerned about others being out to get her that she would be admitted to hospital again. Once the baseline was established, a mastery and pleasure activity schedule was set up with increased levels of activity on alternate days, in order to test her hypothesis that activity would only make her feel worse. Following the experiment, the results of the behavioural experiment showed Danielle that her mood was at its lowest when she was in her room doing nothing. Conversely, the times when she had arranged to meet with an old friend and take her grandmother shopping were the times her mood had been at its highest. In this way, two lessons were learned from the mastery and pleasure experiment: first, that contrary to her expectations, activity was linked with an increase not a decrease in mood; and second, it began to show that thoughts which affected her behaviour and may have maintained her difficulties might not be factual.

Therefore, activity scheduling is a behavioural technique that is used within a cognitive rationale in order to test out the accuracy of cognitions (in other words, a behavioural experiment). It is not only an exercise in its own right, but also used to test out the accuracy of the reasons that people give for not engaging in activities in which they may have engaged prior to the onset of their difficulties. Once this has been done, the course of treatment should be obvious to both therapist and patient.

Another example follows. Janet was referred to the service with a twenty-year history of hearing voices to which she attributed a persecutory explanation. From her problem and goal list, she identified that she would like to tackle her low mood and lack of friends first. However, when therapist and client attempted to look at ways of dealing with this problem initially, no starting suggestions could be found. Janet described that she spent all day sitting on the sofa at her house listening to the voices. She felt that although she hated herself for doing this, she believed that if she were to do more, then the voices would get worse, which would be unbearable and she would, therefore, become even more depressed and possibly suicidal.

Therefore, therapist and patient began to collaboratively devise an experiment to test out Janet's key problem-maintaining cognition of "If I do anything, the voices will get worse and I will get more depressed". It was decided that Janet would rate her activities for one week on an hourly basis, trying occasionally to leave the sofa. Alongside the description of her activities, she would rate the frequency of her voices and the severity of her depression in that hour, using a 0–100 scale.

At the next session, following setting the agenda, the homework set at the previous session was reviewed. The activity data and ratings showed that the voices were at their most frequent when Janet was lying on the sofa and that this also corresponded with her highest depression ratings. The therapist and Janet then spoke about the implications of this homework and possible lessons that could be learned. Janet thought that the homework had shown that activity did reduce the frequency of the voices and had simultaneously improved her mood.

She further commented, however, that she was unsure as to whether she wished to continue to increase her levels of activity, despite this, as "I'm not sure that it's right for a 61 year old to still be doing things". Such cognitions may then lead the therapist and patients to begin to consider this thought, its implication for other aspects of Janet's life, its accuracy and ways in which it might be tested.

Setting up behavioural experiments

Before setting up behavioural experiments, it is important to consider the following questions:

- What is the thought that you need to test out?
- What would be a good way of finding out what you need to know?
- Exactly what information is needed?
- How might this be measurable during an experiment?

For example, if a patient is concerned that if she tells a friend that she has been in a psychiatric hospital recently, then her friend will be disapproving, the experiment set-up must be clear about the possible outcomes in a measurable and behavioural format and the meaning of each outcome. That is to say, in this case, what would the friend actually be *seen* to do, and how would this show her disapproval? It is important to look at definable and measurable outcomes, rather than relying on felt senses, when working with clients who often have a tendency to mind read.

It is important, when designing an experiment, that the therapist and patient are explicit as to what the predictions of the experiment are – based on the thought that the experiment is testing out. Also, it is useful to look at difficulties that may be encountered in the course of the experiment, and ways in which they can be surmounted. It is important to keep a written record of predictions and the format of the experiment because it can be easy to negate the outcome of the experiment without a hard copy of the predictions and the meaning of this or alternate outcomes. Greenberger and Padesky (1995) recommend attention to each of these considerations. An example of a behavioural experiment record sheet is provided in the appendix, which can be useful for this purpose.

After the experiment, the outcome should be assessed with respect to the following questions.

- How does the outcome relate to your negative automatic thought?
- How much do you believe that thought now?
- To what extent were your original predictions confirmed or disconfirmed?
- On the basis of the experiment, what is the most realistic and helpful view of the situation?
- What could I do next to further test out this thought or to consolidate my new view? Are any action plans needed?

Behavioural experiments specific to individuals with psychosis

Behavioural experiments can be used to gather more information and test out or strengthen beliefs regarding the following events.

Volition in relation to voices

The clients' ability to act on their own wishes is often underestimated because of voices that are perceived to be powerful and omnipotent (Chadwick & Birchwood, 1994). It is not uncommon for clients who hear voices to believe that they are unable to act in accordance with their own wishes if this is not in accordance with what the voices tell them. Therefore, therapist and patient can begin working together to devise experiments that allow the client to test this out in a way which the client feels comfortable with.

If I show weakness, I will be attacked

It is very common for paranoid patients to believe that if they show any sign of weakness then they will be attacked. This weakness may be defined in terms of exhibiting anxiety sensations, looking unconfident, being physically vulnerable (e.g. being short or slightly built) or even being different (e.g. looking like a psychiatric patient or being bald). It can be very useful to conduct behavioural experiments to test out such assumptions. Sometimes the therapist may have to do the experiment first (observed by the patient), in order to allow the patient to feel that it is safe enough to take such a risk. We have often had to go to supermarkets or busy streets and make ourselves appear vulnerable (usually by lying down or visibly shaking), and none of us have yet been assaulted (touch wood).

The reaction of others

Patients may have spent much time out of normal social contact and, as a result, may have a range of social concerns. They may also have concerns about the reactions of others following the stigmatisation of their diagnosis or their presentation with the side-effects of neuroleptic medication. An example of a completed behavioural experiment form in relation to this is shown in Figure 9.1.

Using public transport

Again, the client may have a whole range of more or less usual concerns about using public transport. Following the use of cognitive techniques (e.g. alternative problem formulations, understanding the role of cognitions in problem mainten-ance and evaluating the evidence supporting and not supporting the cognitions), the client and patient may devise a series of behavioural experiments to either gain more information if required or help the client move from an intellectual to an emotional belief in the new evidence based belief.

Belief to be tested If I talk to normal people, they will think I am mad Belief 80%					
Experiment to test belief	Given old belief what do you predict?	What might make the experiment difficult	How might we solve this problem?	What was the result of the experiment?	Does this fit with the original prediction?
Talk to woman in KwikSave while paying for shopping about the weather and general things.	She will look at me as if I am mad and will refuse to talk back to me. She may even ask the security guards to escort me out of the shop.	If the store is very busy I won't waste her time if there is a long queue.	As I normally go every other day and I have the time, I will walk past and go in when it doesn't look too busy	I said to the woman that the rain was really heavy. She smiled at me and told me she got so wet on the way to work, she had to dry her shoes with the hand dryer in the staff room.	No, if she thought I was mad she would not have been so friendly to me.
Alternative belief There is no reason for people to think that I am mad if I am friendly and talk to them Belief 70%					

Figure 9.1 Behavioural experiment form

Consequences of voices and disobeying the voices

As with volition, patients may have distressing beliefs about the consequences of disobeying the voices, or they may worry about what hearing voices means in and of itself. Again, behavioural experiments can be useful to help the client begin to test out such concerns.

Robert was a 45-year-old man referred with a seventeen-year history of auditory hallucinations. He described that his voices mainly told him to fall out with his mother (with whom he was very close) and not to go out. Robert reported that the voices would bother him only during the evening. On further questioning, Robert described how the voices were present only while he was in the house, but he was unable to leave the house because the voices told him not to.

During the course of sessions, Robert was provided with normalising information regarding the occurrence and aetiology of auditory hallucinations. We used this information within sessions to explore the likelihood of different explanations for the voices and, therefore, the effect of disobeying the voices. When asked what would happen if he disobeyed the voices and went out when the voices told him not to, Robert replied that he was fearful that he might become a "violent axe-wielding schizophrenic – like you hear about on the news and in the papers".

We used the rest of the session to look at the evidence supporting and the evidence not supporting this belief. Robert described his belief in this statement as falling from 95 to 20 per cent, but he still felt that it was true. We began to look at ways in which we could find out more information regarding the truth of this statement and devised a hierarchy of experiments designed to test this belief.

Negative symptoms

Behavioural experiments, and particularly activity scheduling, can be very useful as interventions for negative symptoms such as anhedonia, apathy and avolition, as has been outlined above.

Behavioural experiments for core beliefs

Rather than testing immediate predictions, behavioural experiments can also be set up to test patients' views of themselves, the world and others. For example, Janet was referred with a long history of auditory hallucinations, which she ascribed to an unseen craft overhead. She was unsure as to who was behind her tormenting her but believed it to be the police, neighbourhood watch, relatives or an old solicitor she had previously had contact with when selling her house. Janet reported that she was constantly plagued by voices, which called her lazy, fat, a thief, and no good, and they warned others that she was a thief. Janet was provided with normalising information regarding the occurrence of auditory hallucinations in an attempt to help her understand why her life experience might make voice hearing more likely. We then listed each of the explanations for the cause of the voices, and considered the plausibility of the mechanism in each case.

Examining the content of the voices and her beliefs as to why she was being punished, it became clear that her beliefs about being "bad" and "having done the worst things in the world" led to her maintenance of her delusional beliefs. Therefore, client and therapist agreed to examine this belief further and looked in more detail at those events in Janet's past, which she saw as the basis of this belief. Janet had married her present husband while already pregnant. Her father had been very angry with her and had called her the black sheep of the family and told her she had brought shame on him and the household. Janet also described how forty years previously, she had been plagued by noisy neighbours and, after many attempts at reasonable discussion, her frustration had led her to steal a garden gnome from her neighbours' back garden. Unfortunately, she was caught disposing of it after attempts to put it back had failed and was branded a thief by the neighbours. While at work, Janet had again dealt with frustrations at work by stealing things from a colleague. She had not been accused, or questioned, but felt that this showed her to be a truly bad person. Janet also reported that she had had bad thoughts about people and had talked about them behind their backs with her husband in previous years.

We began to look at her beliefs that "what I did was the worst thing anyone could have done", or more importantly, the fact that this had become "I am the worst person in the world". Initially, we used a continuum approach to help evaluate the accuracy of this belief (see Chapter 10 for details). In order to complement the work done with the continuum, a survey was devised for both therapist and Janet to ask friends and colleagues in order to gain a more accurate estimate of how often such misdemeanours were committed. This was done because part of Janet's evidence for viewing herself as bad was that "no one else does things like that". It was decided that both Janet and the therapist would each ask ten people to fill in the questionnaire (mentioning that they could, if they preferred, omit their name). Janet predicted that no one of the twenty surveyed would have stolen anything, and only one or two (at most) would have slept with someone they were not married to at the time or talked about people behind their back. The survey form is shown in Figure 9.2. As expected (by the therapist), the

First name, age and gender	Have you ever stolen anything? (Tick for yes)	Have you ever had sex with someone to whom you were not married at the time? (Tick for yes)	Have you ever talked about someone behind their back? (Tick for yes)

Figure 9.2 Survey form

vast majority of respondents replied positively to all of the items. Janet was extremely surprised by this, and it helped her to re-evaluate her belief.

A word of warning: how to prevent behavioural techniques being used as safety behaviours

As mentioned earlier, although some of the behavioural techniques used in cognitive therapy may be similar to those used in behaviour therapy, there are some very important differences in their use. Behavioural techniques are utilised within a cognitive rationale; namely, to test out the accuracy of negative automatic thoughts, images, underlying assumptions or core beliefs.

Other behavioural techniques

The following categories of behavioural techniques require great care that they are utilised only as behavioural experiments to test out cognitions that are shown by the formulation to be important in problem maintenance. Other uses of these techniques may cause them to be adopted as safety behaviours, and hence, develop a role in future problem maintenance.

Distraction

This can be used as a powerful behavioural experiment to help socialise the patient to the cognitive model of affect and symptom maintenance. Often that patient will report reduced anxiety or other difficulties while distracted from their problematic cognitions or voices. This can be used, for example, to show the patient the relationship between cognition and affect.

Distraction can, however, be used as a safety behaviour if key metacognitive concerns regarding thoughts, emotions and internal mental processes are not addressed. The client may use distraction as a safety behaviour believing that it is this that is keeping him or her safe from impending madness, death or disaster.

Focusing

Similar to above, the experiment can be used to show links with cognition or disprove worries about the consequences of voices. Some patients, however, use this as a safety behaviour (e.g. "If I focus all my attention on my voices, I won't lose control and go mad").

Relaxation

Relaxation is often taught as part of CBT without a cognitive rationale. It is fairly common to see patients who have had this experience and currently use relaxation exercises as safety behaviours. It may prevent disconfirmation of problematic cognitions, as the patient may believe, "If I didn't do this when I was anxious, then I would definitely go mad" or "If I didn't use this to get rid of my anxiety, then people would see I was weak and attack me". The teaching of relaxation may be seen as a sign that anxiety symptoms are dangerous and must be stopped from escalation. If relaxation is to be taught, the clinician must be clear of its rationale. What cognitions does the formulation tell us that teaching such skills would help evaluate and alter? An example of this would be that, if the patient believed his or her physiological symptoms to be the result of rays beamed down by aliens, then an experiment where relaxation may reduce symptomatology may help the patient to discover alternative explanations.

Action plans

Cognitive therapy is not about positive thinking, but about realistic and accurate thinking. Therefore, a balanced thought may well show that situations and past actions are not what they should have been or are not ideal. If this is the case, and the client's balanced thought shows that there is truth in the original interpretation of the event, then something must be done to help change the event (if possible). For example, if someone has had a written warning to say that his or her accommodation is at risk, and there is little satisfactory housing elsewhere, then the therapist may need to undertake an action plan to help outline ways in which the person can take steps to stay in the flat. Action plans are used to solve problems that have been identified. They should be specific and should include coping plans for possible problems, a set time to begin, and record progress made. Similar to behavioural experiments, written action plans, records and problem solving strategies are useful and can be incorporated into a record sheet. Action plans often consist of planning with patients to deal with situations that have been difficult in a more effective manner. This can involve increasing skills, breaking tasks down into smaller chunks, learning to problem solve, identifying others in the environment who may be able to offer assistance, and using role-play to identify and rehearse strategies to be implemented in difficult situations.

Summary

Behavioural tasks offer some of the most important and powerful tasks in cognitive therapy. Although they may be behavioural in nature, their aim within cognitive therapy is to promote cognitive change. Therefore, great care must be taken in promoting a cognitive rationale for behavioural tasks and in modifying the techniques to render them suitable. While such techniques can be extremely powerful, incorrect usage can result in reduced effectiveness or, more seriously, in the creation of safety behaviours preventing disconfirmation of problem maintaining cognitions.

Chapter 10

Schema change methods

The terms schema, schema change and schema modification have commonly been used in cognitive therapy and schemas have been defined in a variety of ways by a variety of authors. Interest in schemas and their change within cognitive therapy has increased over recent years, with the development of cognitive approaches for difficulties held over longer periods and for disorders of a more severe and enduring nature, such as personality disorders and psychotic disorders. Within the field of cognitive therapy for psychosis, such work may prove invaluable, due to the nature of the early experiences which may commonly be found within this client group and the difficulties caused to one's view of oneself and others by living with such difficulties for a number of years. It is also likely that, as in other Axis I disorders, people's core beliefs, which underlie vulnerability to psychopathology, may not be amenable to change using methods devised for working with negative automatic thoughts (Mary Shinner, personal communication, 2001). It is also important to be able to employ schema change methods with psychotic patients, as such core beliefs are often reflected in the content of their voices, or are implicated in the development and maintenance of their unusual ideas.

A schema was initially described as a knowledge structure that guides information processing and the implementation of action in response to certain stimuli (Bartlett, 1932, cited in Safran, 1990a). Definitions of schemas which have been offered more recently include the following from Beck et al. (1979): "a schema constitutes the basis for screening out, differentiating and coding the stimuli that confront the individual" (p. 13). Beck et al. (1979) go on to describe schematic beliefs as specific rules that govern information processing and behaviour.

Beck et al. (1990) highlight the need for the prudent use of various tools and the need for great flexibility in approach. The main aim of cognitive therapy with these more severe and enduring disorders is to "develop new schemas and modify old ones" (p. 80). They do not underestimate the difficulties associated with achieving schema change, and advocate treatment using various modes of intervention in sequence and in parallel: "Given the importance of the schematic changes the schemas are difficult to alter. They are held firmly in place by behaviour, cognitive and affective elements. The therapeutic approach must take a tripartite approach" (Beck et al., 1990, p. 10)

Beck's (1976) model of emotional disorders (described in much greater detail in Chapter 2) suggests that experience leads people to form assumptions or conditional beliefs (e.g. "*If* others see what I am really like *then* they will reject me") or rules (e.g. "I must always do what other people ask me to") or schemata about themselves and the world. Schemata are sets of beliefs (unconditional beliefs, e.g. "I am worthless") and assumptions, which may be encoded alongside other emotive material. These are subsequently used to organise perception and to govern and evaluate behaviour (Beck, 1964). The individual's cognitions (automatic thoughts, images and memories) are based on attitudes or assumptions that have been developed from previous experiences.

A consideration to bear in mind when using schema change methods

Certain techniques have been adapted for use as schema change techniques that have long been used as an integral part of routine cognitive therapy for Axis I disorders, such as behavioural experiments and Socratic dialogue. It is important, therefore, to note that their effectiveness as schema change procedures is difficult to partial out from their effectiveness at modifying other levels of cognition found within emotional disorders. However, it may not be unreasonable to assume that they contribute to the success of treatment for various disorders (e.g. depression, panic disorder, social anxiety, obsessive-compulsive disorder, psychosis) by altering different levels of cognition.

There is some preliminary evidence that imagery rescripting is a successful strategy for reducing the symptoms of post-traumatic stress disorder in adult survivors of childhood sexual abuse (Schmucker, Dancu, Foa, & Niederee, 1995). Beyond this, however, specific evidence for the effectiveness of individual schema change procedures is not readily available. The therapy provided in these cases would be likely to be composed of a number of different schema change procedures, rendering it difficult to determine the effectiveness of any specific strategy. However, the relevance of working with imagery with psychotic patients is apparent. Recent research (Morrison et al., 2002b) shows the prevalence of relevant imagery implicated in distressing psychotic experiences to be approximately 75 per cent.

In summary, the development and application of the majority of schema change strategies, although innovative and exciting therapeutically, has yet to be accompanied by sufficient research demonstrating effectiveness. Until this can be established, therapists may need to utilise the techniques with caution, and perhaps not before those strategies that have been demonstrated to be effective have been attempted. In other words, it is important to try to intervene at the maintenance level prior to using schema-focused interventions; not only is this parsimonious, but also it is more likely to result in a quick success. If you become stuck when working at the maintenance level, however, it is often necessary to conduct schema level interventions. It can also be useful to employ schema level interventions for the purposes of relapse prevention, as many core beliefs and underlying assumptions are vulnerability factors for future episodes of psychosis or other kinds of psychological dysfunction.

Provision of a rationale for schema work: the prejudice model

Padesky (1993a) developed a useful strategy to help clients see how their belief operates much like a prejudicial belief, with incoming information being processed differently according to whether it is consistent with, or contradicts, the existing belief. This technique can be applied most easily to unconditional schematic beliefs, such as "I am unlovable", or "I am bad", which Padesky argues are like self-prejudice. It entails the examination of this processing style in the maintenance of a specific prejudicial belief held by someone known to the client, but using a belief with which the client disagrees. The use of this analogy allows the illustration of how a process of ignoring, distorting or making an exception of incoming contradictory information, versus the ready acceptance of confirmatory information, serves to maintain a belief, even when it is not true. See Figure 10.1.

Once clients understand the concepts, they can be encouraged to think about how they would go about changing this other person's prejudicial belief (such as repeatedly presenting the person with contradictory information, so it cannot be construed as an exception, and preventing them from ignoring or distorting it). This process has the additional benefit of allowing the client to consider how difficult and lengthy changing a long-held and extreme belief might be. This is helpful when the model is applied to the client's own belief, in preparing him or

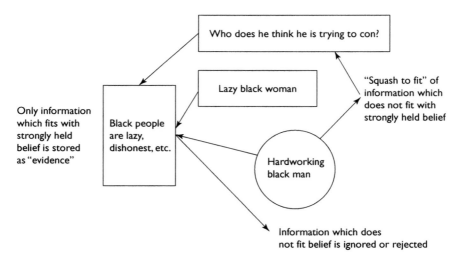

Figure 10.1 Example of the prejudice metaphor

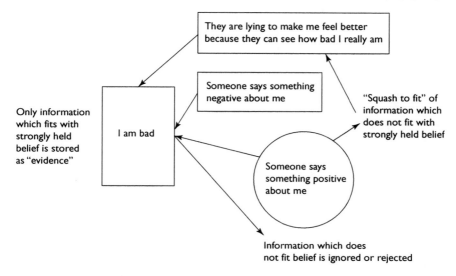

They are lying to make me feel better
because they can see how bad I really am

Someone says something
negative about me

Only information
which fits with
strongly held
belief is stored
as "evidence"

I am bad

"Squash to fit" of
information which
does not fit with
strongly held belief

Someone says
something positive
about me

Information which does
not fit belief is ignored or rejected

Figure 10.2 Personalised example of the prejudice metaphor

her for the process of change (see Figure 10.2). Other techniques such as diaries and positive data logs (described in more detail later in the chapter) can then be used to document evidence against the belief, or, perhaps more constructively, in support of an alternative, more functional belief. This procedure is likely to take a very long time; it is suggested that a minimum of six months is likely to be required in order to see changes in fixed unconditional schematic beliefs (Shinner, personal communication, 2001).

Early techniques: Socratic dialogue and behavioural experiments

Beck et al. (1979) describe a number of cognitive and behavioural techniques for modifying depressogenic assumptions, which can be construed as conditional schematic beliefs (often written in "if . . . then . . ." form, or as rule statements). These include questioning and discussion in therapy sessions to illustrate the illogic and inconsistencies of clients' assumptions. Beck et al. (1979) appear to see this as sufficient for some clients, but acknowledge that, for others, more work is needed. They describe, with examples, the use of a range of behavioural experiments to test out problematic assumptions. One example, if an assumption is a "should" statement, is to then guide the client towards seeing the value of suspending the belief temporarily (and, therefore, acting against it) and seeing what actually happens. Beck et al. (1979) discuss the possible value of helping clients to see their problematic beliefs as unhelpful or unattainable "personal contracts", or as self-fulfilling prophecies, and promote suspending beliefs in order to test the consequences of acting against them. This involves "acting as if" the belief does not exist in order to test the outcome of behaviours which may result if this rule was not operational. For example, if you held the belief, "I am a failure", you might never engage in any activity that had any element of potential evaluation as a result of this. However, if you acted as if this belief did not exist, you might be able to engage in such activities and the outcomes could be used as evidence regarding the belief.

Beck and colleagues also advocate the use of positive data logs, the introduction of the notion of beliefs on continua rather than black or white, the listing of the advantages and disadvantages of dysfunctional assumptions, and the examination of their long-term versus short-term utility with the client. These are described in more detail later in the chapter and illustrated using case examples.

McGinn and Young (1996) reinforce Beck's early emphasis on behavioural experiments as a vital supplement to cognitive techniques. They state that, although cognitive techniques serve to weaken schematic beliefs, they may continue to be triggered by external events, and clients may continue to behave in ways that reinforce them. A process of collaboratively identifying behavioural experiments, which test out original and alternative schematic beliefs, along with specified predictions of the outcome, and a subsequent review of the acquired evidence, is frequently required to achieve schematic change. Young (1994) describes a strategy of devising a hierarchy of new behaviours that expose the client to situations that contradict problematic schematic beliefs in some way. He also describes behavioural pattern breaking as an important component of change, in an attempt to reduce maintenance, compensation and avoidance behaviours that may be serving to maintain original schematic beliefs.

Helping clients view the advantages and disadvantages of different beliefs

In order to ensure collaborative working when challenging beliefs and to prevent falling into the trap of trying to change minds rather than guiding discovery, it is important to establish the advantages and disadvantages of clients' beliefs. It is also very important for both client and therapist to be aware of the positive and negative roles such beliefs play in the client's life. Once the advantages and disadvantages have been elicited, work can begin to see where the balance of favour falls and whether an alternative belief (which can be written to maintain as many of the advantages of the old rule as possible, without the disadvantages of the old rule) might be more useful. See Chapter 8 for an example of examining the advantages and disadvantages of a belief.

Historical testing

The aim of this cognitive technique (described by Beck, 1995; Padesky, 1994; Young & Behary, 1998) is to give clients an opportunity to re-evaluate a lifetime of evidence supporting a schematic belief and to search for counter-evidence. This is performed by breaking their life down into chunks (for example of five years), and within each period, experiences that seem to support the problematic belief can be recorded, and then questioned and re-evaluated using Socratic dialogue. A search is also made for experiences that do not support the schematic belief, and these, too, are recorded. Summaries are made at the end of each chunk, and an overall summary is drawn up at the end of the process. These various summaries are likely to contain the seeds of an alternative schematic belief.

This process may appear to be relatively straightforward to the therapist, but can be extremely difficult for the client. As with all schema change procedures, this strategy needs to be paced very carefully; such a review may take place over a number of sessions.

For example, Ruth (a 39-year-old woman) had a long history of psychotic symptoms. She was highly distressed by her voices and believed that they were the devil talking to her and goading her into wrongdoing. She believed that he was here "to tempt her" because she was intrinsically bad and flawed as a person. Her evidence for this was largely historical in nature. She had been constantly compared unfavourably with her brother as a child and was treated with cruelty while her brother was spoilt. During the evenings she would be left in her room, while her brother was allowed to mix and dine with her mother. Her mother would often tell her that she should not have been born and was rotten to the core. Together, the therapist and Ruth began to look at what appeared to Ruth to be overwhelming evidence for her badness and flawed persona. Events that had been taken as evidence were questioned as to whether they provided evidence as to her badness or had another explanation. Other life experiences that did not fit with her beliefs about herself were also obtained. The results of this historical test can be seen in Figure 10.3.

Use of pie charts

Using pie charts can be a very useful strategy if schematic beliefs represent or reflect inappropriate conclusions regarding past events. This is particularly useful for challenging self-blame for childhood sexual or physical abuse, which is an all-too-common experience for people with psychosis (for a review see Read, 1997). This cognitive method is similar to that used to challenge specific kinds of anxiety-related negative automatic thinking within the context of obsessive-compulsive disorder. It entails the construction of a "pie", the whole of which represents the cause of a negative event. A list of all possible causes is developed collaboratively with the client (such as other people, environmental events, cultural influences, etc., possibly including the client) and slices of the pie are allocated according to how much the client thinks each factor caused the event (see Chapter 8 for some examples). Clients should be encouraged to allocate slices to all other factors before themselves, particularly if inappropriate self-blame is a problem. A common outcome of this procedure is for there to be little room in the pie for

	I am bad and flawed. Belief 100%	
Age	Evidence supporting	Evidence NOT supporting
0–5	In care on three occasions	Returned to same foster family on each occasion as they liked having me
	Unwanted by mother	Mother had psychiatric problems
		Lots of pictures with me and my grandma
5–10	Still bedwetting	So do lots of children and I was upset a lot
	No friends	I wasn't allowed to mix with friends after school and I had no confidence so kept myself to myself
		My brother says I was a lovely little girl
10–15	Mum said it was my fault that Grandma died	Grandma loved me and even if I was bad, that couldn't make Grandma die
	Failed the 11 plus	It's not surprising I did less well at school than my brother as he was much less unhappy
		Used to talk to our neighbour Sue who said I was sweet
		First aid monitor at school
15–20	Beaten up by my first boyfriend	He had been in prison for violence
	Took lots of speed	I took drugs because I felt bad about myself but this is not the same as being bad
		Had a friend
20–25	First hospital admission: told I was "schizophrenic"	Being ill and being bad are different
		It is not surprising I have had some mental health problems given the shit I've been through
		Did voluntary work in a shop
		My brother said he would like me to move in with him
25–30	Another admission under section	This was a stressful period in my life
		Still doing voluntary work when well enough
		Took swimming lessons
30–35	Made homeless	The landlord had to sell the house, it was not because of me: the other tenants had to leave as well
		Started attending drop-in and playing badminton
35–39	Fight on the ward	Other woman who was ill started on me
		Back in contact with my brother
		New supported housing

Figure 10.3 Historical test

self-blame, and clients can begin to work towards reattributing negative events from the past.

Use of criteria continua

This technique, described by Padesky (1994), has a number of aims. First, it provides a baseline against which to measure change. Second, it provides a framework for change (by implying that change is possible). Third, it allows a systematic identification and accumulation of information that challenges the client's problematic schematic belief and supports alternatives. Finally, it aids interim goal setting as a client works towards desired changes.

The method begins with the identification of alternative, adaptive schematic beliefs that clients would like to endorse, if they did not hold their existing, problematic belief. An adaptive continuum is constructed, with the absence of the positive characteristic related to the belief at one end, and its greatest possible presence at the other (e.g. "not at all lovable" and "could not be more lovable"). Current ratings on this scale are obtained (these are usually very low), and the client can, at this stage, be asked to rate other people, including extreme examples, on the same scale. This activity alone can serve to change the client's self-rating, as it introduces the notion of relativity, and it will be impossible for the client to maintain an extremely low initial rating if extreme examples are used.

Objective criteria for obtaining a high rating on the scale are then discussed, using the people they have placed higher than themselves on the scale. Client and therapist can agree a list of these criteria, and for each of these a new sub-continuum is constructed. Clients then rate themselves on each of these criteria continua, and are likely to rate themselves as higher on these than they did on the original, overall scale. Clients are then encouraged to re-rate themselves on the overall scale, taking into account this new information. This procedure will sometimes result in an immediate (if reluctant!) increase in self-rating, but may not be sufficient to obtain an emotional shift linked with an enduring activation of an alternative schema. Consequently, diaries and positive data logs may be needed to record examples of the relevant characteristics, if they are present already and the clients are simply not processing them due to attentional bias. As with the other techniques described, the use of criteria continua may take a considerable time to elicit change, and clients need both to be prepared for this, and to be encouraged by their therapist on an ongoing basis.

For example, Janet believed her voices to be beamed down from satellites by lawyers or police as the result of her stealing a garden gnome from next door when she was first married (as described in Chapter 9). She reported that much of the distress afforded to her came from the voices telling her that she was bad, a statement that she very much endorsed. On attempting to review the evidence regarding the accuracy of such a statement, Janet found it extremely difficult to come up with any evidence that did not support her belief.

Therapy proceeded with the outlining of the prejudice metaphor for the maintenance of strong beliefs and the relationship that this had with the maintenance of our own negative self-beliefs. Janet described herself as totally bad, and, as the voices told her, felt herself to be one of the worst people in the world. Again, her evidence for this was based primarily on the theft of the gnome much earlier in her life, and also by the fact that her father, due to her premarital pregnancy, had forced her marriage to her husband. Janet was helped to rate these events on a continuum and began to evaluate the badness of her actions along a continuum containing other bad events:

0	100
Not bad at all	Worst thing anyone could do

On this line, Janet was encouraged to rate the bad actions of famous people throughout history and to add crimes in the newspapers and theoretical misdemeanours. Once the line was complete with a number of different "bad" actions marking the continuum from 0–100, Janet was asked to place each of her actions on the line. Janet found it impossible to place any of the events on which she based her "badness" at a position higher than 20.

Use of orthogonal continua

Similar to continua mentioned previously, the orthogonal continua technique, also described by Padesky (1994), fulfils the same aims of providing a baseline to measure change and a framework for change, and allows the systematic accumulation of challenging information. It allows clients to plot these data on orthogonal axes to evaluate and challenge the accuracy of underlying assumptions (in the "if . . . then . . ." form).

For example, John (a 33-year-old man) believed, "If I let anyone know that I am nervous then they will beat me up", and, in general, "If people appear anxious, then they will be beaten up". This belief prevented John from leaving his home at any time, as he was certain his anxiety would be spotted and, therefore, he would be set upon. An orthogonal continuum was constructed to help John view his concerns diagrammatically and evaluate how this fitted with experience from his life and the lives of others he knew (see Figure 10.4).

The following questions were asked to help John plot points on the orthogonal continua, which may help him to assess the accuracy of his belief:

• Is there anyone in the past who knows about your anxiety? Have they ever beaten you up?
• Is there anyone at present that knows about your anxiety? Have they ever beaten you up?

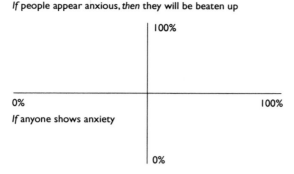

Figure 10.4 Orthogonal continua

- Do you know anyone who is not at all anxious but has been beaten up?
- Does a display of confidence always prevent people from being beaten up?
- Can you think of any circumstances where someone else has shown their anxiety and not been beaten up?
- When people are beaten up, are other factors ever involved?
- Do you know other people who suffer from anxiety? Do they always look as anxious as they feel? What happens to them? Have they been beaten up?

This information can also be used to design behavioural experiments to test such conditional assumptions (see Chapter 9).

Survey methods

Survey methods can be very useful when dealing with patients' misperceptions of the world or to gather evidence as to their concerns. This technique involves encouraging the patient to gather answers to a set of questions by asking people around them. The advantage of this is that they can select the group whose answers will mean the most to them. See Chapter 9 for a survey that was conducted with Janet in relation to her view of herself as bad.

Positive data logs

When clients have been introduced to the prejudice metaphor, positive data logs can be introduced to the client as a way of obtaining and storing information to fit with an alternative, less negative belief. Once a negative core belief (e.g. "I am a failure") has been identified, and its maintenance has been understood using the prejudice metaphor, the client can be asked about an alternative belief they would like to hold. For example, "If you were not a failure, what would you like to be instead?" Once an alternative self-belief has been generated, which is acceptable to the client, work can begin to elicit information that is consistent with this new belief. This can be done by asking the client "Has anything happened today which fits with (new belief) or has anything happened today which if it happened to someone else, you would think fitted with (new belief)?" It is imperative that written records are kept of this information and that this is continued over a considerable period of time. This positive data log represents the alternative core belief, which the client may be unable to represent internally at present, and for which, without the positive data log, evidence has in the past been either discarded or adapted to fit with the old negative belief.

After Janet had been introduced to the prejudice metaphor as a way of understanding how negative self-beliefs maintain themselves and how information that is incongruent with such beliefs is ignored or distorted, positive data logs were introduced. This involved using the idiosyncratic developmental formulation to help identify the core beliefs that were important in maintaining Janet's low self-esteem, and those that best reflected the content of the voices. These included "I am bad" and "I am stupid". Janet was then asked: "If you were not bad and stupid, then what would you like to be?" She identified, "I am OK" and "I can do some things adequately", as the beliefs that she would like to develop. Janet was then asked to keep data of all daily activities past and present, which she could use as evidence for these new beliefs. She was asked to include things she had done that, if done by other people, she would regard as evidence that they were OK and could do some things adequately, in order to prevent distortion or avoidance of positive personal information.

Worksheets or flashcards

Worksheets or flashcards are means of linking current experiences of affect with existing schematic beliefs, and challenging them in an ongoing and systematic way. They can be used in conjunction with other methods to ensure that the skills developed during therapy are put into practice. One example is Judy Beck's Core Belief Worksheet (Beck, 1995), which allows the documentation of original and alternative core beliefs, the extent to which each is believed, and an accumulation of evidence that supports the alternatives. Young's (1994) schema therapy flashcard (also described in Young & Behary, 1998) includes four components. These are acknowledgement of current feelings, identification of schematic belief or beliefs that account for them, reality testing and behavioural self-instruction. Flashcards are particularly important for people with psychotic experiences as they often have problems with memory (either due to medication, preoccupation with psychotic experiences or cognitive deficits).

Imagery modification or rescripting

The utilisation of imagery in cognitive therapy to achieve schema change has become popular since the early 1990s (e.g. Beck, 1995; Hackmann, 1997; Layden, Newman, Freeman, & Morse, 1993; Schmucker, Dancu, Foa, & Niederee, 1995; Wells & Hackmann, 1993; Young & Behary, 1998). Edwards (1989, 1990) has attempted to provide a conceptualisation of an imagery modification technique, utilised in Gestalt therapy, within a cognitive framework. He describes imagery as providing "a special kind of access to cognitive structures" (Edwards, 1989, p. 284) and, in its representation of beliefs and assumptions, as an important tool for the challenging and restructuring of them. The aim of the strategy seems to be the examination of schema in their developmental context, leading to the restructuring of important past events and therefore the modification of schematic beliefs that are derived from them. Use of imagery rescripting within therapy allows the examination of assumptions and the experience and expression of strong emotions in a contained and safe environment. As used within a cognitive framework, the primary aim of these procedures is change in perspective, rather than catharsis, and unlike more dynamic psychotherapy, the content of this work is negotiated in advance. Layden et al. (1993) have described a sequence of prompts for eliciting and modifying unconditional schematic beliefs, developed in childhood, utilising imagery. Components of this include the selection of critical early events, either directly via problematic memories, or via linking back from current experiences of high affect, the elaboration of the child's perceptions and responses to the event, and the challenging of that perception. This is done using the client as an adult in the image, or another trusted adult. The final element is the re-enactment of events by the client so that the outcome is empowering for him or her. Schmucker and colleagues (Schmucker & Niederee, 1995; Schmucker et al., 1995) have developed imagery rescripting procedures for childhood sexual abuse survivors, with three components. These are detailed imaginal exposure to traumatic early memories to allow emotional processing to occur, the utilisation of the adult self in the imagery to "save" the child, challenging schematic beliefs related to vulnerability such as helplessness or powerlessness, and fostering a sense of mastery, and the provision of nurturing by the adult self to the child self to challenge schematic beliefs related to the self, such as worthlessness, unlovability or badness.

Interpersonal techniques and the use of the therapeutic relationship

Safran (1990b) proposes that the core structures that need modification in order to achieve long-term change are "interpersonal schemas" which are embedded in "cognitive-interpersonal cycles". The former is defined as "a generic knowledge structure based on previous interpersonal experiences that contains information relevant to the maintenance of interpersonal relatedness" (Safran, 1990a, p. 87).

Cognitive interpersonal cycles are defined as "an unbroken causal loop through which maladaptive expectations and dysfunctional behaviours maintain one another" (Safran, 1990a, p. 87). Safran (1990b) suggests that the therapist becomes a participant-observer in the therapeutic context, and utilises his or her own emotions and "action tendencies" to generate hypotheses regarding the client's interpersonal style. The major objective is for the therapist to intervene in a way that elicits new and more adaptive behaviour from the client. In the long term, this enables them to elicit different responses from other significant people outside the therapeutic relationship, and as a consequence, to build up a range of new interpersonal experiences. These objectives are initially achieved by the therapist identifying his or her own emotional reactions to the client. A hypothesis of interpersonal theory is that the probability that the therapist's reaction to a client parallels the reactions of others increases with the intensity and rigidity of the client's dysfunctional style. Hence, with individuals with more severe and enduring difficulties, it could be expected that there would be a high correlation between the reactions of the therapist and the reactions of others to the client. The therapist must, therefore, attempt to unhook him or herself from any emotional reaction, and intentionally refrain from carrying through the automatically elicited action tendency. This, it is hypothesised, will provide a new interpersonal experience for the client, and consequently elicit new, more adaptive interpersonal behaviour (Safran, 1990b). A second method within this framework is for the therapist to provide "meta-communicative feedback" regarding their own reactions, and the specific (often subtle) verbal and non-verbal client behaviours that elicit them. This allows the client and therapist to decentre from the cognitions, emotions and behaviours, and consequently enables examination, reformulation and the opportunity for testing the predictions of dysfunctional interpersonal schemas. Such strategies can be useful for dealing with emotions aroused by suspiciousness, negative symptoms or thought disorder in patients.

Core beliefs and the content of voices

The strategies that have been outlined in this chapter can be applied to address the content of voices in exactly the same way as they can be used in relation to beliefs. For example, Joe (a 24-year-old man) heard voices telling him that he was evil and bad. The therapist and Joe used a historical test of his life, a badness continuum, a survey regarding what constituted badness and a positive data log in order to gather evidence and systematically challenge what the voices were saying.

Summary

This chapter has begun to outline some of the schema change techniques that have been used over recent years. This is by no means intended to be an exclusive and exhaustive list, but is rather intended to present some of the techniques that may help to change some of our more strongly held cognitions. There is no doubt that there is scope for other techniques to be used or adapted from other therapeutic modalities and translated into a cognitive framework. However, as mentioned earlier, care must be taken to ensure that research keeps pace with the application of techniques, and as yet, this has failed to be the case with schema-focused therapy.

Chapter 11

Negative symptoms

In this chapter, we consider the role that cognitive therapy may have in helping people who are experiencing the "negative symptoms" of psychosis. Our discussion will be necessarily tentative, as cognitive therapists have so far devoted very little attention to these kinds of difficulties, preferring instead to focus on positive symptoms such as hallucinations and delusions. We begin by defining what negative symptoms are. The conventional view that these symptoms reflect a basic (almost certainly organic) deficit that is a core feature of schizophrenia will be considered alongside some ideas about how it might be possible to understand these difficulties from a psychological perspective. We shall argue that, in the case of many patients, negative symptoms are often exacerbated by depression, social isolation, a lack of reinforcement, over-medication, the trauma of hospital admission, and other sequelae of positive symptoms. Indeed, other marginalised groups in society, for example the long-term unemployed, often appear to experience phenomena similar to those classified by psychiatrists and psychologists as negative symptoms. We shall conclude by presenting some ideas about how these factors might be addressed in a formulation-based approach to the treatment of individual patients and present a case study that illustrates this approach.

What are negative symptoms?

The concept of negative symptoms was introduced into psychiatry by Tim Crow (1980) and subsequently elaborated by other researchers, notably Nancy Andreasen (1989) in the United States. Crow borrowed the term from the nineteenth-century neurologist Hughlings Jackson, who used it to describe the deficits experienced by neurological patients. Jackson believed that these deficits were the consequence of the loss of higher mental functions, whereas the abnormal behaviours sometimes observed in neurological patients reflected a consequent failure to inhibit primitive mental functions. Adapting this idea, Crow argued that negative symptoms are characterised by an absence of behaviours that are desirable, in contrast to the positive symptoms, which are characterised by the presence of behaviours and experiences (for example, hallucinations and delusions) that would preferably be absent. According to Crow's original hypothesis, the two types of symptoms are the product of different neuropathological processes – abnormal functioning of the dopamine system in the case of positive symptoms and neurodegeneration in the case of the negative symptoms.

Even the most enthusiastic biological psychiatrist would concede that this account is no longer adequate. It is fair to say that the dopamine theory of schizophrenia has not lived up to its early promise, and convincing evidence of abnormal dopamine pathways in the brains of schizophrenia patients has proved elusive (Carlsson, 1995). Nor is it clear that neuropathological findings initially attributed to the negative symptoms, for example, enlarged cerebral ventricles, really are specific to these symptoms (Woodruff & Lewis, 1996). However, the observation that delusions and hallucinations on one hand, and the negative symptoms on the other, tend to cluster together into syndromes has survived empirical investigation, albeit with at least one important caveat. Most studies that have attempted to address the question, "Which symptoms go together?" (for example, by using the statistical technique of factor analysis) have identified at least *three* main groups of symptoms rather than Crow's original two: positive symptoms, negative symptoms and symptoms of cognitive disorganisation (mainly attentional difficulties and thought, language and communication disorders) (Andreasen et al., 1995; Liddle, 1987). It is clear from these and other studies that positive and negative symptoms do not correlate with each other (McKenna, 1994). Interestingly, studies of psychotic patients with diagnoses other than schizophrenia, for example patients with diagnoses of psychotic depression or bipolar disorder, have revealed the same three groups of symptoms (Toomey, Faraone, Simpson, & Tsuang, 1998), as have studies of schizotypal traits in ordinary people (Bentall, Claridge, & Slade, 1989; Vollema & van den Bosch, 1995). As these findings appear to hold up in cross-cultural comparisons (Reynolds, Raine, Mellingen, Venables, & Mednick, 2000) it seems likely that the distinction between positive, negative and disorganisation symptoms reflects three main ways in which the experiences of psychotic patients vary, although we should be careful not to jump to the conclusion that the negative symptoms therefore all have the same underlying cause.

Despite the unambiguous evidence of a negative symptom cluster, researchers have differed when listing the individual symptoms belonging to it. For example, affective flattening (absence of emotion), alogia (poverty of content of speech) and avolition (lack of will) are listed as negative symptoms in DSM-IV (APA, 1994). Nancy Andreasen (see Andreasen, 1989; Andreasen et al., 1995) also includes anhedonia (the inability to experience pleasure), apathy and attentional impairment as negative symptoms, while DSM-IV subsumes anhedonia under the heading of associated features of schizophrenia.

Affective flattening refers to the lack of emotional expression seen in some psychotic patients. Andreasen's Schedule for the Assessment of Negative Symptoms (SANS) lists seven main indicators of this symptom: unchanging facial expression expression ("the patient's face appears wooden, mechanical, frozen"), decreased spontaneous movements, paucity of expressive gestures, poor eye-contact, affective non-responsivity ("failure to smile or laugh when prompted"), inappropriate affect, and lack of vocal inflections. It is important to note that these indicators all concern the *expression* of emotion, rather than subjective emotional experience. In a remarkable case study, Bouricius (1989) has described the example of her own son, who was consistently rated as suffering from severe affective flattening by mental health professionals, but whose diaries revealed a vivid and tormented emotional life. A number of investigators have studied the relationship between affective flattening and subjective emotions more systematically, for example by observing patients and asking them to report their emotions when watching emotionally stimulating film clips, and have consistently reported that subjective emotion in affectively flattened patients is quite normal (Berenbaum & Oltmanns, 1992; Ellgring & Smith, 1998; Kring, Kerr, Smith, & Neale, 1993). This finding has at least two important implications for the cognitive-behaviour therapist. First, despite appearance to the contrary, emotional disturbance may be an important problem for many negative symptom patients. Second, lack of emotional responsivity by the patient when discussing particular topics should not necessarily be taken as evidence that those topics are psychologically unimportant.

The SANS lists several indicators of *anhedonia*: a lack of recreational interests and activities, a lack of sexual interest and activity, an inability to feel intimacy and closeness, and inadequate relationships with friends and peers. These indicators all refer to sources of social pleasure (hence, the SANS describes this symptom as anhedonia-asociality), but it is clear that some people also report an absence of pleasure from physical activities and stimuli (for example, fine food or beautiful scenery: Chapman, Chapman, & Raulin, 1976). Studies have consistently shown that these symptoms are not restricted to schizophrenia patients, but are also widely experienced by patients suffering from emotional disorders, especially depression (Blanchard, Bellack, & Mueser, 1994; Harrow, Grinker, Holzman, & Kayton, 1977; Katsanis, Iacono, & Beiser, 1990). As might be expected, when anhedonic patients are questioned about their experience of emotion, they report low levels of positive emotion. However, they also report higher than normal levels of negative emotion (Blanchard, Mueser, & Bellack, 1998), suggesting that anhedonia is not simply an absence of emotion. Therapists should therefore be alert to the possibility that the experiences of anhedonic patients reflect similar processes and issues to those commonly encountered in the depressed patient.

The three indicators of avolition or *apathy* listed in the SANS are poor grooming and hygiene, lack of persistence at work or school, and lack of physical energy. The apathetic patient is usually instantly recognisable from his or her presentation at initial assessment, although therapists should be aware that energetic relatives or other carers are sometimes able to mask the unkempt appearance that would otherwise prevail. Again, it is clear that these signs can be observed in patients who are not psychotic. Fatigue, lack of drive and a loss of interest in appearance are often seen in severely depressed patients, for example.

Four indicators of *alogia* are listed in the SANS: poverty of speech, poverty of content of speech, blocking of speech and increased latency of verbal responses. Poverty of speech refers to a lack of overall speech production, so that the patient observed with this difficulty seems hard or even impossible to engage in conversation. Poverty of content of speech, on the other hand, refers to speech that is vague and relatively lacking in meaning. Paradoxically, these signs may appear to be negatively correlated as patients with poverty of speech may not say enough to allow the clinician to determine that the content of speech is deficient. Although poverty of speech may be evident in depressed patients, longitudinal studies indicate that the course that this symptom follows may differ between diagnostic groups. Depressed patients treated in hospital typically show a reduction in poverty of speech as their treatment progresses whereas negative symptom schizophrenia patients, after discharge from the hospital environment, may show an exacerbation of this symptom (Ragin, Pogue-Geile, & Oltmanns, 1989).

At this point it is appropriate at this point to say something about the significance of the apparent similarity between negative symptoms in patients with a diagnosis of depression and those with a diagnosis of schizophrenia. In fact, this has been a topic of some dispute between researchers, some of whom have preferred to emphasise the similarities whereas other have emphasised differences. A longitudinal study of schizophrenia patients, for example, (Harrow, Yonan, Sands, & Marengo, 1994) found that treatment with neuroleptic medication was associated with high level of depression and anhedonia, suggesting that these two symptoms may be linked. In contrast, other researchers have reported that depression correlates more with positive symptoms than negative symptoms (Norman & Malla, 1991) and that no difference in the level of negative symptoms can be found between psychotic patients who are concurrently depressed and those who are not (Hirsch et al., 1989). Unfortunately, this debate has been obscured by treating both negative symptoms as homogeneous phenomena ("lumps"). From the evidence we have described already, it is evident that negative symptoms are heterogeneous and the same can almost certainly be said for the symptoms of depression (Pilgrim & Bentall, 1999; Snaith, 1995). The appropriate question to ask, therefore, is to what extent do the same psychological processes contribute to specific symptoms of depression and specific negative symptoms? Whereas a comprehensive answer to this question must lie some distance in the future, cognitive-behaviour therapists may address it in their patients by constructing adequate formulations of their patients' symptoms.

Negative symptoms as an intrinsic disease process

Research on negative symptoms has been dominated by the assumption that they are intrinsic features of an underlying psychotic disease process, coupled with the uneasy recognition that very similar looking difficulties are quite frequently observed in patients who are demoralised, anxious or depressed, or can be consequences of various aspects of psychiatric care (for example, neuroleptic treatment or institutionalsiation). Faced with this dilemma, some researchers have argued that it is important to identify those negative symptoms that are *true* features of schizophrenia.

This approach has been taken by William Carpenter and his colleagues, who have attempted to identify a schizophrenia *deficit syndrome* (Carpenter, Heinrichs, & Wagman, 1988). The symptoms which they believe often meet these requirements are restricted emotion as indicated by a lack of facial expression, gestures and vocal inflection, diminished subjective emotional experiences, poverty of speech, loss of interests, a diminished sense of purpose and reduced social drive. According to Carpenter, it is possible to establish that these symptoms are enduring features of illness by excluding likely extrinsic causes such as depression or drug side-effects. Carpenter argues that this can be achieved with a high degree of reliability if information about the development of the illness is obtained from a suitable informant, for example a close relative of the patient (Kirkpatrick, Buchanan, McKenney, Alphs, & Carpenter, 1989).

However, this approach seems to suffer from two important limitations. First, it involves what the behaviourist psychologist B. F. Skinner used to refer to as the *formalistic fallacy* – the assumption that all examples of the same class of behaviour (in this case behaviours subsumed by the definition of the deficit syndrome) have the same cause. Apparently similar behaviour by two different patients may well have different causes, which is why a formulation-based approach to treatment is necessary. Second, Carpenter's attempt to define intrinsic features of schizophrenia by *excluding* probable environmental causes assumes without any real justification an exclusively biological account of the illness. The discovery of a morbid physiological process that plays a causal role in some negative symptoms would be much more convincing evidence of a deficit syndrome, but this has yet to be achieved.

Of course, it is possible that some negative symptoms are relatively stable traits that persist over many years, which is what Carpenter's deficit syndrome concept attempts to capture. Longitudinal research has confirmed that some negative features found in psychotic patients predate the onset of florid psychotic symptoms. For example, it has been found that levels of anhedonia in schizophrenia patients correlate with evidence of poor social functioning before the onset of a recognisable illness (Katsanis, Iacono, Beiser, & Lacey, 1992). However, even this observation does not preclude the possibility that environmental factors play an important role in the development of these symptoms. It is not difficult to imagine environmental factors that might lead to social isolation, for example, or that social isolation might increase a person's vulnerability to developing a full-blown psychotic illness.

These arguments lead us to conclude that, from the viewpoint of the cognitive therapist, at least, the attempt to distinguish between a deficit syndrome and other negative symptoms is unhelpful. When attempting to design psychological treatments, it is more useful to ask *to what extent* different environmental factors may influence different types of negative symptoms, and to try and identify psychological processes that might mediate these influences. This kind of analysis should allow us to identify opportunities for intervention.

Does the environment influence negative symptoms?

Social isolation

Social isolation and an absence of stimulation have been identified as likely influences on negative symptoms by some researchers. Indeed, during the 1960s and 1970s, this type of influence was assumed by most psychiatrists and psychologists, and provided one argument for demolishing asylums and placing patients in the community. Wing and Brown (1970), for example, studied patients who had been subjected to long periods of hospitalisation, and concluded that increasing patients' opportunities for meaningful stimulation should remediate what are now known as negative symptoms, although they also cautioned that over-stimulating patients might cause an exacerbation of positive symptoms. Other commentators have noted similarities between the behaviour (or lack of behaviour) of highly institutionalised patients and people who have suffered long-term unemployment or imprisonment. The observation that work opportunities improve the long-term prospects of institutionalised patients suggests that this comparison may have some validity. Interestingly, there is historical evidence that the outcome of psychotic illness tends to improve during periods of economic growth in which job opportunities are relatively abundant (Warner, 1985).

During the course of an assessment interview, the therapist should enquire about the opportunities for social stimulation available to the patient. The discovery of impoverished social networks might lead the therapist and patient to engage in a problem-solving exercise with the aim of finding ways of increasing opportunities for social contact and social skills learning. If social isolation or lack of stimulation are causing negative symptoms for a particular patient, it is important to assess and formulate the factors that have led to this. For example, one person may be socially isolated because of her social anxiety, whereas another may be isolated due to his concerns about the stigma of mental illness. Other patients may be isolated simply because they have moved to another district and have no way of meeting new people. Clearly, the formulation of the causes of social isolation or lack of stimulation will determine the appropriate treatment strategies.

Trauma and PTSD

Another possibility raised by some researchers is that the *trauma* associated with the emergence of positive symptoms and subsequent hospitalisation sometimes plays a role in the development of negative symptoms. McGorry et al. (1991) have suggested that the negative symptoms of schizophrenia may be related to symptoms of PTSD, such as emotional numbing (which sounds similar to flat affect) and avoidance (which could manifest itself in a similar way to apathy). There is certainly a growing body of evidence to suggest that people with psychosis can develop PTSD in relation to both hospital admissions and their psychotic symptoms (Frame and Morrison, 2001; McGorry et al., 1991; Shaw, McFarlane & Bookless, 1997). For example, it is very common for patients to experience traumatic memories, flashbacks and nightmares about their time on an acute psychiatric ward, and some negative symptoms may emerge as a coping response to this (due to fears of another admission). It is also common for people to be traumatised by their hallucinations or delusions; for example, if you believe, with total conviction, that you are being persecuted by a government agency, then this is likely to be as capable of producing PTSD as if it were really happening. Again, PTSD symptoms such as avoidance and emotional numbing would make sense in such circumstances. Other negative symptoms of PTSD, such as affective constriction, estrangement from others, difficulty concentrating, feelings of derealisation, detachment and general neglect, can also be seen to significantly overlap with the negative symptoms of psychosis. If PTSD is implicated in the development or maintenance of negative symptoms, then intervention strategies derived from a cognitive understanding of PTSD (e.g. Ehlers & Clark, 2000) are likely to be useful. These could include evaluating beliefs about the intrusive symptoms of PTSD, examining the personal meaning of the event that resulted in traumatisation and modifying unhelpful behavioural responses (such as safety behaviours).

Early experience

It is likely that other environmental factors influence the development of negative symptoms but, in the absence of appropriate research, it is only possible to guess what these may be. Speculating, it is possible to think of many ways in which adverse or unsatisfactory early experiences might place the future psychotic patient on a life trajectory that culminates in social withdrawal, an inability to express emotion or a lack of motivation. For example, an absence of suitable social opportunities during critical stages of development might possibly have this effect. The observation that patients who have grown up in rural areas (where social isolation is more common) are more likely to exhibit negative symptoms than those raised in urban areas is consistent with this hypothesis (Varma et al., 1997). Alternatively, it is possible that some patients withdraw from social relationships as a consequence of experiencing punishing social encounters during early life. Consistent with this hypothesis, Blanchard et al. (1998) found that social anxiety in schizophrenia patients correlated with social anhedonia (failure to obtain pleasure from social relationships) but not physical anhedonia (the inability to experience physical pleasure). In an earlier study, Penn, Hope, Spaulding, and Kucera (1994) found that self-reported social anxiety and anxiety observed during a role-play correlated with negative symptoms but not positive symptoms in schizophrenia patients. Incorporating the role of early experience in a formulation of negative symptoms can be important, and can help to normalise such experiences.

Psychological mediators of environmental influences

Environmental factors must influence negative symptoms by affecting psychological processes involved in motivation and emotion. Unfortunately, these processes have hardly been studied in patients with negative symptoms. However, if particular psychological mechanisms could be identified, this would present some obvious opportunities for psychological intervention. The following thoughts about likely mechanisms are necessarily speculative but should provide helpful avenues to explore with individual patients.

Depression

Given the apparent overlap between some negative symptoms and some features of depression, one obvious possibility is that those processes known to be involved in depression may be implicated. For example, people who are depressed typically hold negative beliefs about themselves. They often have dysfunctional standards for evaluating their own achievements (Beck, 1976) and believe themselves to fall far short of their ideals (Higgins, Bond, Klein, & Strauman, 1986). Often, depressed people also interpret events in a pessimistic fashion, attributing negative events to causes that are internal (located in the self), global (likely to affect all areas of life) and stable (likely to persist long into the future) (Abramson, Metalsky, & Alloy, 1989; Abramson, Seligman, & Teasdale, 1978; Alloy et al., 1999). It is therefore possible that similar biases in the interpretation of events may play a role in the apparent apathy and social withdrawal evidenced by the patient with negative symptoms. Perhaps their pessimism is so great that some patients feel that there is no point in seeking out reinforcement, constructing plans for the future, or acting on them. For simplicity, we can call this the *depression/ demoralisation hypothesis*. If depression appears implicated in the experiencing of negative symptoms, it is again important to develop a case conceptualisation to understand this. Treatment strategies should be derived from this but are likely to include activity scheduling (as described in relation to negative symptoms in Chapter 9) and the identification and challenging of negative automatic thoughts about self, world and future.

Self-efficacy

A second, related possibility is that patients with negative symptoms, especially avolition/apathy, do not believe that their actions are likely to lead to successful outcomes. In a substantial programme of research, Albert Bandura (1997) has shown that an individual's decisions and motivation to act are heavily influenced by these kinds of beliefs, known as *self-efficacy expectations*. It is important to recognise that this theory is not as circular as it at first appears; numerous studies by Bandura and others have shown that manipulating an individual's self-efficacy expectations results in changes in actual behaviour. For example, in an experiment by Cervone and Peake (1986), the researchers measured the extent to which psychologically healthy participants would persist at a difficult and repetitive task. Self-efficacy expectations were manipulated by asking people how many times they thought they would complete the task in two stages. First, the participants were asked an "anchoring" question, which was either "Do you think you can do the task more than four times?" or "Do you think you can do the task more than sixteen times?" This was followed by the open question: "How many times do you think you will do it?" The anchoring question influenced the participants' estimates on the open question, so that those given the high anchor typically made higher estimates than those given the low anchor. These estimates were in turn reflected in the participants' actual performance on the repetitive task.

It would not be surprising if people who had suffered a severe disruption to their life because of psychiatric hospitalisation had low self-efficacy expectations. Relatively brief illnesses might have this effect, especially if patients are educated to believe that they have an incurable and lifelong condition by well-meaning psychiatric staff (in our experience a common occurrence). However, only one study has so far collected evidence relevant to this *self-efficacy hypothesis*. As part of a larger study, MacCarthy, Benson, and Brewin (1986) asked psychotic patients to complete a questionnaire measuring their beliefs about the difficulty of daily tasks. Patients who were described as chronically ill estimated the tasks to be much more difficult than acutely ill patients, suggesting that they had much lower self-efficacy expectations.

Self-efficacy expectations, and other beliefs about the self, should be assessed during the course of a cognitive-behavioural interview. This could include the therapist asking about the patient's perception of the likelihood that they would succeed in a series of simple behavioural tasks. In the event that pessimistic expectations are detected, the therapist could negotiate a series of simple and achievable goals, which will form the subject of behavioural experiments designed to test the validity of the patients' expectations.

Anxiety

If, as we have speculated earlier, social anxiety plays a role in some negative symptoms, cognitive and behavioural processes involved in anxiety may also be worth examining in negative-symptom patients. Anxious people tend to be hypervigilant for stimuli relating to their anxiety (Eysenck, 1992), but we are aware of no studies that have investigated vigilance for social stimuli in patients with negative symptoms. The thought processes of anxious people tend to be dominated by themes of threat (Beck, 1976) but, again, the content of thoughts associated with negative-symptom patients has not been studied. Clearly, such thoughts ought to be explored by therapists working with negative-symptom patients, as beliefs about apparently impending but actually unrealistic threats might easily be challenged using conventional cognitive-behaviour therapy techniques. Similarly, avoidance characterises anxiety disorders such as social phobia, agoraphobia and PTSD, and the reduction of avoidance, and the testing of beliefs underlying it, using behavioural experiments is likely to be of use.

Survival strategies and safety behaviours

It is also possible that negative symptoms may develop as safety behaviours or survival strategies. As mentioned earlier, early experience may have a role in negative symptomatology. For example, if a patient was raised in an environment where taking pleasure in something was frowned upon, such as a strongly religious or puritanical family, it may be that not experiencing or expressing pleasure could be useful, and help to avoid emotional or physical punishment. In addition to being functional in the past, it is often the case that negative symptoms may be functional in the present. For example, many patients have experienced being admitted to hospital or having their medication increased following getting upset in front of a mental health professional; therefore, they may develop flat affect in order to prevent their feared outcome of readmission or medication increases. If this is the case, then useful strategies for treatment can include examining the advantages and disadvantages of the behaviour (both in the past and the present), conducting behavioural experiments in order to test the accuracy of such beliefs, and considering alternative strategies for preventing feared outcomes (if the fear is a realistic one).

The effects of drugs on negative symptoms

The possible impact of pharmacological interventions on negative symptoms merits special consideration. Whereas the impact of the social environment on negative symptoms has been almost completely ignored by researchers, the effects of drugs are quite well understood. When Henri Laborit, a French naval surgeon, first suggested that the experimental antihistamine later known as chlorpromazine might have useful psychiatric effects, he was moved by the observation that surgical patients receiving it exhibited a curious psychic indifference to their environment (Shorter, 1997). Leading researchers who worked on the development of neuroleptic drug treatment during the 1950s, for example Jean Delay and Pierre Deniker in Paris and Heinz Lehmann in Quebec, all noted this effect, some even suggesting that the new antipsychotic drugs produced a chemical lobotomy (Cohen, 1997). Although this idea is not taken seriously by most psychopharmacologists now, the existence of a *neuroleptic induced deficit syndrome* (NIDS) is widely recognised (Lewander, 1994). Typically, patients experiencing this syndrome feel lethargic and lacking in motivation, so that the demands of ordinary life may seem almost insurmountable. Evidence that this may be the price that some patients have to pay in order to enjoy the clinical benefits of neuroleptic treatment was obtained in a randomised clinical trial of maintenance neuroleptic therapy, in which Crow, MacMillan, Johnson, and Johnstone (1986) took the unusual step of recording the participants' achievements during the study period. Whereas those given drug treatment suffered fewer relapses, they also achieved less than patients receiving placebo medication. Consistent with this finding, a five-year longitudinal investigation of a large cohort of psychotic patients (Harrow et al., 1994) found that, even when controlling for initial symptoms, patients taking neuroleptics experienced higher levels of depression and anhedonia than those who refused them. It is also possible that the use of illicit drugs (particularly opiates and cannabis) may lead to conditions such as apathy and flat affect, which may be viewed as negative symptoms.

In addition to the well-documented effect of neuroleptic medication on motivation and emotion, it seems likely that these drugs can exacerbate negative symptoms by several indirect pathways. Patients receiving these drugs often experience extra-pyramidal side-effects such as Parkinsonian symptoms (severe shaking and stiffness), dystonias (uncontrollable muscle movements) and akathisia (a subjective state that combines dysphoria, extreme feelings of restlessness and an inability to act). (For a more detailed account of these and other neuroleptic side-effects, see Day & Bentall, 1996.) Although the more recently developed atypical neuroleptics (for example, clozapine, respirodone and olanzapine) are less likely to produce these side-effects, it is still quite common to see patients who are affected by them. Weight gain, another neuroleptic side-effect, is just as likely to be experienced by patients taking atypical neuroleptics as by patients taking the long-established typical medications. Allison et al. (1999), found that, on average, patients taking olanzapine put on 4.45 kilogrammes during their first ten weeks of treatment. Although these kinds of side-effects are distressing in their own right, they may also interfere with the patient's ability – or willingness – to engage in social activities. For example, severely overweight patients, or patients who feel that their Parkinsonian symptoms are unsightly, may feel embarrassed by their appearance, or may find some types of activities too exhausting. The remedy for such a lamentable situation is obvious, but may be difficult to bring about in health services in which biological theories of psychosis predominate. However, sharing an idiosyncratic formulation that implicates antipsychotic medication in the production of negative symptoms may be helpful in changing prescribing behaviour. Other useful strategies (all of which should be formulation driven) include the involvement of advocates, the sharing of information regarding medications with patients, and role-playing discussions about medication with the patients to help them maximise their chances of getting their desired outcome.

The patient's medication should be reviewed with the aim of determining whether the dose of neuroleptic medication received is excessive (research shows that total doses equivalent to more than 350 mg/day of chlorpromazine can rarely be justified: Bollini, Pampallona, Orza, Adams, & Chalmers, 1994). The patient's experience of neuroleptic side-effects can also be assessed using the Liverpool University Neuroleptic Side Effect Rating Scale (LUNSERS: Day et al., 1995), a brief questionnaire that can be completed even by severely disabled patients. As we have already noted, the obvious remedy for a psychiatrist's excessive pharmacological zeal is obvious, but the diplomatic skills of Machiavelli may be required in order to bring this about. Consulting with a sympathetic psychiatric pharmacist may be appropriate in this situation.

Case example

Luke (a 25-year-old man) was referred because of negative symptoms including flat affect, apathy and avolition. He had been bullied at school, and hit by his parents when he got upset at home. Both these experiences led him to believe that expressing emotions was dangerous, so he tried to keep a "blank expression" from an early age. This belief was later reinforced by his experiences of being admitted to hospital against his will, which he attributed to having shown that he was upset. His apathy and avolition seemed to be related to his lack of opportunities for meaningful activity, as he spent all day on his own in the flat, and was reluctant to go out because this caused him to experience anxiety. If he went out, he would worry that he was going to relapse once he noticed any anxiety sensations (as his community psychiatric nurse had told him to avoid stress, because stress was bad and could cause relapses) and would have intrusive memories of times when he had been acutely psychotic in the past. He would, therefore, go home and avoid going out in future. The case formulation that was developed, based on the cognitive model outlined in Chapter 3, is given in Figure 11.1.

Intervention strategies were guided by the formulation. These included education about thought suppression, and behavioural experiments to evaluate the accuracy of this information. Activity scheduling was used in order to challenge his belief that he could not experience pleasure or achievement in his own flat, and his catastrophic beliefs regarding the likelihood of relapse were identified and challenged using an examination of the evidence regarding past relapses and non-relapses, and behavioural experiments in which he increased his busyness without having a relapse. The advantages and disadvantages of his beliefs about expressing emotions were also considered, and behavioural experiments were used to evaluate their accuracy.

Summary

It can be seen that adopting a single symptom-focused approach to the negative symptoms of psychosis is likely to produce a better understanding of the underlying mechanisms than will a syndrome-focused approach. There are likely to be multiple pathways to each of the negative symptoms, which make the use of an idiosyncratic case conceptualisation all the more important and necessary. Factors that should be considered in developing such a formulation include depression, anxiety, PTSD, early experience, social isolation, beliefs, safety behaviours and over-medication. The selection of intervention strategies will be based on the formulation.

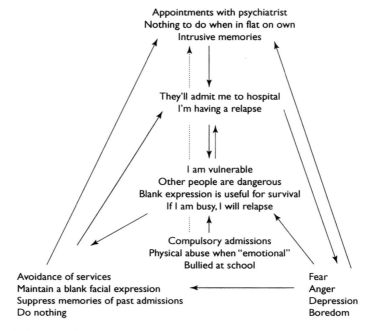

Figure 11.1 A case formulation

Part III

Implementation and maintaining process

Chapter 12

Problems associated with psychosis

People attempting to make a recovery from psychosis may experience associated psychological problems and difficulties such as anxiety, depression, substance abuse and personality problems. We use the term *associated* rather than the more conventional (and medical) co-morbid after Bermanzohn, Porto and Siris (1997), and with regard to the clinical difficulty in actually unravelling the chronology of psychological problems in people with psychosis. Social phobia, post-traumatic stress disorder (PTSD), depression and other psychological difficulties can arise in a person affected by psychosis, and it may not always be helpful (or correct) to understand such phenomena as the *inevitable* sequelae of psychosis itself, and enjoying the status only of epiphenomena in terms of clinical foci. Such problems may precede psychotic episodes and may even be implicated in the development of psychosis through increasing personal vulnerability to psychotic experiences. For other people with psychosis, psychological problems may arise as a result of trying to make an adjustment to psychosis in the face of unhelpful and stigmatising beliefs held about psychotic illness and psychological problems. The process of psychiatric treatment itself, including (but not exclusive to) involuntary treatment, may be implicated in the development of psychological problems such as PTSD (Frame and Morrison, 2001; McGorry et al., 1991). Experience of psychosis may also lead to underlying psychological difficulties becoming more pronounced and disabling. Other problems may emerge as a consequence of short-term attempts to cope with psychotic phenomena including substance abuse and alcohol problems.

Given the range of possibilities in terms of the chronology and aetiology of supposedly mild to moderate psychological difficulties, and personality disorders, in people with psychosis, we consider it more accurate and helpful to regard these as associated rather than as co-morbid problems. This is to ensure that these distressing and potentially disabling problems experienced by people with psychosis are given due consideration in therapeutic endeavours. People with psychosis may have problems with anxiety and depression without reaching a diagnostic threshold for any specific disorder. Therapists and people with psychosis may still wish to devote time to these difficulties, given their potential to arrest normal development (and the recovery process), particularly among young people in the stage of development sometimes known as "early adult transition" (Jackson, Edwards, Hulbert, & McGorry, 1999).

In this chapter we examine the prevalence of other psychological problems among people with psychosis, in particular problems with anxiety, depression, substance abuse and personality disorders. With reference to Chapters 4 and 5, we consider the assessment of people with such difficulties within the context of psychosis. Reference to appropriate approaches to the formulation of such associated problems within the context of psychosis will be made, and an example provided of a formulation of a person with psychosis and associated problems of anxiety. Standard cognitive therapy treatment procedures will be briefly described and possible modifications to such standard procedures for people with psychosis and associated disorders will be discussed.

Other psychological difficulties among people with psychosis

Although the prevalence of anxiety disorders, depression and other psychological problems is high among people with psychosis, services have historically been poor at targeting such disorders for effective treatment. In part, this has been due to the neglect of people with psychosis by most psychological therapists and researchers (until recent times). Perhaps part of this neglect is also associated with the undue pessimism concerning outcome in psychosis, which has limited therapeutic endeavour and creativity. Conceptual confusion has also existed concerning the nature of psychological difficulties such as anxiety and depression within psychosis, with many therapists, and psychiatric orthodoxy, regarding such problems as completely dependent on the psychotic illness itself. This frequently led to assumptions that efforts aimed at treating such disorders were fruitless, at best, and possibly counter-productive. As the unifying concept of schizophrenia begins to unravel in the light of new research into the psychological processes and mechanisms that may account for specific psychotic symptoms (see Chapters 1 and 3), such an approach is clearly no longer adequate.

The alternative to such an approach is to formulate the difficulties of people with psychosis at the level of the person, utilising psychological formulations and treatment strategies when they have been empirically validated and appear to apply to the person being helped. What we are suggesting is that therapists simply utilise empirically validated psychological treatment approaches, where they exist, for disorders such as panic disorder and depression in people with psychosis, if they seem applicable to the formulation. As the rest of this book illustrates, we do not believe that therapists must assume that psychosis is so different that nothing they have learned in the treatment of mild to moderate disorders or the treatment of personality disorders will apply. We maintain that viewing psychosis as very different is based on unhelpful (and probably unscientific) assumptions about the nature of psychotic experiences. In fact, there are a huge number of similarities between cognitive therapy for psychosis and that for other disorders.

Therapists will also be confronted by problems or disorders that people with psychosis experience for which there are not as yet clearly empirically validated treatments (e.g. personality disorders). Our approach in this case is, again, to adopt the same therapeutic position as a therapist as we would if the person did not have a psychotic disorder. We employ psychological approaches that may have utility and, at least, have face and conceptual validity (and where the formulation does not suggest such approaches are contra-indicated). Occasions will arise, when working therapeutically with people with psychosis, where problems or disorders exist that are not easily pigeon-holed into diagnostic categories such as panic disorder or social phobia. Indeed, this is also often true in other settings and services where people do not have a psychotic disorder (e.g. primary care services). The task of the therapist in such situations is to utilise a case conceptualisation as a template for understanding and treating the precise psychological processes that are causing distress to the person with psychosis. Therapists will need to be aware, therefore, of the precise psychological processes that maintain disorders such as panic disorder (catastrophic misinterpretation of normal phenomena) in order to apply the template to an untypical presentation. Experience of the cognitive-behavioural treatment of such disorders or problems in a less complex client group will be highly beneficial for therapists intending to work with people with psychosis.

Prevalence of associated disorders within psychosis

Symptoms of anxiety are very common among people with psychosis. Siris (1991) has estimated that panic and anxiety symptoms occur in about 60 per cent of people with a chronic psychosis. Jackson et al. (1999) note that social phobia is very common among their client group (people with early psychosis) and that PTSD is also quite common, especially for people who have been treated involuntarily. They also suggested that obsessive-compulsive disorder was quite rare among their early psychosis population in Australia, whereas Bermanzohn et al. (1997) found 30 per cent prevalence of OCD among a small sample of people with chronic psychosis. Our own clinical experience, both within a chronic population and an early psychosis population, suggests that anxiety disorders are common among people with psychosis and frequently go completely undetected and untreated.

Depression is very common among people with psychosis, and while it may abate with positive symptoms among some people, chronic depression related to experiences of psychosis is very common. About 10 per cent of people with psychosis die as a result of suicide (Department of Health (DoH), 1994) and it appears that this is linked to problems such as depression and associated hopelessness. Such is the scale of the problem of depression and affective symptoms within psychosis that one of the early trials of CBT for psychosis targeted affective symptoms as one of the main goals of therapy (Garety, Kuipers,

Fowler, Chamberlain, & Dunn, 1994). It has been estimated that up to 65 per cent of people who have had a psychotic episode will experience a major depressive episode within three years (Johnson, 1981). A study by Birchwood et al. (2000) found that 70 per cent of 105 patients with a diagnosis of schizophrenia had depression during their acute psychotic phase, and that 36 per cent developed post-psychotic depression following recovery from positive symptoms. This suggests that the treatment of depression should be a routine consideration for cognitive therapists working with people with psychosis in a formulation-driven manner.

Several studies have examined the development of PTSD following psychosis. Shaw, et al. (1997) found that 52 per cent of forty-five inpatients qualified for a DSM-IIIR diagnosis of PTSD (APA, 1987). McGorry et al. (1991) found that 46 and 35 per cent respectively of thirty-six patients qualified for a DSM-III (APA, 1980) diagnosis of PTSD at four and eleven months following discharge. A lower, but still significant, rate of PTSD (11 per cent) was reported by a study of an inpatient sample of psychosis sufferers in Finland (Meyer, Taiminen & Vuori, 1999). Rates similar to the Australian studies (51 per cent) were found among a larger sample (n = 105) people with schizophrenia receiving community care in Berlin (Priebe, Broker, & Gunkel, 1998); however, this study did not take traumatic experiences other than psychiatric treatment into account, which may have confounded results. Frame and Morrison (2001) studied sixty adults with psychotic illness in acute psychiatric wards, using survey and semi-structured interview techniques, in hospital, and four to six months later; 67 and 50 per cent of the sample reported clinically significant PTSD symptoms at time one and follow-up respectively. Psychotic experiences (as opposed to other traumas and hospital experiences) accounted for 52 per cent of the variance in PTSD scores in a multiple regression analysis after residual psychotic symptoms were controlled for statistically. This study used parallel forms of self-report measures to attempt to separate out the differential contributions of psychosis, hospitalisation and other traumas, but this may have been confusing for some participants. Another study examining thirty-five first episode psychotic patients found similar levels of post-traumatic stress symptomatology (intrusions and avoidance) in this sample to that found in survivors of a shipping disaster (Jackson, 2000). Jackson concluded that PTSD is a relevant concept for people recovering from first episode psychosis, but that it needs to be viewed within a wider framework of normal adaptation to the realities of psychosis. Similarly, there are many studies demonstrating a high level of traumatic life events in people with psychosis. For example, Mueser et al. (1998) found lifetime prevalence of major traumas to be 98 per cent in a sample of patients with severe mental illness, and Read (1997) demonstrated a very high level of childhood sexual and physical abuse in people with psychosis. Clearly, PTSD symptomatology should be assessed in people with psychosis, and treatment strategies should be derived from the formulation.

Substance abuse problems among people with psychosis are also quite common and represent a further challenge for therapists attempting to do cognitive therapy for people with psychosis. A study at the Maudsley hospital in England (Menezes et al., 1996) found that 36 per cent of patients with a severe mental illness such as schizophrenia or depression also had problems with substance misuse. Linszen and Lenior (1999) state that their review of studies of substance abuse among young people with psychosis give a prevalence rate of between 25 and 60 per cent, and they point out that the incidence and prevalence of substance abuse is high among adolescents and young adults generally. They suggest that, given that the peak time of onset for psychosis is adolescence/young adulthood, substance abuse problems among people with emerging or early psychosis should be regarded as a normal phenomenon in clinical work with this population. Mueser, Rosenberg, Goodman & Trumbetta (2002) also point out that substance abuse is common in patients with PTSD, and suggests that this may be one way in which PTSD and psychosis may exacerbate each other. The function of substance misuse should be considered, as should its relationship with other difficulties, and this information should be incorporated into the case conceptualisation and the planning of interventions.

People with personality disorders seldom present directly to services or clinicians with such problems clearly identified. It is far more common for problems with personality to emerge as therapy progresses, or perhaps fails to progress. Personality disorders can be described at the simplest level as the continuation into adult life of behaviours that were once developmentally appropriate but no longer are (e.g. dependence on others for meeting basic needs). In order for individuals to meet formal criteria for a personality disorder, they must be characterised by "an enduring pattern of inner experience and behaviour that deviates markedly from the expectations of the individuals culture, is pervasive and inflexible, has an onset in adolescence or early adulthood, is stable over time and leads to distress or impairment" (APA, 1994). Clinical clues to the existence of treatment-confounding personality disorders include reports of lifelong problems by significant others or self, non-compliance with therapy, lack of progress in therapy not otherwise adequately explained, poor awareness of the effects of their behaviour on others, the person having been sent for therapy by others, and personality problems seeming natural or normal to the affected person (Freeman & Jackson, 1998). Of course, the existence of any (or even all) of the above factors is insufficient for clinicians to conclude that the person they are trying to help has problems with a personality disorder. However, such factors may serve to alert the clinician to consider the possibility as part their evolving formulation (see Chapter 5). In the treatment of psychosis, and perhaps especially early psychosis, problems with personality disorder can be difficult to detect and treat. Given that the peak age of onset of psychosis is at the time when many young adults are experimenting with issues of dependence and independence, it may delay, or even prevent, the development of personality in the affected person. This can lead to difficulties in life that may, if not successfully treated, become entrenched as problems across several domains of life, possibly independent of psychotic illness. Such entrenched problems may eventually be given the label of a personality disorder. Psychotic symptoms may also occur in people who were vulnerable to such difficulties because of a pre-existing personality disorder. Freeman and Jackson (1998) talk about the bi-directional influences of personality disorders and problems such as anxiety and depression. Within the care and treatment of people with psychosis, it is appropriate to recognise that it may interact with personality problems and sometimes generate focal problems such as panic disorder, social phobia or depression. Problems with depression or anxiety disorders may also influence psychotic symptoms and personality problems (where they exist). Potentially, this complex three-way interaction can also be seen against the background of substance abuse, which appears to be almost ubiquitous within the culture for young people. Prevalence rates for the numbers of people with psychotic disorders and associated personality problems are rarely quoted within the literature, perhaps as a consequence of the compartmentalised and hierarchical thinking about these disorders that has prevailed until very recently. A study in Spain (Rodriguez-Solano & Gonzalez de Chavez, 2000) found that 85 per cent of forty patients with a diagnosis of schizophrenia met criteria for a pre-morbid personality disorder (the most common being avoidant, schizotypal and paranoid). It is clear from such studies, and from clinical experience, that therapists can expect to work with people struggling with problems of both psychosis and personality in their day-to-day clinical work.

Treatment

General considerations

Considering variations to procedures from generic cognitive therapy can assist the treatment of disorders associated with psychosis, such as those highlighted earlier. For example, while certain procedures are common to starting therapy, such as the development of a shared problems and goals list, the way this is actually done in therapy may (or may not) need to be different depending on what associated problems of psychosis the person is also experiencing. Disorder specific treatment approaches will then need to be developed and implemented in line with the formulation, and should be based on empirical models and effective treatments of such disorders where they exist. Space precludes detailed description of the cognitive models for the treatment of social phobia, panic disorder, PTSD, depression, personality disorders and substance abuse, but brief reference will be made to such models and treatments, and references for more detailed descriptions of such treatment will be provided.

Starting therapy

A starting point for therapy within a cognitive model is the establishment of a shared idiosyncratic formulation of the problem or disorder with the person experiencing difficulty (see Chapter 5). This is an essential prerequisite for any effective treatment, as the ethos of cognitive therapy is collaborative empiricism and its overt aims include enabling the person presenting with difficulties to become his or her own therapist. Formulation with people with psychosis can have special considerations, but an overriding point to bear in mind is that many people with psychosis may never have considered a psychological understanding of their difficulties. Indeed, they may have received clear messages from mainstream mental health services that their problems are best understood from a purely biological or even genetic perspective. The common tasks of the early stages of cognitive therapy with clients presenting with any given disorder will be to explicitly socialise the person to a cognitive model, to establish a problems and goals list and to develop a maintenance level formulation that attempts to account for the person's target difficulties utilising the cognitive model previously shared. We agree with Jackson et al. (1999) that the techniques used in therapy with people with psychosis are similar to those used in working with people with less severe disorders, but that the pace may need to be slower and the techniques may need to be simplified. Before any effective treatment can take place for clients with psychosis who are also experiencing anxiety disorders, depression, problems with substance misuse or even personality disorders, it is essential that the steps described above are carried out adequately. Failure to appropriately engage people with psychosis in a sound therapeutic relationship is a rate-limiting step (Kingdon, 1998) and no amount of cognitive techniques will compensate for this. If clients with psychosis also present with problems with substance abuse, or even personality disorder, then the therapist will need to be both patient and opportunistic in order to achieve the steps outlined above. Particular problems that may be experienced with people who are also abusing substances can include

- problems associated with intoxication
- missed appointments
- poor concentration as a result of substance abuse
- intolerance of psychological and physical discomfort
- uncertainty without the use of substances or alcohol.

These difficulties can be resolved using a combination of boundary setting, negotiation, contracting and behavioural experiments, all of which should be guided by the preliminary formulation.

People with psychosis and personality difficulties also present a special challenge to therapists attempting to accomplish the early tasks of cognitive therapy. Problems within the therapeutic relationship may be experienced, with the specific difficulty likely to be linked to the type of personality disorder that the person is experiencing alongside their psychosis. Typically, problems with trust and dependency may emerge and can be a challenge to therapists trained exclusively in standard cognitive models, which have sometimes paid little attention to relationship factors and managing the therapeutic relationship within therapy. Here is a clinical example of the first interaction between a therapist and a person with problems with psychosis and personality disorder:

Therapist: Hello, it's nice to meet you. My name is Jo Bloggs ...
Patient: You don't really think it's nice to meet me, do you?

Such a response at the very first interaction between the person with psychosis and personality disorder and the therapist can be a real challenge for a therapist and requires the ability to think on your feet. These factors simply emphasise the importance of conducting a thorough assessment and developing a shared formulation.

Depression and anxiety within the context of psychosis can also present special problems in the starting therapy phase of cognitive therapy. Clients with anxiety problems and psychosis may have difficulties in attending sessions. This is especially likely if a patient has significant social anxiety or agoraphobic symptoms and appointments are held at busy generic health centres. Conversely, patients who have experienced trauma as a result of treatment by psychiatric services may avoid appointments held in mental health centres or acute units with many triggers to memories of traumatic events of admission to a psychiatric facility. Clearly, a therapist would not be surprised if a patient with PTSD would not attend a first session at the site of the trauma, yet we may be inadvertently asking just that. Sensitivity to the case history and flexibility regarding venue prior to the first appointment may help maximise engagement for such clients.

People with depression and psychosis may find the early stages of therapy difficult as a result of their negative thoughts concerning the likelihood of any progress being made in therapy. A lengthy history of problems with psychosis and associated depression may make it difficult for clients to suspend their disbelief that this new approach has anything to offer them. Awareness of such perceptions by therapists may at least help the person with psychosis and depression feel understood by the therapist – a crucial step to further engagement. In addition, the use of activity scheduling or the identification and challenging of hopeless or depressed thoughts may be of use, and ensuring a quick success early in therapy is vital.

Therapist factors in the early stages of cognitive therapy

Working with people with psychosis is challenging for cognitive therapists. When people with psychosis also present with problems of anxiety, depression, substance abuse or personality, therapists can feel overwhelmed by the complexities of formulation and treatment. Cognitive therapists should practice what they preach in such circumstances, and monitor the frequency and effects of their own thinking on their in-session behaviour with clients (see Chapter 7 for an example). Creating a permissive atmosphere within peer supervision, where therapists can express such perceptions honestly, is a useful first step in maintaining therapist motivation and appropriate levels of optimism. It is also important to remind ourselves of Freeman's (1999) work with complex cases, and, specifically, his recommendation that goals within therapy are proximal. It is often helpful to ensure that the goals that are aimed for in therapy are not too ambitious, and that the timescale is appropriate. It can also be useful to check that we are not buying into the received wisdom of the psychiatric system, which encourages hopelessness among clinicians working with people with psychosis.

Formulation

Therapists need to be aware that the notion of a psychological formulation is likely to be a completely new one to people with psychosis. Therapists need to remind themselves that (as stated in Chapter 5) a psychological formulation should be dynamic and may very well start simply before developing to encompass a more global perspective on the clients' difficulties from a psychological perspective.

For example, Carl (a 34-year-old man) hears voices and experiences panic attacks. Both of these were highlighted on his problem list. In the early sessions it was useful to develop a simple maintenance formulation identifying the links between voices and panic attacks (see Figure 12.1). While such a formulation is clearly a very simple one, asking a person to consider a possible relationship between voices and panic symptoms for the first time is an important step in therapy. It can lead on to a discussion of the links between thoughts, feelings and emotions, and has an evidence-based treatment associated with it (i.e. cognitive therapy for panic). A normalising model, in which the relationship between voices and high levels of anxiety, distress and arousal, in the general population can also be discussed. From such a formulation, a therapist can guide a person to considering the assessment of this relationship as a homework task, utilising diaries and

Figure 12.1 Formulation of relationship between voices and panic attacks

recording forms. A record form was used with this client to investigate the possible relationship between voices and panic. It simply involved rating the frequency of and distress about both voices and panic on a daily basis using 0–100 visual analogue scales. This quickly revealed that there was a strong association between the two symptoms.

Simple homework tasks like these should be considered as a means of increasing the likelihood of successful homework experiences, and engaging the client's interest and enthusiasm in a collaborative, scientific venture. By collecting data in this manner, as part of a formulation-driven approach to therapy, more sophisticated and (hopefully) accurate formulations can be developed, which more precisely highlight the relationship between anxiety and positive symptoms, and thus guide therapy.

Therapists have an understandable tendency to prefer complex and sophisticated formulations to relatively straightforward and easy to understand formulations. The temptation to perhaps overcomplicate the picture to demonstrate our competency and how hard we have worked is very human, but it will not do our patients any favours. It is, of course, the person with the problem that really needs to understand the formulation as a basis for action, and something that a lay person can understand is what is required. Formulations are for clinical use, and therapists need to find ways of explaining relationships between thoughts, feelings and behaviour, that ensure that such conceptualisations are understandable and translate into action. Using the patient's own language and terminology is a good starting point.

Psychological formulations are difficult and people with relatively mild to moderate disorders in primary care settings sometimes struggle to adopt a psychological perspective. With people experiencing psychosis, perhaps complicated by problems with anxiety disorders, depression, substance abuse or personality problems, a psychological conceptualisation that attempts to capture the relationships between these variables is a big challenge. Therapists need to avoid feeling overwhelmed by this challenge, allow the relationships to emerge through the therapy sessions, where appropriate, and be honest about parts of the picture they do not understand or the direction of the relationship between variables. Openly asking the person with psychosis about the relationship between psychotic symptoms and depression, for example, is highly appropriate. Sharing dilemmas with patients can be very useful, and there are many benefits of such a collaborative approach. These include facilitation of "psychological mindedness", demonstration of the therapist's position of unconditional positive regard (which may increase self-esteem) and empowerment in the therapeutic process itself (again likely to increase self-esteem). Padesky's (1993b) differentiation between setting out to change minds and true guided discovery is also useful to keep in mind.

None of the above is to imply that the therapist does not have to work too hard. Working with people with psychosis and other difficulties can be likened to hiking without a map; therapists need to be constantly reading the terrain to ensure that potentially fruitful looking diversions are not fraught with further difficulties. Above all else, the emerging formulation should be actively reviewed in supervision throughout therapy to ensure contra-indicated actions (that may become clearer when the full formulation emerges) are not taken or advocated.

Active treatment

We can expect some difficulties in getting to the active stage of therapy with people with psychosis and other disorders. The associated problems of people with psychosis may generate particular difficulties in just proceeding with engagement, socialisation, problem/goal identification and formulation. People with personality problems and psychosis may find the interpersonal intimacy that is a part of all therapy too demanding. Obviously, therapist flexibility is strongly indicated in terms of length and frequency of sessions, but this very flexibility can mitigate against progress in therapy. In therapy with people with psychosis and associated problems, consideration will need to be given to how an intervention aimed at one symptom may have effects on other symptoms. This is not dissimilar to working with people with psychosis without major associated problems, whereby consideration of the possible functional nature of symptoms needs to take place before symptoms are targeted (e.g. in patients with paranoid delusions that may serve a protective function in relation to self-esteem). In the case of people with psychosis who do have other associated problems, this consideration of the costs, benefits and risks of intervention is even more complex (and necessary).

In some cases, the exact relationship between variables such as psychotic symptoms and depression will be unclear despite the best efforts at formulation, and often they will exist within a vicious circle in which it is impossible to tell which came first. Therapists confronted with such a vague and uncertain clinical picture and a person with psychosis desperate for help with key psychotic symptoms may have to rely on frequent monitoring of non-target symptoms while intervention proceeds, in the absence of a more comprehensive idiosyncratic formulation or clear generalised empirical data. Of course, the effects of an intervention on another seemingly independent symptom should be information that helps to develop the formulation. It may not always be possible (or desirable) to wait until a sophisticated, longitudinal multifaceted formulation is available before any intervention is attempted. Compelling clinical and therapeutic reasons do exist that lead the therapist and patient to attempt an intervention on a key symptom prior to the complete picture of how one symptom may affect another being fully available. Therapists retain responsibility for interventions generated and suggested in therapy sessions, and clearly cannot proceed with an intervention if they believe it to be contra-indicated. However, when working with people with multiple and complex problems, therapists should challenge disabling rules that they may have about therapy such as: "Unless I know and can articulate all aspects and relationships of this persons problems I cannot intervene in any way". A more flexible rule could be: "Working with people with complex and multiple problems requires the therapists to maintain an awareness of contra-indicated interventions; however, interventions designed to target a particular symptom can generate useful information about other aspects of the persons problem and can be usefully understood (by therapist and affected person) in that context". Ensuring that patients are involved in all decisions about the selection of change strategies can also minimise the possibility of an unwanted outcome.

Ending therapy

While people who have experienced a psychotic episode should continue to be followed-up by services for some time after the initial episode, even where they are making good progress and are not experiencing problems with symptoms, cognitive therapy is a time-limited activity and should, therefore, come to an end at some point. Within our programme, therapists work within a nominal therapy envelope of twenty-four sessions (usually using renewable six or ten session contracts), but are able to offer more sessions to an individual if they can justify doing so to their peers in supervision. We acknowledge that therapy may sometimes need more than twenty or thirty sessions, but also want to ensure there are good formulation-based reasons for offering extra sessions, and therefore protect both the therapist and the person with psychosis from unlimited and possibly unproductive sessions. At the outset of therapy, the time-limited nature of cognitive therapy should be discussed with the person with psychosis. This is usually presented to the person with psychosis as a therapy that has been found to be helpful to many people who have had some similar experiences, and that is effective over a set number of sessions but not as an open-ended therapy. Contracts of six sessions at a time are usually agreed, with associated goals that are realistic and achievable within the specified time-frame. Clearly, people with psychosis and other associated problems, such as personality problems, may find working within a set time-frame challenging. However, it is possible to achieve things in time-limited therapy even for people with psychosis and problems with their personality as long as both therapist and client are clear about time-frames and appropriate, proximal goals. Therapists can find it difficult to end therapy for a variety of reasons, and when working with people with psychosis the reasons can include a strong desire to be more helpful to the patient. This can be especially true if the person with psychosis will have their needs met by a generic mental health team that does not have a specialist resource dedicated to people with psychosis and may have an extremely medical model. Therapists must avoid substituting themselves for the perceived or real failings of the mental health system. Good supervision should help to prevent this, and possibly highlight more productive ways in which the general mental health system can be facilitated to provide the very best services for people with psychosis. For example, sharing a formulation with the multidisciplinary team or keyworker or case manager, and providing training in the understanding of psychosis from a psychological perspective can help reduce such concerns (see Chapter 15 for further details).

Summary

People with psychosis may experience associated problems such as anxiety disorders, depression, substance abuse and even personality problems. In fact, such complications are extremely common, and can be much more problematic for the affected person than the actual symptoms of psychosis. An overvalued and misunderstood medical approach has tended to emphasise the psychotic symptoms as being core with anxiety problems and depression simply being reactions to the psychosis. Accordingly, many mood problems experienced by people with psychosis are not acknowledged or targeted for treatment by mental health professionals. While treating associated problems alongside the psychosis can be complicated, the basic tools of good psychological therapy can be utilised as the therapist would if the person did not have psychosis. Good supervision, therapist flexibility and interpersonal sensitivity, along with an awareness of empirical templates from the psychological treatment of anxiety disorders and depression, comprise the basic therapeutic toolkit that will enable therapists to offer effective therapy to people with psychosis and associated problems.

Chapter 13

Relapse prevention and management

There is one basic principle to remember when working with patients to develop strategies to identify, minimise and resolve relapse – collaboration. The patient and therapist are joined by a common objective, which is for the patient to achieve and maintain an optimum level of functioning. There may be a subtle difference in how each party is approaching this objective, since the patient who has recovery in view may not want to address relapse until improvement is likely and the patient who has recovered may doubt the relevance of it.

Normalising relapse

Relapse prevention with the focus on self-monitoring begins with establishing a normalising rationale for why relapse may occur and being clear about the different stages which may be part of the relapse process (Spencer, Murray, & Plaistow, 2000). Decatastrophising relapse and focusing on the notion that a lapse does not have to become relapse can instil a sense of optimism and hope for the future.

People who have had distressing and traumatic experiences as a result of psychosis want to avoid its recurrence, but not all of them want to invest in the type of relapse prevention outlined. For some individuals who have made significant improvements, their preferred way of coping with the possibility of relapse is not to talk about their experiences, even with the therapist. These people "just want to get on with their lives" and not be reminded of what happened. This is more likely to be the case for patients who have been specifically referred for relapse prevention, rather than those for whom relapse prevention is part of the overall cognitive therapy process. The therapist is advised to develop a rudimentary formulation for symptom or problem development and resolution, and to share data about relapse rates and possible consequences for the individual. The patient's strategy for dealing with relapse should be evaluated within a cognitive framework.

An integral part of this framework can be the utilisation of the "developmental model of change" (Prochaska & DiClemente, 1992), helping the therapist to identify the individual's change state in relation to relapse. Appropriate strategies can then be used to help people to reach the "think" stage, and subsequently move on to the "determination" (to work on the problem) stage and further. It is important to introduce the concept of relapse prevention or management early in therapy, rather than put it on the agenda at the end of what is seen as the active treatment phase (Blackburn & Davidson, 1995).

Identifying stressors and triggers

No two individuals will identify the same range of stressors and triggers that contribute to relapse. There is no universal concept of a range of general factors which, when in place, will result in relapse for any individual. Specific factors such as sleep deprivation, isolation and bereavement, for example, may cause an increase in, or return of, psychotic symptoms, but not for all patients, and not each time they occur. No single event will generate the same response in all the people who experience it. Consider the person sitting in a vehicle that has broken down on the way to an anxiety-provoking event, which is scheduled to take place at an exact time in front of a number of people (some of whom will be supportive and some hostile), and realises she will be an hour late. Each individual's response is dependent on the meaning and perceived consequences of the event. The prospective bridegroom who will miss his wedding may be distraught or delighted; the anxious conference presenter who no longer has to present may be overjoyed at avoiding further anxiety or disappointed that she did not have the chance to overcome it; the criminal scheduled to be executed may be relieved that it will be delayed, or distressed that the whole process he has been through that day will be repeated. It is the personal meaning of an event, or series of events, in terms of internal and external consequences for the individual that will decide their affective, physiological and behavioural responses (Beck et al., 1979). This concept is central to cognitive therapy, and should be remembered when attempting to prevent relapse.

The formulation is the starting point for identifying stressors and triggers. The critical incident(s) and the preceding period will help the patient and therapist to establish the development of symptoms and to explore the connection between events and consequences (Birchwood, 1995). If a longitudinal formulation was developed in therapy, then the patient will be aware of the development of core beliefs and underlying assumptions, and should be able to understand the relationship between events or experiences, evaluations and outcome.

For example, David (discussed on pp. 120–121) was able to understand, through his formulation (see Figure 13.1), how he had developed his psychotic symptoms and what the possible triggers were for this process repeating itself. This informed his relapse prevention plan, which incorporated monitoring for events that could activate his core beliefs and regular rating of these beliefs.

Emphasis may be placed initially on events where there is a physiological trigger for problems. It is often easier to help the patient understand the connection between a physical state and symptoms because it is a relationship that most people can relate to in a concrete way and will, almost certainly, have experienced. These

Early experiences

- little love or affection from parents
- scapegoated within family
- grandfather asked David (age 6) to do something for him, which David did not do, and grandfather died a few days later
- David had a strong belief that he had caused or contributed to the death

Assumptions formed

- I am responsible for bad things that happen
- I must do things right to prevent bad things happening
- If I am responsible for bad things then people will reject me

Core beliefs

- I am unlovable
- I am bad

Critical incidents

- relationships with parents and siblings deteriorated
- blamed for "breaking up the family"

Assumptions activated/psychotic symptoms emerge

- I have caused something bad to happen
- I am responsible for other bad events
- believed he had caused a major fire in which many people died
- began to engage in repetitive behaviours to reduce or prevent bad things

Consequences

- high levels of anxiety
- constant ruminations about blame
- most of time spent engaging in rituals (covert and overt)
- depressed
- paranoid – police would find out he was to blame and arrest him
- prescribed high doses of antipsychotic medication

Figure 13.1 David's case formulation

experiences can be easily translated into the normalising approach and the therapist can share his or her responses to similar experiences.

Some of the commonly reported critical physical incidents are:

- lack of sleep
- too much sleep
- medication effects – too much, too little, stopping medication suddenly, side-effects
- physical illness
- drug or alcohol consumption.

It is important to locate the true source of factors that contribute to relapse. One can mistakenly identify a relationship between events and assume it is causal when it is actually a consequence of a preceding factor. For example, a patient who describes disturbance in his sleep pattern may have been experiencing high levels of anxiety for a few days following a confrontation with family members. It is likely to be more effective to focus on the cause of the sleep disturbance rather than to devise strategies to cope with its consequences. There may chains of incidents that can be identified as leading up to relapse, which can be conceptualised as pathways or roads. It is possible to expand upon this well used metaphor, and to see the goal of maintaining well-being for a specific length of time as the destination for a journey. Figure 13.2 shows a checklist of essential maintenance and monitoring activities that should be considered.

Formulation

By focusing on the formulation it may be possible to identify both specific and generalised factors that contribute to the development of relapse. An individual may have distinct areas of vulnerability and a number of stressors may be linked by the consequences they produce. For example, the following vulnerabilities, stressors and consequences were identified by Henry (previously mentioned on pp. 120–121).

Vulnerabilities

- Tendency to jump to conclusions without considering the evidence for alternative explanations
- Having no one to discuss concerns with
- Isolated for much of the time
- A sense of social exclusion
- Past persecution related to cultural background.

Start of journey

Check:

- Destination decided
- Route roughly worked out
- How many hours per day driving
- Full tank of fuel
- When the rest periods will be
- When regular checks will take place

* * Remember to take into account

- Age of the vehicle
- Optimum performance of vehicle
- Experience level of driver
- Familiarity with route
- Contingency plans for when the unexpected occurs

At planned stops

Check:

- State of vehicle
- How vehicle has performed over last section
- Has the route been followed
- Do any amendments need to be made to the journey plan
- The vehicle and driver are ready to move on

When the unexpected happens

Check:

- Possible causes
- Possible responses
- What has worked in the past
- What is likely to be the best option
- Who can help you resolve this if you can't do it alone
- What has been learned from this

Nearing destination

Check:

- How far you have come
- What have you learned
- What needs to be done differently
- What is possible
- What the next destination is

Figure 13.2 Checklist

Stressors

- Confrontation with neighbours
- Drop in mood
- Increased cannabis use (although he was using this to reduce anxiety)
- Preoccupation with past persecution
- Physical health problems – airways.

Consequences: stage 1

- Emergence of low-level paranoid thoughts
- Sleep pattern disturbance
- Aware of "voices murmuring in the distance"
- Staying in bed for long spells during the day
- Increase in cannabis use.

Consequences: stage 2

- Sharp increase in paranoid thoughts
- Shouting at neighbours and people in the street
- Experiencing frank persecutory auditory hallucinations
- Contemplating revenge on people who are persecuting him
- Stop taking medication
- Severe depression
- Suicidal ideation.

Consequences: stage 3

- Admission to inpatient unit under Mental Health Act
- Increase in medication.

There is not necessarily a clear linear progression through the stages. This merely outlines some of the signposts and routes that have characterised Henry's previous journeys to relapse. Some of the negative consequences that become stressors may have been introduced as coping strategies or safety behaviours by the patient. For example, Henry increased his cannabis use to reduce the anxiety he experienced as a result of the content of auditory hallucinations, and stayed in bed to avoid making noise that might have led to further confrontation with his neighbours. He had not realised that these actions were contributing to the problem because he focused on the short-term gain and did not consider possible negative effects. When stressors occurred, he did not have a range of strategies that were functional both in the short and long-term; rather, he simply followed well-trodden pathways for dealing with problems without actively making a decision. The following excerpt from therapy illustrates this:

Therapist: What do you do when your mood gets low?
Henry: I stay in bed and try to feel better, get over it.
Therapist: Does it work?
Henry: Sometimes, not always.
Therapist: When it doesn't work do you stop doing it?
Henry: Well there's nothing else I can do?
Therapist: What else have you tried to do?
Henry: Well, nothing much I guess. Doesn't seem like there's much I can do about it anyway, it either gets better or it doesn't.

Henry had not considered alternative strategies because he did not believe that alternatives could exist. The therapist could help him evaluate when his strategy was effective and what the reasons were for that success, and, similarly, when it was ineffective and what the negative consequences of an unsuccessful strategy were. Unsuccessful strategies may simply fail to help the target problem, or may actually contribute to it. For example, not only did lying in bed fail to improve his mood, but also it actually increased his isolation, upset his sleep pattern and increased the amount of time he spent ruminating on past persecutory events (and, therefore, decreased his mood).

Metaphors

The use of metaphors in therapy can help a person translate what may appear to be an abstract concept into concrete terms (Beck, 1976). The most effective metaphors are those that have relevance for the patient; for example, someone who enjoys snooker might use "potting the white" to indicate a stressor. In relapse work, likening the progress through life to a car journey, with the patient represented by the car and relapse represented by the reduced functioning and possible break-down of the car, allows the patient to adopt an objective perspective, and the use of such imagery can be very powerful. Used creatively, metaphor and imagery can provide limitless possibilities for exploration, experimentation and evaluation of the whole process of relapse prevention work.

The car-journey metaphor could be utilised bearing the following points in mind:

- Let patients choose the car that best represents them or how they would like to be (this could be the only time they have an XJ6).
- What condition is this car in right now, what needs to be done to it to make it safe or roadworthy for the journey ahead?
- Do you need a different car – i.e. new underlying assumptions/rules?
- Who might be around to help you on the journey – will there be passengers or any back-seat drivers?
- What routine checks (monitoring symptoms for example) will you need to make?

- Are there things you need to check more often, perhaps on a daily or weekly basis?
- Should you be going to car maintenance classes (booster therapy sessions, support groups, etc.)?
- Make sure you take breaks in the journey, don't push yourself too hard.
- Have you got a decent map – what will you do if you get lost?
- What do you do when a knocking noise suddenly starts – plan for unexpected events?
- Where do you get help – do you ask the bloke next door or go to the garage?

Identifying early warning signs

Indicators that a person is at risk of, or is in the process of, relapsing are not always easily observed by the patient but may be perceived by others, and they are not always negative or unpleasant experiences (Bustillo, Buchanan, & Carpenter, 1995). Herz and Melville (1980) found that 70 per cent of individuals who experienced psychosis and 93 per cent of their families were able to identify non-psychotic and psychotic symptoms that indicated the onset of relapse. The formulation will help locate the very early indicators of possible relapse and identify whether there are early interventions that would arrest the process if they were put in place. Indicators which are perceived as positive or neutral events or experiences may merely act as signposts and not constitute a contributory factor, although they may in fact be causal. These signs will be different for each individual and the therapist must guard against jumping to conclusions on the patient's behalf, and maintain a scientific approach to the retrospective discovery of the early origins and indicators of the relapse process. For example, just because a person smoked cannabis around the time of onset of a psychotic episode, it does not necessarily follow that cannabis caused (or even contributed to) that psychotic episode. For one person, it may well be the case that cannabis use is likely to increase the risk of relapse, whereas for another person using cannabis may be unrelated to their psychosis or, indeed, help to prevent or ameliorate psychosis (we have seen numerous patients for whom cannabis helps them deal with their voices, for example). This idiosyncratic, individualised approach to the identification of triggers is necessary to provide effective relapse prevention, and again highlights the need for a case conceptualisation.

No two relapse processes will be the same for any one person, and while the concept of a 'relapse signature' (Birchwood, 1996) highlights the idiosyncratic nature of relapse, it implies that relapse always follows the same pattern, which is not the case. It is attention to detail within the formulation that will track each episode of relapse from the first signs through to the early stages, throwing up indicators that are not always obvious and signs that at first appear innocuous, but subsequently prove significant. However, Birchwood, Smith, Macmillan, and Hogg (1989) report the most common early warning signs to be sleeplessness, irritability, tension, depression and social withdrawal, all of which are relatively non-specific. Incipient psychosis (fleeting unusual ideas or experiences) is also a common precursor to relapse.

Monitoring

Identifying early warning signs, and later stages in relapse and responses, can involve both the patient and people who have regular contact with the patient. If signs are within the patient's internal state, either physical or psychological, then self-monitoring is appropriate, while others can monitor observable behaviours that the patient may initially be unaware of. Birchwood (1996) describes two distinct stages in the monitoring process, beginning with engagement with the patient in meaningful activity and demonstration that change is possible. The second stage is the identification of specific signs that indicate the relapse process is beginning matched with an appropriate intervention. Emphasis is placed on a shared responsibility (between patient, relatives and services) for detecting early signs of relapse and for appropriately implementing previously defined interventions.

Previous relapse routes, alongside existing vulnerabilities, will indicate what should be monitored, how it should be monitored and the frequency of monitoring required. Initially, it may be useful to group indicators by their system (i.e. cognitive, behavioural, emotional, physiological or environmental). Subsequently, depending on what form the changes take in these factors, a monitoring tool to detect levels of change should be selected or designed. For example, if low mood was an early sign, then the patient may complete a standardised measure of depressive symptoms, or specific items on the measure, to monitor mood change and pick up small shifts that may not be obvious. If depression leads to a quick deterioration in functioning then the frequency of monitoring would be much greater than if it was an indicator of deterioration some time away.

For example, Jason devised a basic system for monitoring factors that would either contribute to relapse or indicate that it could be happening:

Weekly
- hours worked that week
- alcohol consumed that week
- number of times he socialised with his family that week

Monthly
- number of outings and telephone conversations with his daughter.

Of course, the best monitoring strategy will be ineffective if the patient does not remember to do it. It is similar to doing homework in therapy, but in that case patients are motivated towards improving their current situation. Encouraging people to maintain it may be less easy. Most people will take the car to the garage when there is something seriously wrong and they are worried about it breaking down, but the numbers who have the car regularly serviced at the exact mileage it should be done are considerably less.

One strategy to enhance regular monitoring is to link it to another event that takes place in the patient's life with the same frequency. Jason devised a weekly monitoring system for three behaviours and spent time thinking about what he did once a week, without being disturbed or observed, with easy access to measures and enough time to do it properly. He wanted to pair it with an activity that made him feel good and he decided to complete the self-monitoring as soon as he had filled in his football pools coupon. He kept both sets of forms in the same place as an extra reminder and he felt that both activities were increasing the chances that the future could be better. Jason also involved his wife and asked her to let him know whenever she observed specific events such as irritation with her or their daughter and restless behaviour. Another patient decided to involve his son in the monitoring process, and arranged for him to ask set questions and give him feedback during their regular telephone calls.

For some patients an added strategy may be to increase the intensity or frequency of the monitoring when certain signs, which rarely occur, are noted. Material gathered during monitoring will provide a useful source of information for evaluating and revising the relapse prevention/management plan. Regular evaluation and modification, if indicated, are essential to maintain the appropriateness of the process. Data collected will give patients accurate feedback of their functioning and the effectiveness of any strategies they have employed to deal with problematic experiences.

Matching strategies to signs and problems (or preventing lapse from becoming relapse)

The whole point of monitoring signs of relapse is to employ strategies to prevent or minimise the effect of relapse for patients, and the earlier those interventions can be utilised in the process the greater the chance that they will be effective. The formulation may have identified a range of strategies utilised in the past by patients, and treatment will have focused on the resolution of current problems and a comparison of ineffective and effective strategies. For each problem or warning sign patients need to have at their disposal a number of strategies that can be applied, either in a prescribed pattern or matched to the problem dependent on its context.

Relapse management can be likened to a condensed version of therapy but should not be seen as a quick fix. Monitoring identifies problems, goals are set, and appropriate interventions are utilised to work towards the goals. Some problems may need to be resolved by interventions that focus on the presenting problem, while others may need to focus on the cause of the problem, and some may need to do both.

Material generated during therapy, for those patients who have been through active therapy, should be easily accessible to patients to allow them to reflect on the process of problem identification and resolution. Having this material in a folder that is easily accessed, and with specific material that is easily located, increases the likelihood that it will be utilised. Each intervention that is utilised must be continuously evaluated by the patient in order to help him decide the next step in the relapse management process. Contingency plans need to be in place for when interventions do not have the predicted effect. At no point should patients be in any doubt about the next step and they should maintain a sense of being in control of the process rather than being controlled by it. Flow charts that clearly indicate "if this happens then do this" followed by "if this does not work do this or one of these" encourages the person to apply an intervention, evaluate its effect, and then make a decision on the next step based on that evaluation.

Traditionally, interventions applied at the time when early warning signs are noticed have been medical, such as increasing medication or admission to hospital. However, the use of an idiosyncratic case conceptualisation to guide relapse prevention would suggest that the strategies of cognitive therapy will be effective. As suggested earlier, if a core belief is a vulnerability factor, then schema change methods may be helpful in preventing relapse. Similarly, if sleep deprivation is a trigger, then cognitive behavioural methods for improving sleep will be useful, as would an analysis of the causes of the sleep disruption. There is evidence that the delivery of cognitive therapy, targeted at people who are exhibiting early warning signs, reduces relapse by 50 per cent in people with psychotic disorders (Gumley, O'Grady, McNay, Reilly, Power & Norrie, 2003).

Involving other people in the process

For many patients, one of the most difficult decisions to make is when to involve someone else in the process. By involving others, the control over the process may be compromised and most patients will identify a hierarchy of significant others who they would be willing to utilise. Close relatives are not always the first people they want to involve. Although they are the people who know most about the patient and his or her past experiences, the patient may not wish to cause them any concern or may not want them to take control in a way that has happened in the past. Well-meaning relatives may insist that the patient visit their doctor or psychiatrist rather than try to deal with problems themselves. Some relatives may involve other agencies without consulting with patients, and in some cases attempt to have patients admitted to hospital with or without their consent. If relatives are involved in the monitoring process, then it is helpful to have them attend a joint session with the patient in order to discuss this process.

The decatastrophising and normalising of relapse should, where possible, be shared with other professionals and significant others who are part of the patient's life. Similarly, the relapse prevention/management plan should be shared with however many of these people the patient will agree to so that these individuals can encourage the patient to implement strategies outlined and evaluate them.

It is essential to recognise whether someone is part of the answer or part of the problem, and efforts should be made by the therapist and patient to involve others in being part of the answer. Equally, the patient needs to be aware of the criteria that will leave others, including the therapist, with reduced options when responding to or helping with the patient's problems. For many patients, the option of hospital admission is the very bottom of their options list and it takes considerable skill on the therapist's part to use this not as a threat, but as motivation for early intervention. It is also important to help the person recognise that admission may, sometimes, be an appropriate intervention.

Summary

There is no guaranteed answer to relapse. The therapist and patient can only devise strategies that have the best chance of success, and the therapist must be explicit about this. A plan is just a plan and the same applies to maps. They are only a guide to help you get to where you want to be, and they only show the possible routes. Even the national motoring organisations cannot help a person plan for every possible problem; they can only tell the routes according to average speed, scenery, possible hazards and weather conditions. They do not take account of the make and age of the car, how many miles and breakdowns it has had, and how many passengers, difficult or otherwise, it will be carrying. Who knows how they will deal with skids, animals who suddenly appear on the road, diversions and countless other unforeseen obstacles. Relapse prevention can be perceived as an advanced driving course that helps you to develop the skills needed to deal with known and unknown hazards and who to contact at what point. Most vehicular breakdowns can be prevented, but only by regular maintenance, vigilant anticipation of problems, and developing skills to deal with the unexpected. Nobody sets out to have a breakdown on the motorway and be towed to the nearest garage, whether they like it or not, but planning and investment-type behaviour can reduce the chances of this happening.

Chapter 14

Integration of homework into therapy

Why should homework be done (and why devote a chapter to it)?

Homework assignments carried out between sessions are an essential part of cognitive therapy and, in theory, are thought to be central to determining outcome. Beck et al. (1979) described homework as "an integral, vital component of treatment" (p. 272) and recommended that homework assignments should be utilised throughout therapy but, especially in the earlier phases with depressed patients, to "improve level of functioning, counteract obsessive thinking, change attitudes, and give a feeling of gratification" (p. 141). This can be achieved by providing the person with opportunities to collect information, test dysfunctional beliefs and practise new skills. Delusional beliefs will rarely change following intellectual challenging alone (Chadwick et al., 1996), and are more likely to be strengthened rather than weakened if the patient perceives the therapist's stance as confrontational. It is only by experiencing emotions and behaving in different ways that patients can collect new evidence to use in the reappraisal of delusional beliefs (Morrison, 1998b). Glaser et al. (2000) reviewed the available empirical evidence and concluded that patients with schizophrenia who receive CBT that includes homework assignments, improve at least 60 per cent more than those who receive treatment without homework tasks.

There are many effects to be gained from homework, which will enhance both active therapy and relapse prevention. This section will outline the benefits for the individual of being part of the decision-making process which identifies homework and engaging in tasks that are appropriate and relevant.

When one hears the word *homework*, what images, assumptions and emotions does it evoke? Most people, therapists included, will identify some (or all) of the following:

- doing something unpleasant
- having to make time for it
- missing out on something else
- worrying you won't get it right and the consequences of this

- feeling bad if you don't do it
- doing the least amount possible
- feeling resentful that you have to do it
- not seeing the point of it
- having been no good at homework at school
- having only negative memories of homework
- rushing through it to get it over with.

Some people will have more positive memories or expectations, but most of us will focus on the negative when the *H* word is mentioned. The majority of people will associate homework with something written down, which is subsequently marked and has serious consequences contingent upon the mark.

Before negotiating homework with a patient, it is essential to discuss the rationale and make it clear that homework in therapy bears little resemblance to their experiences at school or in other educational establishments. Calling it "work between sessions" or "independent work", especially in the early sessions, may help to minimise negative reactions to the concept.

The rationale for homework

A therapy session is a very brief part of the patient's week, and therapy an even smaller part of their life, so it has to make a powerful impact both within and across sessions. Some changes will happen in session, but they are the small changes that pave the way for the big ones (they are the free samples that persuade the patient to buy the economy size pack and use it). Therapists know that what happens in therapy sessions is important, but what happens outside of them is even more important. *The idea that homework enhances therapy should be replaced by the idea that therapy enhances homework.*

Secondary gains of homework

Patients who do homework are being active, both in the process of therapy and in actually completing a task. There may be a sense of achievement, an increase in the collaborative nature of the therapeutic relationship as patients perceive that they are taking an active part, and a sense of empowerment as they can influence therapy and shape the process. A written record of homework outcomes is a means of helping patients monitor progress and, at the close of therapy, is part of a linear account of change and achievement. It is also a valuable source of information that can be utilised in relapse prevention or management, and a reminder of what works, what strategies are most appropriate, and that change is possible.

Types of homework

There are, essentially, three types of homework. These are information collection, experiments and the practice of new skills. They are not mutually exclusive and any combination may be employed to meet an objective.

Information collection

The collection of information relating to current functioning, thinking and affect states in early sessions not only informs the formulation but also can be used as baseline data when evaluating treatment outcome. This initial information can form part of a wider assessment and help establish, for example, level of risk, medication effects and coping strategies. In some cases, self-monitoring about voices or distressing thoughts can actually reduce the frequency of such symptoms, thus providing therapeutic benefit as well. For example, Ian experienced paranoid delusions and persecutory auditory hallucinations. To test the hypothesis that his cannabis use was exacerbating his symptoms he kept a record of specific symptoms in terms of frequency, duration and intensity while recording the frequency and duration of cannabis use over a seven-day time-frame.

Experiments

These can be used to discover what happens when the patient thinks or behaves differently and, while an obvious outcome may be assumed, there is genuine exploration involved. As outlined in Chapter 9, behavioural experiments are often the most successful way of achieving belief change. For example, Malcolm experienced abusive auditory hallucinations and attended to them for most of the day, arguing with and shouting at the "voices". The homework was to do what he normally did (i.e. attend to the hallucinations) on some days, and on alternate days he would follow an agreed activity plan. Every day he was asked to record information relating to the onset, frequency, duration and content, of the hallucinations.

The practice of new skills

As treatment progresses, the patient may need to put new skills into practice so that they become established; intense repetition is often necessary before this is the case. This may include tasks such as reviewing evidence and generating alternative explanations, as well as trying out new ways of behaving. For example, Jim had become anxious when left to care for his two young daughters in case he obeyed the instructions of the "voices" to "do bad things" or "hurt other people before they hurt you", and had developed strategies to deal with this. He had experimented with a number of strategies and the most effective were to recognise the trigger for what he had, by then, realised were intrusive thoughts, and to challenge the meaning of those thoughts using evidence from past homework. That evidence showed that not only had he never acted on those thoughts, but also he had never been violent towards anyone in his life. The homework task was to increase the time he regularly spent caring for the children alone while practising reviewing the evidence for this belief.

What to choose for homework

The identification of homework tasks usually takes place at the end of the therapy session and is influenced by a number of factors. The clinical problem, the cognitive model, the formulation, the patient's goals for therapy and the issues raised in session, all will give clear indicators of the type of tasks that will be appropriate. Padesky and Greenberger (1995) refer to the three Rs of homework. These are relevant, realistic and responsibility, and can be used to help identify a specific homework task. The tasks must be relevant to the model, formulation and session content, while clearly relating to the patient's idiosyncratic goals. For the tasks to be realistic they must be achievable and significant, not so difficult that the patient fails and not so easy that there is no sense of achievement or change. Responsibility for the tasks must lie in the patient's domain and be under his or her control.

Frequently, there are a number of options for a homework task, all of which would make sense and be useful. If a number of options appear to be appropriate tasks, then it is worth considering which will have the greatest effect in terms of collecting information, testing hypotheses or practising skills. Sometimes, one task will allow patients to do all three and, given that homework is usually difficult for patients, they will gain maximum benefit from it. Mary's homework task was to go into social situations (such as shopping, visiting a friend's house for coffee, or collecting her granddaughter from nursery), and collect information on how many people actually looked at her. Mary usually makes no eye contact with people when out of the house but felt that others were looking at her. This task had multiple benefits:

- it got her out the house, which was useful as she had become increasingly more isolated
- she experienced a sense of achievement at just completing the work
- she gained specific objective information on how many people looked at her
- she was familiarising herself with situations that would eventually be used to test hypotheses.

How to choose homework

Negotiating homework should be a collaborative process. This is illustrated in the following excerpt from a therapy session.

Therapist: On the basis of what we have discussed today, what do you think it would be useful for you to do before the next session?

Patient: I don't know.

Therapist: Well we've looked at what things could be having an influence on the decrease or increase in symptoms and we've got a sort of theory but no facts . . . [leaves opportunity for patient to make a suggestion] . . . is there some way we could progress on this?

Alternating between statements that suggest action and questions that focus on what action might be taken can help the patient generate suggestions that can then be evaluated. Also, brainstorming a range of tasks related to both the agenda items and the patient's goals can inform both parties and lead to evaluation of options. Collaboration is not having the patient decide the homework unilaterally, but rather it is working together on identifying an appropriate task or tasks. Nor is collaboration assigning a task, giving a rationale and then asking, "Do you think that's all right?" Both parties bring expertise; for the therapist it is related to conceptual models and treatment, and for patients it is related to themselves as individuals. This is why homework should not be given a cursory few minutes at the end of the session. Sufficient time must be set aside to explore options, rationales, obstacles and recording methods (see Chapter 6 for agenda setting in relation to homework).

Cognitive therapy is not the only therapeutic setting that may lead to patients agreeing to undertake between-session tasks. Discussion around tasks that patients may have agreed to do in the past, what they did or did not do, and what influenced completion of such tasks, will help to identify problem areas, and strategies to overcome them can be explored in session before the task is attempted. One of the initial stumbling blocks for many patients appears to be that homework often requires them to write something on paper. Reluctance to do so may be related to worries about literacy, worries about other people finding it, or the effect of seeing their problems on paper. Recognising and dealing with such difficulties early in therapy will encourage homework identification and compliance on the patient's part. Developing recording methods that use tick boxes, or providing the patient with a Dictaphone if accurate recording of thoughts is sought, can overcome poor literacy skills.

What if the patient cannot think of a homework task and does not want to do what you have "collaboratively" suggested? You could try consideration of the following:

- checking out if the task(s) meet the three Rs – relevant, realistic, within the patient's responsibility
- checking whether the patient's reasons for not wanting to do certain tasks might just be obstacles that you could collaboratively devise strategies to overcome them rather than absolute refusal

- being explicit about how difficult meaningful homework can be, but also explicitly emphasise the gains to be made
- giving examples of homework that has been done by other patients and what the outcome was.

If appropriate meaningful homework cannot be agreed, then try to get patients to do something, no matter how small, in order to establish a pattern of always being active between sessions. This could, for example, be asking them to read something, listen to an audio tape of the session (which is often vital to combat memory difficulties) or check something out with a professional involved in their care.

For most people, a piece of homework is usually something that is done once. This is another good reason to avoid calling it homework in the first instance. The word reminds most people of past experiences and the good thing about home-work in school is that once the teacher has seen it (however bad the evaluation) you do not have to do it again. In cognitive therapy, the task (especially if it is the practising of new skills) may have to be repeated many times, and patients should be made aware of this. The trick is to balance all the possible "negative" information with the "positive" information in order to help the patient see that effort in homework will produce results, but that effort is always required first.

Practical ways to enhance homework compliance

It is important to ensure that the rationale for undertaking tasks between sessions is explicit in the process of socialising the patient to the model. The patient needs to understand the consequences of doing and not doing these tasks and, as with other parts of the process, may need to have the rationale repeated many times over the course of therapy. Tarrier, Yusupoff, McCarthy, Kinney, and Wittkowski (1998) found that 22 per cent of patients suffering from chronic schizophrenia who dropped out of psychological treatment said they did not understand what was going on.

It is also important to negotiate, and stick to, an appropriate amount of time on the agenda for homework. Always leave more time than you think you will need. Remember that you have to agree the tasks, ensure that the patient understands the rationale for them, and explore the difficulties and highlight the benefits. It is also important to encourage the patient to suggest appropriate homework tasks. This can be done by brainstorming possibilities related to the session, focusing on tasks that will lead to goals being achieved, and reflecting on past successful homework. Always check with the patient that you have a shared understanding of exactly which specific tasks are to be undertaken, the rationale for doing them and the expected gains. Ensure that the patient has written details of the homework tasks and rationale and that they are easily referred to. Using a folder to store session records and homework (both past and current) reduces the chances of either the details being mislaid or the tasks being put off. It is much easier to lose or ignore a sheet of paper than a folder, and a folder appears to enhance the business-like quality of the therapy and the patient's own responsibility within it.

If written details are to be recorded, then it is important to ensure that you furnish the patient with typed grids, templates or other formats in sufficient quantity. Hand-drawn layouts with brief headings are less motivating than formal recording sheets. Pre-prepared formats can be personalised in collaboration with the patient and this too will enhance the likelihood of completion. Make sure that the patient has enough sheets or understands that he or she can follow on using blank sheets. Giving one sheet can lead to the misunderstanding that all the data must fit on it or that homework ends when the sheet is full. Similarly, ensure that the patient understands that, just because there are ten sheets, he or she does not need to complete all ten sheets.

It is important to recognise and address difficulties that the patient may encounter. Asking the question, "What might get in the way of you completing the homework?" will elicit possible problems, as will consideration of past homework performance. The review of the patient's state at the start of the session, and his or her presentation during it, may give the therapist clues to any current obstacles. Patients who experience auditory hallucinations of a command nature may have to deal with "voices" instructing or warning them not to do the homework and be reluctant to share this with the therapist. Patients who experience paranoia may feel confident in the session that the work can be done find that confidence disappears at the point of attempting the work. Written challenges to obstacles, kept with the homework rationale, may help overcome reluctance. Simple techniques, such as establishing what time of day (or what day of the week) would give the best chance of success when doing homework, can be powerful in overcoming a number of obstacles beyond the patient's control. Explore the effects that medication may have. Some side-effects may interfere with the person's ability to remember tasks or the motivation to attempt them. Initially, patients who experience negative symptoms may need to undertake very small tasks in order to establish a pattern of experimentation and change and ensure some success (see Chapter 9 for a description of activity scheduling as a behavioural experiment to test out relevant beliefs). For those patients who have a chaotic lifestyle, homework may be low on their priorities and be superseded by more pressing matters. Using a questionnaire, such as the Possible Reasons for not Doing Self-Help Assignments Questionnaire (Beck & Burns, 1979), may elicit such obstacles and can be used to help in the generation of solutions. Linking homework to the resolution of some of these problems makes optimum use of opportunity and effort.

How to ensure homework is not done

The following tongue-in-cheek consideration of how to ensure that patients will never do their homework may be helpful in illustrating the importance of the preceding information regarding strategies to assist completion of such tasks:

- Make sure the patient has none, or only the vaguest, or, better still, the wrong idea of why homework is an integral part of therapy.
- Leave thirty seconds at the end of each session to agree homework. Don't mention it when you agree the agenda and it will be a nice surprise.
- On the rare occasion when patients have completed the homework, ask them to hand it over, but don't look at it. Rather, put it to one side and never refer to it if you can help it. If you are forced into looking at it, point out everything that was done wrong, or not at all, and suggest that they "could do better".
- Always tell the patient what the homework is, but if you haven't left the usual thirty seconds, tell them to think about it, design a homework of their own choosing and to let you know next time how they got on.
- When patients don't believe they can do the homework, be very reassuring, and mildly patronising if you think you can get away with it, but let them know how annoyed you will be if they don't do it.
- Don't let patients write anything down in therapy or take anything other than blank sheets of paper away if you can help it. You are the therapist, you take the notes and you keep them.
- If patients are really motivated, they will remember everything you say and act exactly on your instructions. If they do not, you have every right to get annoyed with them, be late for sessions, be didactic (they clearly don't appreciate collaboration) and think about discharging them.
- If they have to be given a recording sheet for the homework, make sure you handwrite, on the grubbiest piece of paper you can find (curled corners and the odd footprint and coffee stain add considerably to the effect), no more than three words. There is no limit to the amount of lines and geometric shapes you should use, in fact the less space you leave for writing, the less you will have to talk about at the next session. Never, ever, give out more than one page.
- Don't assume that because your patients have never done any of the homework you have set them that they won't do this one. You're the therapist, you went to the lectures, and you know what comes next in the model. Don't worry; they'll get the hang of it eventually.
- Refuse to accept the notion that your patients have anything more important than therapy in their lives. If you can fit them in for an hour a week then it's not much to ask that they do a bit of homework.

Complementary uses of homework

There are a number of other reasons why homework is an important part of cognitive therapy. It can generate useful information in a variety of ways. For example, issues resulting from homework (completion, attempts or non-attempts) can be used to help set the agenda and identify session targets. Because the formulation is dynamic, the information gained from homework will be incorporated into it and will, in itself, influence further work. If some, or all, of the homework has been completed, then there is an opportunity for the patient to be given positive feedback and credit for their achievements. The concepts of scientific exploration, problem solving and self-efficacy can be discussed and related to the work done. Not doing homework can help identify beliefs about failure, such as "I'll make a mess of it, so what's the point in doing it" or "I couldn't even do the homework, because I'm useless/stupid/weak/a failure".

What to do when patients will not do homework

If a patient has not completed all, or some, of the homework previously agreed, then the therapist needs to know exactly why that is the case so that the issue(s) can be taken into consideration when future homework is negotiated. The patient will often give a reason, or confession, readily, but this may not give the whole picture. Questioning used to gain this information should be of a collaborative nature. For example, "You were pretty confident that you would be able to do the homework and I can see how . . . could stop you doing . . . but I wonder whether there are any other influences that might have made it difficult for you?" It can be a fine line between curious and confrontational, and it is important to maintain collaboration while exploring possible reasons for not completing homework. If the patient perceives the therapist as critical, then the therapeutic relationship will probably suffer.

If the patient does not see the point in doing homework or regularly has problems completing it, then consideration should be given to making it an agenda item (i.e. devoting a whole session to this issue). The therapist should check through the strategies that enhance homework compliance and consider which could be emphasised in the negotiation and evaluation of tasks. Once the obstacles have been identified, both parties should work together to design strategies to overcome them. Sharing information with the person about what other patients find difficult or easy about identifying and doing homework can be useful. If the patient has had negative experiences in attempting to complete homework, then tasks should be agreed that would ensure success. No matter how small a step they may seem, it is movement in the right direction and the opposite of failure. Some homework tasks can be identified and completed in the therapy session, so that the patient experiences the whole process and has a success to build on before an attempt is made between sessions.

Factors that patients say are important

We have asked patients about their experiences of doing homework while undertaking cognitive therapy for psychosis (Dunn, Morrison, & Bentall, 2002). Patients can readily identify reasons why they did or did not do their homework between sessions. The themes that have the greatest influence on completion of tasks are

- insight
- understanding
- rationale
- exhaustion
- explanation
- analysis
- learning
- difficulty.

Some of these were related to therapist factors that increased the likelihood that homework would be attempted and completed. For example, if the therapist gives a clear rationale for both global and specific homework, it is more likely to be attempted. Similarly, the therapist explaining (in terms the patient can understand) the gains to be made from doing homework, and the therapist helping the patient to gain an understanding of how the problem developed and what maintains it, were associated with increased compliance. The patient factors that reduced the likelihood of homework completion included feeling exhausted at the end of a therapy session, or feeling exhausted in general, and anticipating that the homework would be difficult (and therefore putting it off). Not having the energy to undertake the homework was also cited as a reason for not attempting tasks.

Factors that increased homework completion that were identified by patients following the completion of a piece, or pieces, of homework included learning more about their problems, gaining insight into their own problems through experimentation, learning the skill of scientific analysis of problems and realising that they could make changes and progress. The experience of making gains through homework in the initial phase of therapy greatly increased motivation to undertake tasks and to overcome obstacles.

Patients appear to be influenced by a small range of factors, but the individual experience for each patient needs to be examined in detail and used in therapy. Recognition by the therapist that these influences exist for many patients and sharing that information in the early phase, in addition to focusing on the gains the patient has made through homework across the process of therapy, will influence selection of homework tasks, motivation and impetus to complete them.

Homework and the therapeutic relationship

A good therapeutic relationship, or alliance, makes it possible for the patient to accept and follow the treatment protocols, and increases the likelihood of the patient completing homework tasks. A shared agreement on the strategies to be used to achieve therapeutic goals also increases the likelihood of homework task adherence. The better the relationship and the more empathy, trust and genuineness the patient perceives in the therapist, the safer a patient will feel. It is from this safe base that the patient begins to explore and evaluate his or her situation (see Chapter 7 for further discussion).

Some case examples

Two case examples will be given in order to help illustrate the important factors that contribute to homework compliance. Barry was a patient with a high level of homework compliance. He believed that he was Jesus and had been sent down to Earth to save mankind. At its strongest he had rated the level of conviction as 100 per cent and, as the level reduced, he began to feel to feel ashamed of how he had thought and behaved, and he feared that people would avoid him or talk about him. He worried that the level of conviction might increase at any time and he would, once again, behave in a way that would lead him to be treated very negatively by neighbours, friends and family. An interview with him found his level of adherence to homework tasks to be high because of the following factors:

- Homework tasks were specific and were informed by the formulation and therapeutic goals.
- There was a quick socialisation to, and acceptance of, the model and treatment by the patient.
- The concept of homework as an integral part of therapy was introduced with treatment rationale.
- The therapist responded to less than 100 per cent completion of homework with use of humour, followed by a collaborative exploration of reasons why that had happened.
- There was an early homework success in therapy that kept the patient motivated to complete further tasks.
- The patient had confidence in the therapy.
- There was a good therapeutic relationship and the patient had confidence in the therapist.
- The patient listened to audio tapes of the therapy between sessions and kept a copy of all tapes.
- The gains were spelled out before homework and then capitalised on afterwards.
- The patient used a folder to keep handouts, session records and completed homework together.
- The patient kept a written record of each therapy session.
- Exact details of homework tasks were written down by the patient.
- The rationale for homework was always written down.
- Possible obstacles were explored and strategies were devised to overcome them.
- Metaphors were used to illustrate points when discussing the concept of homework. For example, homework as car maintenance, with the therapist as a mechanic who has worked on a number of cars with success and is happy to advise on this one (i.e. the patient). The only way to test the car is to start up the engine then take it for a run, and the only way to keep it in good condition is for the owner (the patient) to invest in it (time, effort and money).

- Imaginal rehearsal of the homework task in session was used in some sessions.
- The therapist's input was played down, increasing the patient's self-efficacy.

Mary was a patient with a low level of homework compliance. She believed that TV cameras were present in her house and that presenters of certain programmes were observing her. She was uncertain of why they were doing this, but they gave her "signs" to let her know that they had seen her do certain things. She also believed that people in the street, and in shops, were watching her and possibly following her but had no idea why or indeed what they may be going to do as a consequence. Her level of adherence to homework tasks was low because of the following factors:

- While there was high compliance initially when homework was simply recording non-distressing data or dealing with low-affect situations, Mary could not tolerate focusing on distressing situations. She believed that moderate or high levels of affect were to be avoided at all costs.
- There was no support at home, and she could not confide in her partner. She believed that if he knew the content of her thinking then he would make efforts to have her readmitted to the inpatient unit.
- She was reluctant to write anything down, either a session record or homework, because it was too distressing to see her problems on paper or on the white board.
- Mary would not allow sessions to be taped because she was worried that her partner would find the tape and use this against her.
- A lot of time was spent recapping and repeating agenda items because she had no written information to refer to between sessions.
- Early benefit gained from global therapy factors (such as warmth, empathy and listening) kept her attending sessions, but she remained reluctant to attempt any meaningful tasks.
- She was fearful of negative consequences of behavioural experiments where there was a possibility of high affect.
- Mary had a lifelong history of poor self-esteem and self-confidence.
- She had been traumatised by hospital admissions and was fearful that experiments may increase her symptoms and lead to admission.

Many of these difficulties are potential targets for cognitive therapy, and could have been worked with in this framework (such as low self-esteem, fear of high affect, avoidance and catastrophic fears of relapse). However, the environmental factors that were involved in the maintenance of her problem would have needed to be tackled first, and she was unwilling or unable to consent to involving her partner in joint therapy sessions or to re-evaluating the advantages and disadvantages of her relationship.

Summary

Homework is an integral part of cognitive therapy for psychosis. It is important to ensure that patients (and therapists) are aware of the need for work to be conducted between sessions. Homework should be agreed collaboratively, and can involve collecting information, experimenting or practising skills. There are many factors that can increase the likelihood of a patient attempting their homework, and sufficient time and effort should be spent on ensuring that these factors are addressed.

Chapter 15

Problems related to service delivery and context

This book describes an approach to understanding psychotic experiences, along with associated methods to help relieve suffering and improve quality of life for people with psychosis from a psychological perspective. The particular psychological orientation described and advocated is a cognitive one. This approach utilises a generic cognitive model of emotional disorders, as well as more specific cognitive models of psychotic experience. These approaches have been offered to people with experiences of psychosis who met DSM-IV criteria for schizophrenia, schizo-affective disorder or delusional disorder (APA, 1994), as an adjunct to treatment as usual within an adult mental health service in Salford and Trafford. The purpose of this chapter is to consider the implementation of such approaches within standard mental health services for people with psychosis, focusing particularly on the culture of adult mental health services within the UK, and the procedures, practices and, perhaps, philosophical changes, that may be necessary in order to *routinely* offer such psychological perspectives and treatment paradigms.

The culture and values of mental health services

The approach to the treatment of people with psychosis by mainstream mental health services has long been largely biological in nature. Indeed, until the early 1990s, the concept of a major psychological contribution to the care and treatment of people with psychosis was almost completely absent from the mental health agenda. Although family approaches have been demonstrated, in a series of randomised controlled clinical trials, to be of great value in reducing relapse rates for people with psychosis (Goldstein & Miklowitz, 1995), even these approaches are not routinely provided by mainstream mental health services. Routine treatment for people with psychosis often involves the prescription of one (or more) of several antipsychotic drugs, and some follow-up in outpatients at irregular intervals, often by a relatively junior (and temporary) member of the treating psychiatric team. Before the early 1990s, most people with psychosis were not on the caseload of a community psychiatric nurse (White, 1990) and received little in the way of rehabilitation from the mental health services. Mental health professionals had been criticised for apparently abandoning those in greatest need (including people with psychosis) in preference to new clients who articulated better their need for help and support from mental health services (Weller, 1989). The move away from those people that mental health services had traditionally focused on so alarmed the authorities, threatening as it did the long-standing thrust of government policy to community care and provision for people with serious mental illness, that the government was forced to offer the strongest possible guidance to prevent this drift continuing (Department of Health, 1990). Some evidence does, now, appear to be available to suggest that mental health services have at least managed to focus back, to some extent, on their priority populations (White, 1995), including people with psychosis. The challenge of offering psychologically informed care and treatment to people with psychosis is at least as big a challenge as ensuring that services focus their attention on such individuals. There are many aspects to this challenge, and it may be useful to review each of them, in turn, prior to providing some guidelines and suggestions on how to overcome such impediments to implementing psychologically informed treatment to people with psychosis.

Challenges to the provision of psychological interventions: the medical model and the mental health team

We would argue that a poorly understood medical model of psychosis, with an exclusive emphasis on the biological basis of psychosis could undermine a more open-minded (and scientific) approach to psychosis. Psychiatrists still carry huge amounts of influence and status within community mental health teams (CMHTs) and services, and an indifferent, or even hostile, attitude to the potential contribution of psychologically orientated approaches from a psychiatrist can cause real problems for other professionals advocating such approaches. If the team member advocating such an approach is from a profession with an historic deferential status to medicine, this can feel like a really major challenge. Of course, such challenges can also come from team members with differing professional backgrounds. It may be that the team has a powerful team leader who is not from psychiatry, and hostility or indifference from this person or any influential player in the team can be difficult to overcome. Evidence from research into the implementation of family intervention in routine services (Fadden, 1997; Kavanagh, 1992) appears to suggest that if individuals have received training in psychosocial interventions (such as family intervention) in isolation from the rest of their team, then routine practice of such approaches is difficult to effect. This is especially so if the members receiving such training are of a fairly junior position or grading within their own professional group (Bradshaw, Richards, Pusey, & Payle, 2001). One potential solution is to try to generate a shared understanding of the individual case using Padesky's (1996) five systems approach. Because this explicitly incorporates biological or physiological information and the social environment, it can be helpful in providing a conceptualisation that everyone in the team can understand and feel that they have a valued role in relation to. It is also, arguably, more predictive in relation to medical interventions than a diagnosis would be. For example, it is generally agreed that antipsychotic medications treat hallucinations, delusions and thought disorder, which are cognitive and behavioural experiences, rather than the illness of schizophrenia, and mood stabilisers treat mood swings (an affective component). The mechanism of action for such medications may be arousal reduction or the restoration of sleep patterns, which are easier to conceptualise using a five systems model than a diagnostic one. Similarly, the five systems model can better account for why services also target issues such as housing, benefits, carers and employment.

There is also an issue in relation to the required shift of resources, funding and power that would be required to deliver psychological services routinely to people with psychosis. Most clinicians would agree that a stress-vulnerability model is an appropriate explanation for psychosis; this implies an interaction between biological and psychosocial processes. If we assume a 50 per cent contribution for each, then services should be structured, and funded, to reflect this. However, the current position is probably more like 90 versus 10 per cent in favour of medically orientated treatments, and the change that is required is unlikely to be greeted with enthusiasm by the medical profession, as doctors are human too, and are, therefore, unlikely to want to give up their hold on power and status. One way to address this is to focus on the needs that are to be met by services, and to reiterate that the services we work in are there to serve the best interests of our patients, as opposed to our own professional interests. Other potential solutions to these difficulties are summarised in the troubleshooting section of this chapter.

Poor clinical management of the mental health team

Organisations that provide mental health services for the population paid for from the public purse have only recently been charged with the responsibility of ensuring that the organisation itself promotes *appropriate* clinical activity to its target populations. This seemingly self-evident responsibility of mental health trusts and other agencies is, in fact, a new concept in the UK public services. Until the government began to talk about, and give, specifically *clinical* responsibilities to trusts and other providers of services, through the concept of clinical governance (as part of its attempt to modernise health services in general), clinical activity within trusts was meant to be self-monitored by professional groups. A series of public scandals, where the total inadequacies of current arrangements to protect the public from powerful, and sometimes dangerous, clinicians and, perhaps, a long-held desire to tackle the inability of public services to manage and control highly autonomous clinical elites, combined to promote the need for tighter controls over public health services activities. The concept of clinical governance was promoted as one such tool in effectively managing health services. However, this concept does represent a real paradigm shift, and cannot be expected to bear fruit in the short term. At the present time, clinicians who have been appropriately trained in psychological approaches to psychosis, including approaches with a growing evidence base (such as cognitive-behavioural approaches), will sometimes find themselves in the frustrating position of working within a mental health team who may be unsupportive or even hostile to their orientation. They may also find themselves without any recourse to a proper clinical management system, which would give their approach the approval and authority the growing evidence base warrants. They may be left to compete with other approaches without such an evidence base for clinical space or funding. More likely, they may experience benign neglect, whereby people with psychosis, who can potentially gain real benefit from such approaches, are simply not referred, or psychological approaches to clinical problems are never properly considered. Many of us have experienced this. A typical example was provided in a ward round where a patient who had been an inpatient for twelve months was being reviewed (several antipsychotics had already been tried unsuccessfully). The clinical psychologist attached to the CMHT suggested that the patient be referred for cognitive therapy, since the studies that have demonstrated its efficacy have largely been conducted with chronic, drug-resistant patients. This proposal was met with laughter by the majority of the staff in the ward round, and no referral was made. Several potential responses can be adopted to this kind of resistance, and are summarised in the troubleshooting section (see pp. 233–235).

Lack of access to supervision and support

For mental health professionals trying to implement cognitive approaches to psychosis after a period of discrete training such as the COPE programme (Manchester University, 2000), problems with ongoing access to appropriate supervision and support may be encountered. Psychological therapists, including clinical psychologists, perhaps on account of their relatively small numbers within mental health services, have often advocated their need to be managed and located in discrete psychological therapy teams or departments, where their unique psychological perspective will not be undermined by other professionals with, perhaps, a more biological orientation. Such arguments are, at times, advanced on the basis of perceived professional self-interest and protectionism, and the "special" status of psychological approaches is often unhelpful to people with psychosis, but the issue of how to maintain minority perspectives within a generic mental health team is a real one. Of course, the question cuts the other way as well, in that separating out psychological therapy skills into a discrete team risks giving the impression that such skills are the preserve of a small number of specialists and need not concern the rest of the mental health team, and makes the dissemination of a psychological perspective more difficult. Clearly, if the large numbers of people with psychosis served by the mental health teams are to have access to potentially 'quality of life' enhancing approaches, such as cognitive behavioural therapies, then these teams must offer such skills as *routine* not specialist treatments. The challenge for those charged with the responsibility of designing and managing contemporary mental health programmes for people with psychosis that are needs based and likely to be effective on a large scale, is not only to maintain the unique perspectives and contributions of appropriately trained psychological therapists, but also to make such perspectives and contributions less unique over time, by helping others within the mental health team to consider such approaches and develop appropriate skills. One potential solution to this is to locate the psychological therapists within a department (or directorate) of psychological services, but to ensure that individual members of staff are allocated to a specifically identified generic service (such as a CMHT or early intervention service). They should conduct their clinical work within that locality in order to be accessible to patients and carers, and have a geographical base with the generic service in order to facilitate the development of a psychological perspective or culture.

The sort of supervision that is required for psychological therapy may, arguably, be different from that which is needed for other aspects of mental health work. Other professionals within the mental health team may not hold supervision in the same esteem as psychologically orientated therapists must, and this can also be a potential source of tension with mental health professionals not trained in psychological approaches. When a mental health professional has recently acquired new skills as a result of a discrete post-qualification training programme, the need to practise and to have excellent supervision arrangements in place is paramount. Confidence can often still be very brittle, or even already low, and the slow change of pace, and, sometimes, the lack of response to treatment, involved in working with people with psychosis needs proper reflection and consideration in a supportive environment in order to prevent demoralisation setting in. Where services are genuinely committed to implementing psychosocial interventions for people with psychosis, including cognitive therapy, they can sometimes be overly ambitious (perversely, given other factors we have noted within the mental health system) about what can be achieved by one or two people in the first year or two after training, and a good and experienced supervisor can help individuals post-training (and the teams they belong to) be realistic about short- and medium-term expectations. This will hopefully help to prevent later disappointment and demoralisation.

Psychological therapy skills such as setting SMART goals (specific, measurable achievable, realistic and time-limited) can be utilised here also. All therapists can struggle to maintain treatment fidelity in the real world of clinical practice from time to time, and this can be a real concern with an evidence-based therapy delivered through a very human medium, such as a meeting between two individuals. Such problems can arise as a result of numerous factors that good access to supervision and support can monitor and help to resolve. Common reasons why therapists can fail to maintain treatment fidelity include role tension between being a therapist and having other responsibilities for the person you are dealing with (e.g. case management or risk assessment) or lack of confidence in the new role of psychological therapist compared to the security of their old role. Unhelpful comments from professional colleagues who do not understand the process of therapy, such as "the person is getting worse after the sessions rather than better" can also be problematic. Genuinely *clinical* audit could make a contribution to the maintenance of treatment fidelity by therapists. For example, the existence of a problem and goals list, a formulation or an attendance record for supervision, could all be the subjects of an audit cycle.

Caseload size and integration

If psychologically trained therapists are to provide evidence-based psychological treatments to people with psychosis within the mental health team, an optimum amount of time needs to be devoted to such activity by the individual offering the treatment and the team as a whole. If individuals' time and caseload are managed within the mental health team, real commitment by the team to such time-consuming (in the short- to medium-term) approaches will need to be given. Continuing with a full mental health team caseload and trying to offer discrete therapies to more than one or two people is likely to be unsuccessful in anything other than the short term. The ability to prioritise the time to provide evidence-based therapies, such as cognitive therapy, may often prove the biggest service-related challenge for many professional staff. Community-based mental health services are under real pressure in many parts of the United Kingdom, especially in inner city areas where elective admissions effectively seem to no longer exist. Some mental health teams are not functionally differentiated, and in effect this can mean that any mental health professional can expect to have to perform a range of sometimes competing roles within any one working day (for example an assessment role, a crisis response role, a short-term treatment role and a case management role). This failure to differentiate functions and roles can make planned, non-crisis work such as a psychological therapy contract almost impossible to commit to, given the likelihood that some crisis or urgent aspect of the professional's role may clash with such a commitment at some stage.

Basic needs come first (and the context/environment really matters)

People with psychosis will have a range of needs, and on occasion some of these needs will be basic ones. While many people with psychosis can meet their basic needs without any assistance, there may be others who need support and assistance in order to do so from time to time. If basic needs are not met, then attempts at psychological therapy are likely to be compromised. Basic needs for housing, warmth, shelter and a minimum amount of money must be provided for in order to facilitate the effective utilisation of therapy. While this is self-evident, we have experienced people referred for therapy who had pressing basic needs that were outstanding. Many people with psychosis also have multiple social problems such as poor housing, a lack of role or meaningful activity, and poverty or racism, while also experiencing stigmatisation. Psychological therapy, while effective with people with psychosis, is not a universal panacea; however, those working in a psychological way can fall into the psychological fallacy of believing it to be so (Scheff, 1975). The needs of people with complex problems, such as psychosis, demand a comprehensive and systematic approach from the mental health system; unfortunately, such an approach is, all too often, lacking. The structure of cognitive therapy can help to identify such problems. Often patients will not have had a large amount of time devoted to the generation of a shared list of problems and corresponding goals, and prompts about such social issues can be useful. However, cognitive therapy for housing or finding a job does not exist, and would not be a good idea for either patient or therapist, so such needs should be referred on when identified. While cognitive therapy for people with psychosis has a growing evidence base suggesting that it is effective, other approaches to helping people with psychosis recover are also important. The care programme approach (CPA) should be a good framework for highlighting such needs, and the patient's keyworker or case manager should be informed and encouraged to make action plans to address them.

The influence of the environment on people with psychosis, and on their chances of making a good recovery, have for too long been neglected by standard mental health systems. Although the focus of this book has been on providing formulation-driven cognitive therapy for people with psychosis, as therapists we fully acknowledge the influence of social and environmental factors on the potential to recover from psychosis (these have been extensively reviewed by Warner, 1994). Providing only cognitive therapy to marginalised or disadvantaged people, without concurrent efforts by the mental health system to address their needs for a valued and meaningful daytime activity (including the possibility of paid work), is poor practice. Therapists should also avoid the temptation of substitutionism – psychological therapists are rarely trained in case management and are usually such a scarce resource that they should resist playing other roles.

Problems can arise in therapy as a result of the fact that, sometimes, cognitive therapy requires two people to work together on quite intimate material. Psychological therapy is an interpersonal process, and problems about the distance or closeness of the therapist and client in relation to gender, sexual orientation, class and ethnic background can intrude into the therapy setting and impede progress. Therapy teams with as much diversity as possible, hopefully reflecting the ethnic/class/gender/sexual orientation of the population to be served, are the ideal. In practice, this is unlikely to be possible, but services providing cognitive therapy for people with psychosis can at least make overt statements about valuing life experiences, including the experience of psychosis itself. Wherever possible, choice of therapist gender (at least) should be offered, consistent with sensitivity to the traumatic life experiences many clients have had before the onset of psychosis. Collaboration with voluntary sector mental health agencies representing such groups as ethnic minorities, young people, lesbian and gay service users, and voice hearers can be useful in considering resolution of these difficulties in service provision.

Family environment

On occasion it may become evident to the therapist that psychological therapy is likely to prove less than optimally effective, given the home or family environment that the person with psychosis is exposed to. With some close friends and family members of people with psychosis, short explanations of the aims of therapy and the methods involved (with the client's consent) may be enough to allow for a suspension of belief, at least allowing the therapy some kind of chance to succeed. With others who are perhaps more ingrained in their attitudes towards the person with the diagnosis, more active family intervention may be required concurrent with, preceding or subsequent to cognitive therapy. Of course, family interventions for people with psychosis should not just be provided where an overt family problem exists; such approaches are preventative and should be provided proactively by mental health services. From the perspective of providing cognitive therapy to people with psychosis, family interventions will certainly need to be provided if the formulation indicates that a maintaining environmental factor (in this case, the family environment) must change in order to give therapy a chance of succeeding. However, while such interventions have been scientifically tested and described many times (Barrowclough & Tarrier, 1992; Goldstein & Miklowitz, 1995), they are seldom provided by standard mental health services. The absence of the provision of standard family intervention packages for the friends and family of people with psychosis may present a real challenge for the person with psychosis and the therapist. The psychological therapist who orientates towards the team, and helps in whatever way possible to support fledgling attempts at providing psychosocially orientated care, may be making a big indirect contribution to the effectiveness of cognitive therapy for people with psychosis. The provision of family interventions should also be informed by psychological approaches to the understanding of psychosis. As highlighted in Chapter 1, the diagnosis of schizophrenia is a fairly meaningless concept (particularly at the individual level), yet many standardised family intervention packages employ a very medical model of schizophrenia and psychosis. Psychoeducational information often tells families that their relative has an inherited brain disease, which can cause guilt and hopelessness in carers and patients alike. Patients who are receiving formulation-driven cognitive therapy will have a very different understanding of their difficulties, so there is great potential for mixed messages. It is, therefore, important to ensure that families are given information that reflects an accurate understanding of psychosis, and incorporates psychological factors, rather than the commonly utilised, somewhat one-sided, medical model. Employing Padesky's (1996) five systems model can be helpful with this.

At times, it can be useful to have joint cognitive therapy sessions with family members or friends present as well as the patient. This is often the case if an environmental factor is implicated in the maintenance of the patient's difficulties. The use of a cognitive framework can be useful in helping achieve resolution of the problem. For example, if a person has the negative symptom of avolition, and is constantly berated by his or her parents for not getting out of bed, a traditional, medically informed approach would be to tell the family that it is a symptom of the illness that is schizophrenia, and therefore should not be criticised. This may be effective in reducing the criticism, but may leave the family vulnerable to reverting back to their old style of interacting. However, if a formulation is shared that explains the patient's reasons for staying in bed, as well as the family's reaction to it, as well as how the two might interact to form a vicious circle, it is likely that behaviour change may be more lasting. It may also have the added benefit that both parties may feel that they understand each other better. See Figure 15.1 for an example of this.

Working collaboratively with people who are detained

On occasion people will be referred for psychological therapy who are detained under the Mental Health Act 1983. While it is uncommon for psychological therapists to play a direct role in decisions to detain and treat individuals, as part of the multidisciplinary team therapists are clearly associated with such decisions from the perspective of the people with psychosis, whether they like it or not. This can challenge the basic philosophical position of cognitive therapy (i.e. collaborative empiricism). Although the numbers of currently detained people who are referred for psychological therapy may be low, being a person receiving mental

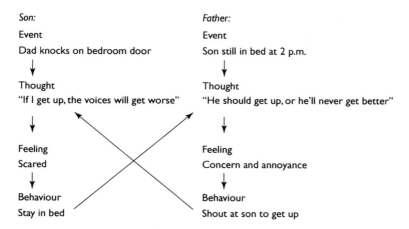

Figure 15.1 A cognitive formulation of a specific family issue

health treatment from individuals who hold the power to compulsorily detain and treat is likely to inform most subsequent interactions with mental health professionals. Psychological therapists are part of the mental health team, even when working in an adjunctive role. We have found no simple way of approaching this potentially problematic issue, other than by being as honest as possible with the affected individual, and negotiating as much flexibility from the rest of the mental health team as safety allows. Sharing awareness of the possibly iatrogenic nature of compulsory inpatient treatment (Morrison, Bowe, Larkin, & Nothard, 1999) with others in the mental health team may allow a fully balanced risk assessment that includes calculating the risk of detention and compulsory treatment as well as the risk of non-intervention into the equation. Normalising responses to hospital admission, such as being traumatised (Morrison et al., 1999) or feeling pathologised (Rosenhan, 1973), can be useful. It can also help to act as an advocate within the system for patients who are admitted against their will, and often an easily agreed shared goal can be getting out of hospital. The therapist can find out what the blocks to discharge are (e.g. refusal to comply with medication or risk to self or others) and these issues can then be collaboratively examined.

Overcoming the challenges

Since we started to write this book, the UK government has identified the need for early intervention teams for people with emerging and early psychosis (Department of Health, 2001). The implementation guide provided suggests that the following principles of care are adopted by such teams:

• culture, age and gender sensitive
• family orientated
• sustained engagement
• treatment in least restrictive setting possible
• service is age appropriate
• educational, employment and other social needs focused upon
• symptom not diagnosis focused
• focused on population of about 1 million.

Some of these principles relate specifically to the needs of people with early psychosis, although it appears to us that many of them are relevant and appropriate for people with a longer problem history. A specific programme of care for all people with psychosis, like the early intervention teams suggested for people with early psychosis, with a dedicated consultant psychiatrist, care co-ordinator and therapist, time could help overcome many of the problems highlighted earlier. Until such a time, we offer the following suggestions of how to overcome service delivery and contextual problems in providing cognitive therapy in routine settings for people with psychosis. These have been developed over time, largely through trial and error, in order to help with the goal of promoting psychologically literate and aware care and treatment for people with psychosis, and they appear to us to have been useful.

Staff should have dedicated time

For the reasons outlined earlier, it is important that staff have dedicated time, and ideally be full time in their role as psychological therapist for people with psychosis. Ideally this should be a team that is an adjunct to existing services, or be sited within a multidisciplinary team that is genuinely dedicated to meeting the social, medical and psychological needs of people with psychosis or early psychosis.

Have entry and exit criteria

If the service is a dedicated one, the target population should be clearly defined and the entry and exit criteria should be operationalised. This should not be done solely on the basis of diagnosis, given the reservations expressed in Chapter 1, and the Department of Health's (2001) recommendations to embrace diagnostic uncertainty. This could be done using a combination of diagnosis and/or presence of certain symptoms (e.g. hallucinations, delusions or thought disorder), possibly with the caveat that they cause distress. In practice, this means accepting patients who would be eligible for DSM-IV diagnoses such as bipolar disorder, psychotic depression and borderline personality disorder, as well as drug-induced psychoses. Exit criteria should be defined in terms of time and functional outcomes, and clear discharge pathways should be explicit.

Have explicit aims and objectives

It is important for team members and service users that those responsible for the provision of cognitive therapy have clearly defined, explicit aims and objectives. It is often helpful to have a philosophy of care that is similarly explicit, in order to help develop these aims and objectives. It is important that these are viewed as dynamic, as opposed to set in stone, but that any changes are made in consultation with service users and other stakeholders such as commissioners, carers' groups, CMHT staff and managers.

Be a multidisciplinary psychological therapy service

Our therapists were from two different professional backgrounds (clinical psychology and mental health nursing) and we often noted that this seemed to diminish professional rivalries or tensions within the multidisciplinary CMHTs concerning our role. Where therapists are appropriately qualified, we aim to achieve a mixed economy of professional people with diverse backgrounds in order to offer evidence-based psychological therapy to people with psychosis. Having people from diverse backgrounds as psychological therapists in the same therapy team also paid other dividends. For example, some of our therapists had been trained in different therapeutic orientations as well as cognitive therapy, which was helpful on occasions. Some of our therapists had worked within the mental health teams in other trusts as care co-ordinators and understood the psychiatric system and its pressures on front-line staff well, and made any constructive criticism to the system more palatable and credible.

Be open and supportive to others who show interest

Our programme has an overt goal to offer a unique psychological perspective within the mental health teams concerning people with psychosis. One of the trusts we work within had no access to any clinical psychology input within the mental health teams themselves, and the availability of psychological therapies within the primary care teams was not accessible to clients receiving care and treatment from the secondary mental health services. Mental health staff within the services had long considered themselves to be denied training opportunities and in some ways considered their area a poor relative of the adjoining big city services. However, we found the vast majority of the mental health service staff to be open and interested in our work and perspectives. We consciously cultivated this by doing talks and presentations about our approach and providing some basic training and awareness raising regarding cognitive therapy. One of our therapists even facilitated a psychosis and cognitive therapy supervision group when requested to do so by the team to which he was attached, in order to encourage other professionals to consider cognitive perspectives on clinical problems. In retrospect, it was probably inappropriate to provide this kind of supervision to people largely untrained in any kind of psychological approaches, but the individuals attending the group quickly drew the conclusion that they needed training rather than supervision. The supervision meetings had opened some eyes to the potential of psychological therapies in psychosis and the willingness of our therapist to attempt to provide such a forum, despite their concerns, demonstrated an openness and transparency that was very helpful in encouraging referrals and teamworking. When working within a multidisciplinary team with low levels of awareness and knowledge of cognitive approaches to psychosis, the therapist who is open to other team members about their approach and techniques (where confidentiality permits) will go a long way.

Use your psychological toolkit to help with teamwork goals

We have discussed the problems that can be experienced when attempting to promote a psychological understanding and treatment paradigm for people with psychosis. Problems of powerful individuals being indifferent or even hostile to psychological approaches can be compounded by the historic and still contemporary failure to properly clinically manage public mental health services. Understanding the system in which the therapist operates can be crucial in tactically advancing a psychological approach and establishing goals that are realistic and achievable, given the context, rather than overly ambitious goals. Such a contextual understanding of the situation confronting the therapist in his or her goal of promoting a psychological understanding of psychosis within the multidisciplinary mental health team can aid the identification of appropriate strategic actions. For example, it may be necessary to ask senior people within the organisation to advocate the organisations commitment to such approaches in the context of clinical governance and evidence based practice. Working at understanding the context within which the therapist must work can be seen as the organisational equivalent of a formulation, allowing the therapist to predict what may need to change to allow any success with psychologically orientating the mental health team to people with psychosis. Making such a formulation explicit, complete with boxes and arrows, can be very helpful in choosing which intervention is likely to be successful in achieving the goals (since each arrow represents a causal relationship that may be amenable to change, directly or indirectly).

Troubleshooting

There follows a list of common difficulties that are encountered when trying to deliver cognitive therapy to people with psychosis. We have tried to list several possible solutions for each one.

The mental health system will not fund such services

- Draw attention to relevant policy documentation (e.g. National Service Framework)
- Encourage users and carers to approach commissioners and senior managers
- Conduct an audit of psychological need in people with psychosis
- Contrast existing service provision and the messages it entails with those that are possible with a psychologically informed service.

The mental health team fails to refer people, in general, for psychological therapy

- Share evidence of effectiveness
- Have a dedicated team or protected time; knowing you will be sitting on your backside doing nothing can be a powerful motivator for referrals
- See each team member and discuss caseload/potential referrals
- Accept self-referrals
- Target family doctors and other primary care services and encourage them to refer

- Target voluntary sector services and educational institutions and encourage them to refer
- Offer team some training in cognitive approaches to psychosis
- See team manager about the problem
- Reflect on own approach to teamwork in supervision.

The mental health team will not refer a specific person for psychological therapy

- Ask for the specific rationale that contra-indicates cognitive therapy in this case
- Share evidence of effectiveness
- Highlight unmet need via CPA
- Present the "suck it and see" argument
- Accept self-referrals
- See the team manager about the problem
- Reflect on own approach to teamwork in supervision.

Personal caseload mitigates against providing therapy

- Share evidence of effectiveness of psychological therapy
- Set up an experiment with your time with clearly auditable outcomes
- Share non-provision of evidence-based therapy with managers/users/carers
- Discuss the need to reorganise or prioritise work with immediate colleagues
- Ask managers for a three-year plan to offer evidence-based therapy.

CPA is ineffective, which affects likelihood of success with CT

- Include a line in all assessment letters about "will be happy to attend next CPA"
- Copy all letters to keyworker/care co-ordinator/case manager
- Assume helpfulness and commitment of care co-ordinator as starting point
- Learn about local CPA and how it is monitored
- Consider whether it is appropriate to take on a role as care co-ordinator
- Ask for CPA meetings to be held regularly
- Write to care co-ordinator identifying unmet needs
- Encourage patients and carers to demand CPA reviews, and inform them of what they should expect
- Understand (but do not accept) difficulties of co-ordinating good standards of care.

Constant organisational restructuring is current priority

- Do not wait until reorganisation or restructuring is completed (it probably never will be!)
- Find senior forum to press need to offer evidence-based psychological therapies
- Maintain or develop important clinical allies
- Encourage service users and carers (both individually and through voluntary sector organisations to request evidence-based psychological therapies)
- Take opportunities to meet with senior potential allies early
- Provide solutions to the new managers and leaders, rather than more problems.

Summary

Providing psychological therapy routinely to people with psychosis appears to be more complex than it perhaps ought to be. Once appropriately trained in cognitive therapy, the therapist has to ensure that she or he has good access to continuing supervision and help the rest of the mental health team to make appropriate use of their new skills. This is sometimes difficult because mental health teams are made up of people with differing perspectives on the treatment of psychosis. Even though the therapist offering cognitive therapies to people with psychosis has a good evidence base with which to justify their approach, the culture of many mental health services is not always empirical or scientific. Alliances may need to be built with managers, users and carers, in order to get evidence based psychological therapies in place, in accordance with organisational responsibilities such as clinical governance. The size of this clinical, organisational and political agenda is such that a reasonable level of seniority or change management experience may be helpful in implementing it.

Appendices

Mastery and pleasure form

	Monday	Tuesday	Wednesday	Thursday	Friday	Saturday	Sunday
7–8 a.m.	M= P=	M= P=	M= P=	M= P=	M= P=	M= P=	M= P=
8–9 a.m.	M= P=	M= P=	M= P=	M= P=	M= P=	M= P=	M= P=
9–10 a.m.	M= P=	M= P=	M= P=	M= P=	M= P=	M= P=	M= P=
10–11 a.m.	M= P=	M= P=	M= P=	M= P=	M= P=	M= P=	M= P=
11–12 p.m.	M= P=	M= P=	M= P=	M= P=	M= P=	M= P=	M= P=
12–1 p.m.	M= P=	M= P=	M= P=	M= P=	M= P=	M= P=	M= P=
1–2 p.m.	M= P=	M= P=	M= P=	M= P=	M= P=	M= P=	M= P=
2–3 p.m.	M= P=	M= P=	M= P=	M= P=	M= P=	M= P=	M= P=
3–4 p.m.	M= P=	M= P=	M= P=	M= P=	M= P=	M= P=	M= P=
4–5 p.m.	M= P=	M= P=	M= P=	M= P=	M= P=	M= P=	M= P=
5–6 p.m.	M= P=	M= P=	M= P=	M= P=	M= P=	M= P=	M= P=
6–7 p.m.	M= P=	M= P=	M= P=	M= P=	M= P=	M= P=	M= P=
7–8 p.m.	M= P=	M= P=	M= P=	M= P=	M= P=	M= P=	M= P=
8–9 p.m.	M= P=	M= P=	M= P=	M= P=	M= P=	M= P=	M= P=
9–10 p.m.	M= P=	M= P=	M= P=	M= P=	M= P=	M= P=	M= P=
10–11 p.m.	M= P=	M= P=	M= P=	M= P=	M= P=	M= P=	M= P=
11 p.m.–12 a.m.	M= P=	M= P=	M= P=	M= P=	M= P=	M= P=	M= P=

Example: mastery and pleasure activity rating schedule

Instructions: in each hourly slot, at the end of each hour, write a description of what you did in that hour.

Also rate in that hour:

M= i.e. how much of a sense of achievement (mastery) did doing what you did give you on a 0–100 scale (with 0 being no sense of achievement and 100 being the best sense of achievement you have ever felt).

And

P= i.e. how much of a sense of pleasure did doing what you did give you on a 0–100 scale (with 0 being no pleasure and 100 being the most pleasure you could imagine).

Form for generating alternative explanations

Event _____

Anxious or
paranoid
thought

Belief at time ___%

Anxiety at time ___%

Are there any other factors which might explain the actual event?
Write these down, leaving your initial explanation as the last one.

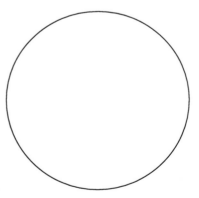

Therapy session record

Name . . . .   Date . . . .

Therapist . . . .

Areas discussed

Conclusions

Work to complete before next session

Reason(s) for doing it

Next session

Date . . . .   Time . . . .   Place . . . .

CLIENTS' GUIDE TO COGNITIVE THERAPY FOR HEARING VOICES: AN INTRODUCTION

Tony Morrison and Sarah Nothard

What is cognitive therapy?

Cognitive means our "thought processes", or literally, to do with our thoughts or the way we think. Cognitive therapy looks at the way our thoughts and beliefs may be linked to our moods, behaviour, physical experiences and to the events in our lives. Cognitive therapy sees these things as being interlinked, but emphasises our thoughts and beliefs as the area to focus on. An example of a different approach would be a medical doctor's emphasis on our physical experiences as the main area of focus.

The thoughts we have about an experience, in other words the way we interpret them, have been shown to have a powerful effect on our emotional (what we feel), behavioural (what we do) and physiological (what our bodies do) responses. This is a central theme for cognitive therapy and is used to work with all types of difficulties or problems.

A common example

You are lying in bed, just about to fall asleep, when you hear a bang in the garden outside. If you think "it's probably just the wind blowing the gate shut", you are likely to feel calm, roll over and fall asleep.

However, if you think "that was a burglar breaking into the house", you are likely to feel scared and anxious. You may hide under the covers, listening out for other noises.

The way these factors are linked can be shown as follows:

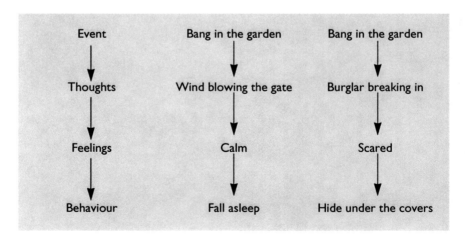

Event	Bang in the garden	Bang in the garden
Thoughts	Wind blowing the gate	Burglar breaking in
Feelings	Calm	Scared
Behaviour	Fall asleep	Hide under the covers

This shows how the same event can be interpreted in different ways. It also shows how the way we interpret things can affect how we feel and what we do.

Cognitive therapy for hearing voices

As we have already discussed, cognitive therapy looks at the links between thoughts, moods, behaviour and physical response. It emphasises how the interpretation we make of an event – the way we think about it – can influence the other factors. This process can be applied to the experience of hearing voices, if we also treat the experience of hearing voices as an event.

An example

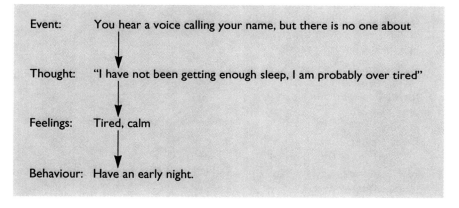

Event: You hear a voice calling your name, but there is no one about

Thought: "I have not been getting enough sleep, I am probably over tired"

Feelings: Tired, calm

Behaviour: Have an early night.

If you did not know that lack of sleep can cause people to hear voices, you might react in a very different way, for example:

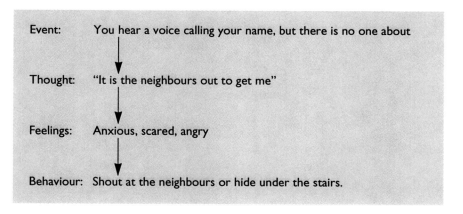

Event: You hear a voice calling your name, but there is no one about

Thought: "It is the neighbours out to get me"

Feelings: Anxious, scared, angry

Behaviour: Shout at the neighbours or hide under the stairs.

Viewing the experience of hearing voices in this way can allow us to look at different explanations of the experience and can help us make sense of the experience.

The stress-vulnerability model

This is a model which has been used to explain the different experiences there are of hearing voices and other unusual experiences. It explains why some people seem more prone to hearing voices. It also explains why people hear voices during different times in their lives. The stress-vulnerability model looks at the roles played by stress and our own individual vulnerability to hearing voices.

This vulnerability or proneness may be influenced by things inherited from our parents, or things we have learnt as we have grown up, or often, a combination of the two. Different kinds of stress appear to be linked to the experience of hearing voices. These include:

- lack of sleep
- isolation
- social withdrawal
- traumatic experiences
- drug taking
- alcohol
- bereavement.

Figure A.1 attempts to show how stress and vulnerability interact and may lead to someone hearing voices.

For example, people with a low vulnerability to hearing voices will need to experience a lot of stress before they hear voices. On the other hand, people with

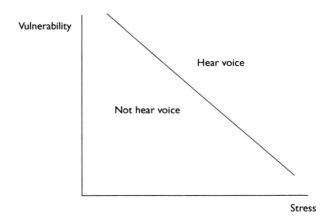

Figure A.1 The stress-vulnerability model applied to hearing voices

a high vulnerability will need to experience only low levels of stress before they hear voices.

Looking at the role that stress plays, we can now see how cognitive therapy can be used to help reduce stress. In cognitive therapy we focus on the interpretations we make about the experience of hearing voices. With our therapist we will learn techniques to test out these interpretations and look for alternatives.

It is important to remember that lots of people hear voices, and many of these are not patients.

If you wish to discuss any of the points raised here, please tell your therapist, who will be able to help you.

Behavioural experiment form

Belief to be tested					Belief %
Experiment to test belief	Given old belief what do you predict?	What might make the experiment difficult?	How might we solve this problem?	What was the result of the experiment?	Does this fit with the original prediction?

Alternative belief:

Belief   %

Interpretations of voices inventory

The experience of hearing sounds and voices when there is nothing there to explain it is a common one. It is particularly common when under stress, falling asleep or waking up. Listed below are a number of attitudes and thoughts that people have expressed about hearing unexpected sounds or voices. There are no right or wrong answers. Please give a response about how you generally feel.

Please read each statement and then circle the number which corresponds to how much you believe this. Please give a response to all the statements.

If I were to hear sounds or voices that other people could not hear, I would probably think that . . .

	Not at all	Somewhat	Moderately so	Very much
1 They are a sign that I am being punished.	1	2	3	4
2 They help me keep control.	1	2	3	4
3 They would make me harm someone.	1	2	3	4
4 They mean I have done something bad.	1	2	3	4
5 They mean that I am close to God.	1	2	3	4
6 They mean I will do bad things.	1	2	3	4
7 They allow me to help others.	1	2	3	4
8 They mean that I have been chosen.	1	2	3	4
9 They make me important.	1	2	3	4
10 They will make me go crazy.	1	2	3	4
11 They mean I will lose control of my behaviour.	1	2	3	4
12 They will take over my mind.	1	2	3	4
13 They have come from the spiritual world.	1	2	3	4
14 They are a sign that I am evil.	1	2	3	4
15 They will harm me physically.	1	2	3	4
16 They mean I am possessed.	1	2	3	4
17 They have to be obeyed.	1	2	3	4
18 They make me special.	1	2	3	4
19 They help me cope.	1	2	3	4
20 They keep me company.	1	2	3	4

continued . . .

continued . . .

	Not at all	Somewhat	Moderately so	Very much
21 I would not cope without them.	1	2	3	4
22 They mean I will harm myself.	1	2	3	4
23 They control the way I think.	1	2	3	4
24 They protect me.	1	2	3	4
25 If I do not obey them, something bad will happen.	1	2	3	4
26 They mean I am a bad person.	1	2	3	4

Thank you

Scoring Key	M factor 1		P factor 2		C factor 3
item no.	1	item no.	2	item no.	10
	3		7		11
	4		9		12
	5		18		22
	6		19		23
	8		20		
	13		21		
	14		24		
	15				
	16				
	17				
	22				
	25				
	26				

Source: © Morrison, Wells, & Nothard, 2000

Revised predisposition scale

Below are a number of statements that people have expressed about personal experiences. Please read each item carefully and say how much you generally agree with it by circling the appropriate number. Please respond to all the items, there are no right or wrong answers. Do not spend too much time thinking about each one.

	Never	Sometimes	Often	Almost always
1 I daydream about being someone else.	1	2	3	4
2 I hear a voice speaking my thoughts aloud.	1	2	3	4
3 A passing thought will seem so real that it frightens me.	1	2	3	4
4 I imagine myself off in far distant places.	1	2	3	4
5 I fantasise about being someone else.	1	2	3	4
6 In my daydreams I can hear the sound of a tune almost as clearly as if I were actually listening to it.	1	2	3	4
7 I hear the telephone ring and find that I am mistaken.	1	2	3	4
8 I hear people call my name and find that nobody has done so.	1	2	3	4
9 I have heard the voice of God speaking to me.	1	2	3	4
10 The people in my daydreams seem so true to life that I think they are real.	1	2	3	4
11 No matter how much I try to concentrate on my work unrelated thoughts always creep into my mind.	1	2	3	4
12 I can see things strongly in my daydreams.	1	2	3	4
13 I can hear music when it is not being played.	1	2	3	4
14 I have seen a person's face in front of me when no one was there.	1	2	3	4
15 I can see the people in my daydreams very clearly.	1	2	3	4
16 My thoughts seem as real as actual events in my life.	1	2	3	4
17 I have a vivid imaginary life.	1	2	3	4

continued . . .

continued . . .

	Never	Sometimes	Often	Almost always
18 I have had the experience of hearing a person's voice and then found that there was no one there.	1	2	3	4
19 When I look at things they look unreal to me.	1	2	3	4
20 I see shadows and shapes when there is nothing there.	1	2	3	4
21 I have been troubled by hearing voices in my head.	1	2	3	4
22 When I look at myself in the mirror I look different.	1	2	3	4
23 The sounds I hear in my daydreams are generally clear and distinct.	1	2	3	4
24 When I look at things they appear strange to me.	1	2	3	4

Source: © Morrison, Wells, & Nothard, 2000

References

Abramson, L. Y., Seligman, M. E. P., & Teasdale, J. D. (1978). Learned helplessness in humans: Critique and reformulation. *Journal of Abnormal Psychology, 78,* 40–74.

Abramson, L. Y., Metalsky, G. I., & Alloy, L. B. (1989). Hopelessness depression: A theory-based subtype of depression. *Psychological Review, 96,* 358–372.

Adler, C. M., Goldberg, T. E., Malhotra, A. K., Pickar, D., & Breier, A. (1998). Effects of ketamine on thought disorder, working memory, and semantic memory in healthy volunteers. *Biological Psychiatry, 43,* 811–816.

Alford, B. A., & Beck, A. T. (1997). *The integrative power of cognitive therapy.* New York: Guilford.

Al-Issa, I. (1978). Sociocultural factors in hallucinations. *International Journal of Social Psychiatry, 24,* 167–176.

Allen, T. E., & Argus, B. (1968). Hyperventilation leading to hallucinations. *American Journal of Psychiatry, 125,* 632–637.

Allison, D. B., Mentore, J. L., Heo, M., Chandler, L. P., Cappelleri, J. C., Infante, M. C., & Weiden, P. (1999). Antipsychotic-induced weight gain: A comprehensive research synthesis. *American Journal of Psychiatry, 156,* 1686–1696.

Alloy, L. B., Abramson, L. Y., Whitehouse, W. G., Hogan, M. E., Tashman, N. A., Steinberg, D. L., Rose, D. T., & Donovan, P. (1999). Depressogenic cognitive styles: Predictive validity, information processing and personality characteristics, and developmental origins. *Behaviour Research and Therapy, 37,* 503–531.

Alpert, M. (1985). The signs and symptoms of schizophrenia. *Comprehensive Psychiatry, 26,* 103–112.

American Psychiatric Association. (1980). *Diagnostic and statistical manual of mental disorders* (3rd ed.) Washington, DC: Author.

American Psychiatric Association. (1987). *Diagnostic and statistical manual of mental disorders – revised* (3rd ed.) Washington, DC: Author.

American Psychiatric Association (1994). *Diagnostic and statistical manual of mental disorders* (4th ed.). Washington, DC: Author.

Andreasen, N. C. (1979a). The clinical assessment of thought, language and communication disorders. *Archives of General Psychiatry, 36,* 1315–1321.

Andreasen, N. C. (1979b). Thought, language and communication disorders: Diagnostic significance. *Archives of General Psychiatry, 36,* 1325–1330.

Andreasen, N. C. (1989). Scale for the Assessment of Negative Symptoms (SANS). *British Journal of Psychiatry, 155*(suppl. 7), 53–58.

Andreason, N. C., & Grove, W. M. (1986). Evaluation of positive and negative symptoms in schizophrenia. *Psychiatrie and Psychobiologie*, 1: 108–121.

Andreasen, N. C., Roy, M.-A., & Flaum, M. (1995). Positive and negative symptoms. In S. R. Hirsch & D. R. Weinberger (Eds.), *Schizophrenia* (pp. 28–45). Oxford: Blackwell.

Arntz, A., & Van den Hout, M. (1996). Psychological treatments of panic dsorder without agoraphobia: Cognitive therapy versus applied relaxation. *Behaviour Research and Therapy, 34*, 113–121.

Ayllon, T., & Azrin, N. H. (1968). *The token economy: A motivational system for therapy and rehabilitation*. New York: Appleton-Century-Crofts.

Baker, C. A., & Morrison, A. P. (1998). Cognitive processes in auditory hallucinations: Attributional biases and metacognition. *Psychological Medicine, 28*, 1199–1208.

Bandura, A. (1997). *Self-efficacy*. New York: W. H. Freeman.

Bannister, D. (1968). The logical requirements of research into schizophrenia. *British Journal of Psychiatry, 114*, 181–188.

Barnard, P. (1985). Interactive cognitive subsystems: A psycholinguistic approach to short-term memory. In A. Ellis (Ed.), *Progress in the psychology of language* (pp. 197–258). Hove, UK: Lawrence Erlbaum Associates.

Barondes, S. H. (1998). *Mood genes: Hunting for the origins of mania and depression*. Oxford: Oxford University Press.

Barrett, T. R., & Etheridge, J. B. (1992). Verbal hallucinations in normals. I: People who hear voices. *Applied Cognitive Psychology, 6*, 379–387.

Barrowclough, C., & Tarrier, N. (1992). *Familes of schizophrenic patients: Cognitive-behavioural intervention*. London: Chapman & Hall.

Bebbington, P. E., & Kuipers, E. (1994). The predictive utility of expressed emotion in schizophrenia. *Psychological Medicine, 24*, 707–718.

Beck, A. T. (1952). Successful outpatient psychotherapy of a chronic schizophrenic with a delusion based on borrowed guilt. *Psychiatry, 15*, 305–312.

Beck, A. T. (1963). Thinking and depression: Idiosyncratic content and cognitive distortions. *Archives of General Psychiatry, 9*, 324–333.

Beck, A. T. (1964). Thinking and depression. II: Theory and therapy. *Archives of General Psychiatry, 10(6)*, 561–571.

Beck, A. T. (1967). *Depression: Clinical, experimental and theoretical aspects*. New York: Harper & Row.

Beck, A. T. (1976). *Cognitive therapy and the emotional disorders*. New York: International Universities Press.

Beck, A. T. (1996). Beyond belief: A theory of modes, personality and psychopathology. In P. M. Salkovskis (Ed.), *Frontiers of cognitive therapy*. New York: Guilford.

Beck, A. T., & Burns D. D. (1979). Possible reasons for not doing self-help assignments questionnaire. In A. T. Beck, A. J. Rush, B. F. Shaw, & G. Emery (1979) *Cognitive therapy of depression: A treatment manual*. New York: Guilford.

Beck, A. T., Ward, C. H., Mendelson, M., Mock, J., & Erbaugh, J. (1961). An inventory for measuring depression. *Archives of General Psychiatry, 41*, 53–63.

Beck, A. T., Rush, A. J., Shaw, B. F., & Emery, G. (1979). *Cognitive therapy of depression: A treatment manual*. New York: Guilford.

Beck, A. T., Emery, G., & Greenberg, R. L. (1985a). *Anxiety disorders and phobias: A cognitive perspective*. New York: Basic Books.

Beck, A. T., Steer, R. A., Kovacs, M. & Garrison, B. (1985b). Hopelessness and eventual suicide: A ten-year prospective study of patients hospitalized with suicidal ideation. *American Journal of Psychiatry, 142*, 559–563.

Beck, A. T., Freeman, A., & Associates (1990). *Cognitive therapy of personality disorders.* New York: Guilford.

Beck, A. T., Wright, F. D., Newman, C. F. & Liese, B. S. (1993). *Cognitive therapy of substance abuse.* New York: Guilford.

Beck, J. S. (1995). *Cognitive therapy: basics and beyond.* New York: Guilford.

Beck, J. S. (1996). Cognitive therapy of personality disorders. In P. M. Salkovskis (Ed.) *Frontiers of cognitive therapy.* New York: Guilford.

Bellack, A. (1992). Cognitive rehabilitation for schizophrenia: Is it possible? Is it necessary? *Schizophrenia Bulletin, 18*, 43–50.

Bentall, R. P. (1990a). The illusion of reality: A review and integration of psychological research on hallucinations. *Psychological Bulletin, 107*, 82–95.

Bentall, R. P. (1990b). The syndromes and symptoms of psychosis: Or why you can't play 20 questions with the concept of schizophrenia and hope to win. In R. P. Bentall (Ed.), *Reconstructing schizophrenia* (pp. 23–60). London: Routledge.

Bentall, R. P. (1996). From cognitive studies of psychosis to cognitive-behaviour therapy for psychotic symptoms. In G. Haddock and P. D. Slade (Eds.), *Cognitive behavioural interventions with psychotic disorders.* London: Routledge.

Bentall, R. P. (2000). Hallucinatory experiences. In E. Cardena, S. J. Lynn, & S. Krippner (Eds.), *Varieties of anomalous experience: Examining the scientific evidence* (pp. 85–120). Washington, DC: American Psychological Association.

Bentall, R. P. (in press). *Madness: Psychosis and human nature.* London: Penguin.

Bentall, R. P., & Kaney, S. (1989). Content-specific information processing and persecutory delusions: An investigation using the emotional Stroop test. *British Journal of Medical Psychology, 62*, 355–364.

Bentall, R. P., & Slade, P. D. (1985). Reality testing and auditory hallucinations: A signal-detection analysis. *British Journal of Clinical Psychology, 24*, 159–169.

Bentall, R. P., & Young, H. F. (1996). Sensible-hypothesis-testing in deluded, depressed and normal subjects. *British Journal of Psychiatry, 168*, 372–375.

Bentall, R. P., Claridge, G. S., & Slade, P. D. (1989). The multidimensional nature of schizotypal traits: A factor-analytic study with normal subjects. *British Journal of Clinical Psychology, 28*, 363–375.

Bentall, R. P., Baker, G. A., & Havers, S. (1991). Reality monitoring and psychotic hallucinations. *British Journal of Clinical Psychology, 30*, 213–222.

Bentall, R. P., Kinderman, P., & Kaney, S. (1994). The self, attributional processes and abnormal beliefs: Towards a model of persecutory delusions. *Behaviour Research and Therapy, 32*, 331–341.

Bentall, R. P., Corcoran, R., Howard, R., Blackwood, R., & Kinderman, P. (2001). Persecutory delusions: A review and theoretical integration. *Clinical Psychology Review, 21*, 1143–1192.

Berenbaum, H. (1999). Peculiarity and childhood maltreatment. *Psychiatry, 62*, 21–35.

Berenbaum, H., & Oltmanns, T. F. (1992). Emotional experience and expression in schizophrenia and depression. *Journal of Abnormal Psychology, 101*, 37–44.

Bermanzohn, P. C., Porto, L., & Siris, S. G. (1997). *Associated psychiatric syndromes in chronic schizophrenia: Possible clinical significance.* Paper presented at the XXVIII Congress of the European Association for the Behavioural and Cognitive Therapies, Venice, Italy, September.

Bhurgra, D., Mallett, R., & Leff, J. (1999). Schizophrenia and Afro-Caribbeans: A conceptual model of aetiology. *International Review of Psychiatry, 11*, 145–152.

Birchwood, M. (1995). Early intervention in psychotic relapse: cognitive approaches to detection and management. *Behaviour Change*, 12, 2–19.

Birchwood, M. (1996). Early intervention in psychotic relapse: Cognitive approaches to detection and management. In G. Haddock & P. D. Slade (Eds.), *Cognitive-behavioural interventions with psychotic disorders*. London: Routledge.

Birchwood, M., Smith, J., Macmillan, F., & Hogg, B. (1989). Predicting relapse in schizophrenia: The development and implementation of an early signs monitoring system using patients and families as observers: A preliminary investigation. *Psychological Medicine, 19*, 649–656.

Birchwood, M., Mason, R., MacMillan, F., & Healy, J. (1993). Depression, demoralization and control over psychotic illness: A comparison of depressed and non-depressed patients with a chronic psychosis. *Psychological Medicine, 23*, 387–395.

Birchwood, M., Iqbal, Z., Chadwick, P., & Trower, P. (2000). Cognitive approach to depression and suicidal thinking in psychosis. 1: Ontogeny of post-psychotic depression. *British Journal of Psychiatry, 177*, 516–521.

Blackburn, I. M., & Davidson, K. (1995). *Cognitive therapy for depression and anxiety.* Cambridge: Cambridge University Press.

Blackburn, I. M., & Twaddle, V. (1996). *Cognitive therapy in action*. London: Souvenir.

Blackburn, I. M., Bishop, S., Whalley, L., & Christie, J. (1981). The efficacy of cognitive therapy in depression: A treatment trial using cognitive therapy and pharmacotherapy, each alone and in combination. *British Journal of Psychiatry, 139*: 181–189.

Blanchard, J. J., Bellack, A. S., & Mueser, K. T. (1994). Affective and social correlates of physical and social anhedonia in schizophrenia. *Journal of Abnormal Psychology, 103*, 719–728.

Blanchard, J. J., Mueser, K. T., & Bellack, A. S. (1998). Anhedonia, positive and negative affect and social functioning in schizophrenia. *Schizophrenia Bulletin, 24*, 413–424.

Blaney, P. (1986). Affect and memory: A review. *Psychological Bulletin, 99(2)*, 229–246.

Bleuler, E. (1950). *Dementia praecox or the group of schizophrenias* (E. Zinkin, Trans.). New York: International Universities Press. (Original work published 1911)

Bollini, P., Pampallona, S., Orza, M. J., Adams, M. E., & Chalmers, T. C. (1994). Antipsychotic drugs: Is more worse? A meta analysis of the published randomized controlled trials. *Psychological Medicine, 24*, 307–316.

Bordin, E. S. (1974). *Research strategies in psychotherapy*. New York: John Wiley.

Bordin, E. S. (1979). The generalizability of the psychoanalytic concept of the working alliance. *Psychotherapy: Theory, Research and Practice, 16*, 252–260.

Bourguignon, E. (1970). Hallucinations and trance: An anthropologist's perspective. In W. Keup (Ed.), *Origins and mechanisms of hallucinations* (pp. 83–90). New York: Plenum.

Bouricius, J. K. (1989). Negative symptoms and schizophrenia. *Schizophrenia Bulletin, 15*, 201–207.

Boyle, M. (1990). *Schizophrenia: A scientific delusion*. London: Routledge.

Bradshaw, T., Richards, D., Pusey, D., & Playle, J. (2001). *Identifying factors that facilitate and impede the implementation of psycho-social interventions in routine clinical practice*. Poster presentation at Fourth International Conference on Psychological Treatments for Schizophrenia, September, Cambridge.

Bremmer, J. D., Randall, P., Scott, T. M., Bronen, R. A., Seibyl, J. P., Southwick, S. M., Delaney, R. C., McCarthy, G., Charney, D. S., & Innis, R. D. (1995). MRI-based measurement of hippocampal volume in patients with combat-related posttraumatic stress disorder. *American Journal of Psychiatry, 152*, 973–981.

Brockington, I. (1992). Schizophrenia: Yesterday's concept. *European Psychiatry, 7*, 203–207.

Brothers, L. (1997). *Friday's footprint: How society shapes the human mind.* Oxford: Oxford University Press.

Brown, G. W. (1984). The discovery of expressed emotion: Induction or deduction? In J. Leff & C. Vaughn (Eds.), *Expressed emotion in families: Its significance for mental health* (pp. 7–25). New York: Guilford.

Burns, D. D. (1980). *Feeling good: The new mood therapy.* New York: Signet New American Library.

Burns, D. D., & Auerbach, A. (1996). Therapeutic empathy in cognitive-behavioural therapy: Does it really make a difference? In P. M. Salkovskis (Ed.), *Frontiers of cognitive therapy* (pp. 135–164). New York: Guilford.

Bustillo, J., Buchanan, R. W., & Carpenter, W. T. (1995). Prodromal symptoms vs early warning signs and clinical action in schizophrenia. *Schizophrenia Bulletin, 21*, 553–559.

Butler, R. W., Mueser, K. T., Sprock, J., & Braff, D. L. (1996). Positive symptoms of psychosis in posttraumatic stress disorder. *Biological Psychiatry, 39*, 839–844.

Candido, C. L., & Romney, D. M. (1990). Attributional style in paranoid vs depressed patients. *British Journal of Medical Psychology, 63*, 355–363.

Carlsson, A. (1995). The dopamine theory revisited. In S. R. Hirsch & D. R. Weinberger (Eds.), *Schizophrenia* (pp. 379–400). Oxford: Blackwell.

Carpenter, W. T., Heinrichs, D. W., & Wagman, A. M. I. (1988). Deficit and nondeficit forms of schizophrenia. *American Journal of Psychiatry, 145*, 578–583.

Cartwright-Hatton, S., & Wells, A. (1997). Beliefs about worry and intrusions: The meta-cognitions questionnaire and its correlates. *Journal of Anxiety Disorders, 11*, 279–296.

Cervone, D., & Peake, P. K. (1986). Anchoring, efficacy, and action: The influence of judgemental heuristics on self-efficacy judgements and behavior. *Journal of Personality and Social Psychology, 50*, 492–501.

Chadwick, P., & Birchwood, M. (1994). The omnipotence of voices: A cognitive approach to auditory hallucinations. *British Journal of Psychiatry, 164*, 190–201.

Chadwick, P., & Birchwood, M. (1995). The omnipotence of voices II: The beliefs about voices questionnaire (BAVQ). *British Journal of Psychiatry, 166*, 773–776.

Chadwick, P., & Lowe, C. (1990). Measurement and modification of delusional beliefs. *British Journal of Psychiatry, 162*, 524–532.

Chadwick, P., & Trower, P. (1997). To defend or not to defend: A comparison of paranoia and depression. *Journal of Cognitive Psychotherapy, 11*, 63–71.

Chadwick, P. D. J., Birchwood, M. J., & Trower, P. (1996). *Cognitive therapy for delusions, voices and paranoia.* New York: John Wiley.

Chambless, D. L., Caputo, G. C., Bright, P., & Gallagher, R. (1984). Assessment of fear of fear in agoraphobics: The Body Sensations Questionnaire and the Agoraphobic Cognitions Questionnaire. *Journal of Consulting and Clinical Psychology, 52*, 1090–1097.

Chapman, L. J., & Chapman, J. P. (1988). The genesis of delusions. In T. F. Oltmanns & B. A. Maher (Eds.), *Delusional beliefs* (pp. 167–183). New York: John Wiley.

Chapman, L. J., Chapman, J. P., & Raulin, M. L. (1976). Scales for physical and social anhedonia. *Journal of Abnormal Psychology, 85*, 374–382.

Chapman, L. J., Edell, E. W., & Chapman, J. P. (1980). Physical anhedonia, perceptual aberration and psychosis proneness. *Schizophrenia Bulletin, 6*, 639–653.

Claridge, G. S. (1987). The schizophrenias as nervous types revisited. *British Journal of Psychiatry, 151*, 735–743.

Clark, D. A., & Steer, R. A. (1996). Empirical status of the cognitive model. In P. M. Salkovskis (Ed.), *Frontiers of cognitive therapy*. New York: Guilford.

Clark, D. M. (1986). A cognitive approach to panic. *Behaviour Research and Therapy, 24*, 461–470.

Clark, D. M. (1988). A cognitive model of panic. In S. Rachman & J. Maser (Eds.), *Panic: Psychological perpectives*. Hillsdale, NJ: Lawrence Erlbaum Associates, Inc.

Clark, D. M. (1996). Panic disorder: from theory to therapy. In P. M. Salkovskis (Ed.), *Frontiers of cognitive therapy*. New York: Guilford.

Clark, D. M., & Fairburn, C. G. (1997). *The science and practice of cognitive therapy*. Oxford: Oxford University Press.

Clark, D. M., Salkovskis, P. M., Hackmann, A., Middleton, H., Anastasiades, P., & Gelder, M. (1994). A comparison of cognitive therapy, applied relaxation and imipramine in the treatment of panic disorder. *British Journal of Psychiatry, 164*, 759–769, URLJ: bjprcpsych org/

Clark, D. M., & Teasdale, J. D. (1982). Diurnal variation in clinical depression and accessability of memories of positive and negative experiences. *Journal of Abnormal Psychology, 91*, 87–95.

Clark, D. M., & Wells, A. (1995). A cognitive model of social phobia. In R. G. Heimberg & M. R. Liebowitz (Eds.), *Social phobia: Diagnosis, assessment, and treatment* (pp. 69–93). New York: Guilford Press.

Cohen, D. (1997). A critique of the use of neuroleptic drugs in psychiatry. In S. Fisher & R. P. Greenberg (Eds.), *From placebo to panacea: Putting psychiatric drugs to the test* (pp. 173–228). New York: John Wiley.

Cooklin, R., Sturgeon, D., & Leff, J. P. (1983). The relationship between auditory hallucinations and spontaneous fluctuations of skin conductance in schizophrenia. *British Journal of Psychiatry, 142*, 47–52.

Coon, D. W. (1994). Cognitive-behavioural interventions with avoidant personality: A single case study. *Journal of Cognitive Psychotherapy, 8*, 243–253.

Corcoran, R., Mercer, G., & Frith, C. D. (1995). Schizophrenia, symptomatology and social inference: Investigating "theory of mind" in people with schizophrenia. *Schizophrenia Research, 17*, 5–13.

Cox, D., & Cowling, P. (1989). *Are you normal?* London: Tower Press.

Crow, T. J. (1980). Molecular pathology of schizophrenia: More than one disease process? *British Medical Journal, 280*, 66–68.

Crow, T. J. (1986). The continuum of psychosis and its implication for the structure of the gene. *British Journal of Psychiatry, 149*, 419–429.

Crow, T. J., MacMillan, J. F., Johnson, A. L., & Johnstone, E. C. (1986). The Northwick Park study of first episodes of schizophrenia. II: A controlled study of prophylactic neuroleptic treatment. *British Journal of Psychiatry, 148*, 120–127.

Cutting, J., & Murphy, D. (1990). Impaired ability of schizophrenics, relative to manic or depressives, to appreciate social knowledge about their culture. *British Journal of Psychiatry, 157*, 355–358.

David, A. S. (1994). The neuropsychological origin of auditory hallucinations. In A. S. David & J. C. Cutting (Eds.), *The neuropsychology of schizophrenia* (pp. 269–313). Hove, UK: Lawrence Erlbaum Associates.

Day, J. C., & Bentall, R. P. (1996). Neuroleptic medication and the psychosocial treatment of psychotic symptoms: Some neglected issues. In G. Haddock & P. D. Slade (Eds.), *Cognitive-behavioural interventions with psychotic disorders* (pp. 235–274). London: Routledge.

Day, J. C., Wood, G., Dewey, M., & Bentall, R. P. (1995). A self-rating scale for measuring neuroleptic side effects: Validation in a group of schizophrenic patients. *British Journal of Psychiatry, 166*, 650–653.

Department of Health (1990). *Community care in the next decade and beyond.* London: HMSO.

Department of Health (1994). *Key area handbook: Mental illness* (2nd ed.). London: HMSO.

Department of Health (2001). *The Mental Health Policy Implementation Guide.* London: HMSO.

Dickins, W. T., & Flynn, J. R. (2001). Heritability estimates versus large environmental effects: The IQ paradox resolved. *Psychological Review, 108*, 346–369.

Dobson, K. S. (1989). A meta-analysis of the efficacy of cognitive therapy for depression. *Journal of Consulting and Clinical Psychology, 57(3)*, 414–419.

Docherty, N. M., Evans, I. M., Sledge, W. H., Seibyl, J. P., & Krystal, J. H. (1994). Affective reactivity of language in schizophrenia. *Journal of Nervous and Mental Disease, 182*, 98–102.

Docherty, N. M., Hall, M. J., & Gordinier, S. W. (1998). Affective reactivity of speech in schizophrenia patients and their nonschizophrenic relatives. *Journal of Abnormal Psychology, 107*, 461–467.

Drury, V. M., Robinson, E. J., & Birchwood, M. (1998). "Theory of mind" skills during an acute episode of psychosis and following recovery. *Psychological Medicine, 28*, 1101–1112.

Dunbar, R. (1997). *Grooming, gossip and the evolution of language.* London: Faber & Faber.

Dunn, H., Morrison, A. P., & Bentall, R. P. (2002). Patients' experiences of homework tasks in cognitive behavioural therapy for psychosis: A qualitative analysis. *Clinical Psychology and Psychotherapy, 9*, 361–369.

Edwards, D. (1989). Cognitive restructuring through guided imagery: Lessons from Gestalt therapy. In A. Freeman, K. Simon, H. Arkowitz, & L. Bentler (Eds.), *Comprehensive handbook of cognitive therapy.* New York: Plenum.

Edwards, D. (1990). Cognitive therapy and the restructuring of early memories through guided imagery. *Journal of Cognitive Psychotherapy: An International Quarterly, 4*, 33–49.

Ehlers, A., & Breuer, P. (1995). Selective attention to physical threat in subjects with panic attacks and specific phobias. *Journal of Anxiety Disorders, 9(1)*, 11–31.

Ehlers, A., & Steil, R. (1995). Maintenance of intrusive memories in posttraumatic stress disorder. A cognitive approach. *Behavioural and Cognitive Psychotherapy, 23(3)*, 217–249.

Ellason, J. W., & Ross, C. A. (1997). Childhood trauma and psychiatric symptoms. *Psychological Reports, 80*, 447–450.

Ellgring, H., & Smith, S. (1998). Affect regulation during psychosis. In F. W. Flack &

D. J. Laird (Eds.), *Emotions in psychopathology: Theory and research* (pp. 323–335). New York: Oxford University Press.

Ellis, A. (1962). *A guide to rational living*. New York: Prentice Hall.

Ellis, H. D., & Young, A. W. (1990). Accounting for delusional misidentifications. *British Journal of Psychiatry, 157*, 239–248.

Elman, J. L., Bates, E. A., Johnson, M. H., Karmiloff-Smith, A., Parisi, D., & Plunkett, K. (1999). *Rethinking innateness: A connectionist perspective on development*. Cambridge, MA: MIT Press.

Ensum, I., & Morrison, A. P. (in press). The effects of focus of attention on attributional bias in patients experiencing auditory hallucinations. *Behaviour Research and Therapy*.

Eysenck, M. W. (1992). *Anxiety: The cognitive perspective*. Hove, UK: Lawrence Erlbaum Associates Ltd.

Fadden, G. (1997). Implementation of family interventions in routine clinical practice following staff training programs: A major cause for concern. *Journal of Mental Health UK, 6(6)*, 599–612.

Falloon, I., & Talbot, R. E. (1981). Persistent auditory hallucinations: Coping mechanisms and implications for management. *Psychological Medicine, 11*, 329–339.

Falloon, I. R. H., Boyd, J. L., McGill, C. W., Williamson, M., Razani, J., Moss, H. B., Gilderman, A. M., & Simpson, G. M. (1985). Family management in the prevention of morbidity of schizophrenia: Clinical outcome of a two-year longitudinal study. *Archives of General Psychiatry, 42*, 887–896.

Fenigstein, A. (1984). Self-consciousness and the over-perception of self as a target. *Journal of Personality and Social Psychology, 47*, 860–870.

Fenigstein, A., & Vanable, P. A. (1992). Paranoia and self-consciousness. *Journal of Personality and Social Psychology, 62*, 129–134.

Fenigstein, A., Scheier, M. F., & Buss, A. H. (1975). Public and private self-consciousness: Assessment and theory. *Journal of Consulting and Clinical Psychology, 43*, 522–527.

Fennell, M. (1989). Depression. In K. Hawton, P. M. Salkovskis, J. Kirk, & D. M. Clark (Eds.), *Cognitive behaviour therapy for psychiatric problems: A practical guide*. Oxford: Oxford University Press.

Flanagan, C. M. (1993). Treating neurotic problems that do not respond to psychodynamic therapies. *Hospital and Community Psychiatry, 44*, 824–826.

Fleming, K., & Green, M. F. (1995). Backward masking performance during and after manic episodes. *Journal of Abnormal Psychology, 104*, 63–68.

Foa, E. B., Ehlers, A., Clark, D. M., Tolin, D. F., & Orsillo, S. M. (1999). The Posttraumatic Cognitions Inventory (PTCI): Development and validation. *Psychological Assessment, 11*, 303–314.

Fowler, D. (2000). Psychological formulation of early psychosis: A cognitive model. In M. Birchwood, D. G. Fowler, & C. Jackson (Eds.), *Early intervention in psychosis: A practical handbook*. Chichester: John Wiley.

Fowler, D., Garety, P., & Kuipers, E. (1995). *Cognitive-behaviour therapy for psychosis: Theory and practice*. Chichester: John Wiley.

Frame, L., & Morrison, A. P. (2001). Causes of posttraumatic stress disorder in psychotic patients. *Archives of General Psychiatry, 58*, 305–306.

Frederick, J., & Cotanch, P. (1995). Self-help techniques for auditory hallucinations in schizophrenia. *Issues in Mental Health Nursing, 16*, 213–224.

Freeman, A. (1999). *CBT for personality disorder*. Paper presented at the British

Association for Behavioral and Cognitive Psychotherapies, Manchester Branch Spring Conference, Manchester, April.

Freeman, A., & Jackson, J. T. (1998). Cognitive-behavioural treatment of personality disorders. In N. Tarrier, A. Wells, & G. Haddock (Eds.), *Treating complex cases: The cognitive behavioral therapy approach*, Chichester: John Wiley.

Freeman, D., & Garety, P. A. (1999). Worry, worry processes and dimensions of delusions: An exploratory investigation of a role for anxiety processes in the maintenance of delusional distress. *Behavioural and Cognitive Psychotherapy, 27*, 47–62.

Freeman, D., Garety, P., Fowler, D., Kuipers, E., Dunn, G., Bebbington, P., & Hadley, C. (1998). The London-East Anglia randomized controlled trial of cognitive-behaviour therapy for psychosis. IV: Self-esteem and persecutory delusions. *British Journal of Clinical Psychology, 37*, 415–430.

Freeman, D., Garety, P. A., & Kuipers, E. (2001). Persecutory delusions: Developing the understanding of belief maintenance and emotional distress. *Psychological Medicine, 31*, 1293–1306.

Freeston, M. H., Ladoucer, R., Gagnon, F., Thibodeau, N., Rheaume, J., Letarte, H., & Bujold, A. (1997). Cognitive behavioral treatment of obsessive thoughts: a controlled study. *Journal of Consulting and Clinical Psychology, 65*, 405–413.

Frith, C. D. (1979). Consciousness, information processing and schizophrenia. *British Journal of Psychiatry, 134*, 225–235.

Frith, C. D. (1992). *The cognitive neuropsychology of schizophrenia*. Hillsdale, NJ: Lawrence Erlbaum Associates Inc.

Frith, C., & Corcoran, R. (1996). Exploring "theory of mind" in people with schizophrenia. *Psychological Medicine, 26*, 521–530.

Frith, C. D., & Done, C. J. (1989). Experience of alien control in schizophrenia reflect a disorder in the central monitoring of action. *Psychological Medicine, 19*, 359–363.

Gallagher, A. G., Dinan, T. G., & Baker, L. V. J. (1994). The effects of varying auditory input on schizophrenic hallucinations: A replication. *British Journal of Medical Psychology, 67*, 67–76.

Gallup, G. H., & Newport, F. (1991). Belief in paranormal phenomena among american adults. *Skeptical Inquirer, 15*, 137–146.

Garety, P., & Freeman, D. (1999). Cognitive approaches to delusions: A critical review of theories and evidence. *British Journal of Clinical Psychology, 38(2)*, 113–154.

Garety, P. A., & Hemsley, D. R. (1994). *Delusions*. London: Psychology Press.

Garety, P. A., Hemsley, D. R., & Wessely, S. (1991). Reasoning in deluded schizophrenic and paranoid patients. *Journal of Nervous and Mental Disease, 179(4)*, 194–201.

Garety, P.A., Kuipers, L., Fowler, D., Chamberlain, F., & Dunn, G. (1994). Cognitive Behaviour therapy for drug resistant psychosis. *British Journal of Medical Psychology, 67*, 259–271.

Garety, P. A., Kuipers, E., Fowler, D., Freeman, D., & Bebbington, P. E. (2001). A cognitive model of positive symptoms of psychosis. *Psychological Medicine, 31*, 189–195.

Gaston, L., & Marmar, C.R. (1994). The California Psychotherapy Alliance Scales. In A. O. Horvath & L. S. Greenberg (Eds.), *The working alliance*. New York: John Wiley.

Gelder, M. (1996). The scientific foundations of cognitive behaviour therapy. In D. M. Clark & C. G. Fairburn (Eds.), *Science and practice of cognitive behaviour therapy*. Oxford: Oxford University Press.

Gelso, C. J., & Carter, J. A. (1985). The relationship in counselling and psychotherapy:

components, consequences, and theoretical antecedents. *The Counselling Psychologist, 13*, 155–244.

Glaister, B. (1985). A case study of auditory hallucinations treated by satiation. *Behaviour Research and Therapy, 23*, 213–215.

Glaser, N. M., Kazantzis, N., Deane, F. P., & Oades, L. G. (2000). Critical issues in using homework assignments within cognitive-behavioural therapy for schizophrenia. *Journal of Rational-Emotive and Cognitive Behavior Therapy, 18*, 247–261.

Goldfried, M. R. (1995). Towards a common language for case formulation. *Journal of Psychotherapy Integration, 5*, 221–244.

Goldstein, M. J., & Miklowitz, D. J. (1995). The effectiveness of psychoeducational family therapy in the treatment of schizophrenic disorders. *Journal of Marital and Family Therapy, 21(4)*, 361–376.

Gomes-Schwartz, B. (1978). Effective ingredients in psychotherapy: Prediction of outcome from process variables. *Journal of Consulting and Clinical Psychology, 46(5)*, 1023–1035.

Goodman, L. A., Rosenberg, S. D., Mueser, K., & Drake, R. E. (1997). Physical and sexual assault history in women with serious mental illness: Prevalence, correlates, treatment, and future research directions. *Schizophrenia Bulletin, 23*, 685–696.

Gorman, J. et al (1984) Response to hyperventilation in a group of patients with panic disorder. *American Journal of Psychiatry, 141(7)*, 857–861.

Gottesman, I. I., & Shields, J. (1982). *Schizophrenia: The epigenetic puzzle.* Cambridge: Cambridge University Press.

Gould, L. N. (1948). Verbal hallucinations and activity of vocal musculature. *American Journal of Psychiatry, 105*, 367–372.

Grassian, G. (1983). Psychopathology of solitary confinement. *American Journal of Psychiatry, 140*, 1450–1454.

Green, M. F. (1998). *Schizophrenia from a neurocognitive perspective: Probing the impenetrable darkness.* Boston, MA: Allyn & Bacon.

Greenberger, D., & Padesky, C. A. (1995). *Mind over mood: A cognitive therapy treatment manual for clients.* New York: Guilford Press.

Grimby, A. (1993). Bereavement among elderly people: Grief reactions, post-bereavement hallucinations and quality of life. *Acta Psychiatrica Scandinavica, 87*, 72–80.

Grove, W. M., & Andreasen, N. C. (1985). Language and thinking in psychosis. *Archives of General Psychiatry, 42*, 26–32.

Gumley, A. I., O'Grady, M., McNay, L., Reilly, J., Power, K., & Norrie, J. (2003). Early intervention for relapse in schizophrenia: Results of a 12-month randomised controlled trial of cognitive behaviour therapy. *Psychological Medicine, 33*, 419–431.

Gumley, A., White, C. A., & Power, K. (1999). An interacting cognitive subsystems model of relapse and the course of psychosis. *Clinical Psychology and Psychotherapy, 6*, 261–278.

Hackmann, A. (1997). The transformation of meaning in cognitive therapy. In M. Power & C. R. Brewin (Eds.), *The transformation of meaning in psychological therapies: Integrating theory and practice.* Chichester: John Wiley.

Hackmann, A., Clark, D. M., and McManus, F. (2000). Recurrent images and early memories in social phobia. *Behaviour Research and Therapy, 38*, 601–610.

Haddock, G., McCarron, J., Tarrier, N., & Faragher, E. B. (1999). Scales to measure dimensions of hallucinations and delusions: The psychotic symptoms rating scales (PSYRATS). *Psychological Medicine, 29*, 879–889.

Haddock, G., Slade, P. D., Bentall, R. P., & Faragher, B. F. (1998). Cognitive-behavioural treatment of auditory hallucinations: A comparison of the long-term effectiveness of two interventions. *British Journal of Medical Psychology, 71*, 339–349.

Haddock, G., Wolfenden, M., Lowens, I., Tarrier, N., & Bentall, R. P. (1995). The effect of emotional salience on the thought disorder of patients with a diagnosis of schizophrenia. *British Journal of Psychiatry, 167*, 618–620.

Harrow, M., & Prosen, M. (1978). Intermingling and the disordered logic as influences on schizophrenic thought. *Archives of General Psychiatry, 35*, 1213–1218.

Harrow, M., Grinker, R. R., Holzman, P. S., & Kayton, L. (1977). Anhedonia and schizophrenia. *American Journal of Psychiatry, 134*, 794–797.

Harrow, M., Yonan, C. A., Sands, J. R., & Marengo, J. (1994). Depression in schizophrenia: Are neuroleptics, akinesia or anhedonia involved? *Schizophrenia Bulletin, 20*, 327–338.

Heilbrun, A. B. (1980). Impaired recognition of self-expressed thought in patients with auditory hallucinations. *Journal of Abnormal Psychology, 89*, 728–736.

Heinrichs, R. W. (2001). *In search of madness: Schizophrenia and neuroscience*. Oxford: Oxford University Press.

Hemsley, D. R. (1993). A simple (or simplistic?) cognitive model for schizophrenia. *Behaviour Research and Therapy, 7*, 633–645.

Herz, M., & Melville, C. (1980). Relapse in schizophrenia. *American Journal of Psychiatry, 137*, 801–812.

Higgins, E. T., Bond, R., Klein, R., & Strauman, T. J. (1986). Self-discrepancies and emotional vulnerability: How magnitude, accessibility and type of discrepancy influence affect. *Journal of Personality and Social Psychology, 41*, 1–15.

Hirsch, S. R., Jolley, A. G., Barnes, T. E., Liddle, P. F., Curson, D. A., Patel, A., York, A., Bercu, S., & Patel, M. (1989). Dysphoric and depressive symptoms in schizophrenia. *Schizophrenia Research, 2*, 259–264.

Hoenig, J. (1982). Kurt Schneider and anglophone psychiatry. *Comprehensive Psychiatry, 23*, 391–400.

Hollon, S. D., & Kendall, P. C. (1980). Cognitive self-statements in depression: Development of an automatic thoughts questionnaire. *Cognitive Therapy and Research, 4*, 383–396.

Honig, A., Romme, M. A. J., Ensink, B. J., Escher, S. D. M. A. C., Pennings, M. H. A., & DeVries, M. W. (1998). Auditory hallucinations: A comparison between patients and nonpatients. *Journal of Nervous and Mental Disease, 186*, 646–651.

Horowitz, M., Wilner, N., & Alvarez, W. (1979). Impact of Events Scale: a measure of subjective distress. *Psychosomatic Medicine, 41*, 209–218.

Horvath, A. O., & Greenberg, L. S. (1986). Development of the Working Alliance Inventory. In L. S. Grenberg & W. M. Pinsof (Eds.), *The psychotherapeutic process: Research handbook*. New York: Guilford.

Horvath, A. O., & Greenberg, L. S. (Eds.) (1994). *The working alliance: Theory, research and practice*. New York: John Wiley.

Horvath, A. O., & Symonds, D. (1991). Relation between working alliance and outcome in psychotherapy: A meta-analysis. *Journal of Counseling Psychology, 38(2)*, 139–149.

Huq, S. F., Garety, P. A., & Hemsley, D. R. (1988). Probabilistic judgements in deluded and nondeluded subjects. *Quarterly Journal of Experimental Psychology, 40A*, 801–812.

Ingram, R. E. (1990). Self-focused attention in clinical disorders: Review and a conceptual model. *Psychological Bulletin, 107*, 156–176.

Inouye, T., & Shimizu, A. (1970). The electromyographic study of verbal hallucination. *Journal of Nervous and Mental Disease, 151*, 415–422.

Jackson, C. (2000). *The trauma of early psychosis: Is PTSD a relevant concept for people recovering from a first episode of psychosis.* Paper presented at the 2nd International Early Psychosis Conference, New York.

Jackson, H. J., Edwards, J., Hulbert, C., & McGorry, P. D. (1999). Recovery from psychosis: Psychological interventions. In P. D. McGorry, & H. J. Jackson (Eds.), *The recognition and management of early psychosis.* Cambridge: Cambridge University Press.

Jakes, I. C., & Hemsley, D. R. (1996). Characteristics of obsessive compulsive experience. *Clinical Psychology and Psychotherapy, 3*, 93–102.

Johns, L. C., & McGuire, P. K. (1999). Verbal self-monitoring and auditory hallucinations in schizophrenia. *Lancet, 353*, 469–470.

Johns, L. C., & van Os, J. (2001). The continuity of psychotic experiences in the general population. *Clinical Psychology Review, 21(8)*, 1125–1141.

Johnson, D. A. W. (1981). Studies of depressive symptoms in schizophrenia. *British Journal of Psychiatry, 139*, 89–101.

Johnstone, E. C., Crow, T. J., Frith, C. D., & Owens, D. G. C. (1988). The Northwick Park "functional" psychosis study: Diagnosis and treatment response. *Lancet, ii*, 119–125.

Kaney, S., & Bentall, R. P. (1989). Persecutory delusions and attributional style. *British Journal of Medical Psychology, 62*, 191–198.

Kaney, S., Wolfenden, M., Dewey, M. E., & Bentall, R. P. (1992). Persecutory delusions and the recall of threatening and non-threatening propositions. *British Journal of Clinical Psychology, 31*, 85–87.

Katsanis, J., Iacono, W. G., & Beiser, M. (1990). Anhedonia and perceptual aberration in first-episode psychotic patients and their relatives. *Journal of Abnormal Psychology, 99*, 202–206.

Katsanis, J., Iacono, W. G., Beiser, M., & Lacey, L. (1992). Clinical correlates of anhedonia and perceptual aberation in first-episode patients with schizophrenia and affective disorders. *Journal of Abnormal Psychology, 101*, 184–191.

Kavanagh, D. J. (1992). Family interventions for schizophrenia. In D. J. Kavanagh (Ed.), *Schizophrenia: An overview and practical handbook* (pp. 407–423). London: Chapman & Hall.

Kay, S. R., & Opler, L. A. (1987). The Positive and Negative Syndrome Scale (PANSS) for schizophrenia. *Schizophrenia Bulletin, 13*, 507–518.

Kay, S. R., Opler, L. A., & Fiszbein, A. (1986). *Positive and Negative Syndrome Scale (PANSS) Rating Manual.* San Rafael, CA: Social and Behavioural Sciences Documents.

Kemp, R., Chua, S., McKenna, P., & David, A. S. (1997). Reasoning and delusions. *British Journal of Psychiatry, 170*, 398–405.

Kendell, R. E., & Brockington, I. F. (1980). The identification of disease entities and the relationship between schizophrenic and affective psychoses. *British Journal of Psychiatry, 137*, 324–331.

Kendell, R. E., & Gourlay, J. A. (1970). The clinical distinction between the affective psychoses and schizophrenia. *British Journal of Psychiatry, 117*, 261–266.

Kinderman, P. (1994). Attentional bias, persecutory delusions and the self concept. *British Journal of Medical Psychology, 67*, 53–66.

Kinderman, P., & Bentall, R. P. (1996). Self-discrepancies and persecutory delusions: Evidence for a defensive model of paranoid ideation. *Journal of Abnormal Psychology, 105*, 106–114.

Kinderman, P., & Bentall, R. P. (1997). Causal attributions in paranoia: Internal, personal and situational attributions for negative events. *Journal of Abnormal Psychology, 106*, 341–345.

Kingdon, D. (1998). Cognitive behaviour therapy of psychosis: Complexities in engagement and therapy. In N. Tarrier, A. Wells, & G. Haddock (Eds.), *Treating complex cases: The cognitive behavioural therapy approach*. Chichester: John Wiley.

Kingdon, D. G., & Turkington, D. (1994). *Cognitive-behavioural therapy of schizophrenia*. Hove, UK: Lawrence Erlbaum Associates Ltd.

Kingdon, D. G., & Turkington, D. (1999). Cognitive-behavioural therapy of schizophrenia. In T. Wykes, N. Tarrier, & S. Lewis (Eds.), *Outcome and innovation in the psychological treatment of schizophrenia*. London: John Wiley.

Kirkpatrick, B., Buchanan, R. W., McKenney, P. D., Alphs, L. D., & Carpenter, W. T. (1989). The schedule for the deficit syndrome: An instrument for research in schizophrenia. *Psychiatry Research, 30*, 119–123.

Klerman, G. L. (1978). The evolution of a scientific nosology. In J. C. Shershow (Ed.), *Schizophrenia: Science and practice* (pp. 99–121). Cambridge, MA: Harvard University Press.

Klimidis, S., Stuart, G. W., Minas, I. H., Copolov, D. L., & Singh, B. S. (1993). Positive and negative symptoms in psychoses: Re-analysis of published SAPS and SANS global ratings. *Schizophrenia Research, 9*, 11–18.

Kovacs, M., & Beck, A. T. (1978). Maladaptive cognitive structures in depression. *American Journal of Psychiatry, 135*, 525–533.

Kovacs, M., Rush, A., Beck, A., & Hollon, S. (1981). Depressed outpatients treated with cognitive therapy or pharmacotherapy: A one year follow-up. *Archives of General Psychiatry, 38(1)*, 33–39.

Kraepelin, E. (1990). *Psychiatry: A textbook for students and physicians. Vol. 1. General psychiatry*. Canton, MA: Watson Publishing International. (Original work published 1899)

Kring, A. M., Kerr, S. L., Smith, D. A., & Neale, J. M. (1993). Flat affect does not reflect diminished subjective experience of emotion. *Journal of Abnormal Psychology, 102*, 507–517.

Kuipers, E., Garety, P., Fowler, D., Dunn, G., Bebbington, P., Freeman, D., & Hadley, C. (1997). The London-East Anglia randomised controlled trial of cognitive-behaviour therapy for psychosis. I: Effects of the treatment phase. *British Journal of Psychiatry, 171*, 319–327.

Kuipers, L., Birchwood, M., & McCreadie, R. D. (1992). Psychosocial family intervention in schizophrenia: A review of empirical studies. *British Journal of Psychiatry, 160*, 272–275.

Layden, M. A., Newman, C. F., Freeman, A. & Morse, S. B. (1993). *Cognitive therapy of bordeline personality disorder*. Boston, MA: Allyn & Bacon.

Leafhead, K. M., Young, A. W., & Szulecka, T. K. (1996). Delusions demand attention. *Cognitive Neuropsychiatry, 1*, 5–16.

Leff, J. P., Kuipers, L., Berkowitz, R., Eberlein-Fries, R., & Sturgeon, D. (1982). A controlled trial of intervention with families of schizophrenic patients. *British Journal of Psychiatry, 141,* 121–134.

Leonhard, K. (1979). *The classification of endogenous psychoses* (R. Berman, Trans.). New York: Irvington. (Original work published 1957)

Lewander, T. (1994). Neuroleptics and the neuroleptic-induced deficit syndrome. *Acta Psychiatrica Scandinavica, 89,* 8–13.

Liddle, P. F. (1987). The symptoms of chronic schizophrenia: A reexamination of the positive–negative dichotomy. *British Journal of Psychiatry, 151,* 145–151.

Linszen, D. H., & Lenior, M. E. (1999). Early psychosis and substance abuse. In P. D. McGorry and H. J. Jackson (Eds.), *The recognition and management of early psychosis.* Cambridge: Cambridge University Press.

Lyon, H. M., Kaney, S., & Bentall, R. P. (1994). The defensive function of persecutory delusions: Evidence from attribution tasks. *British Journal of Psychiatry, 164,* 637–646.

MacCarthy, B., Benson, J., & Brewin, C. R. (1986). Task motivation and problem appraisal in long-term psychiatric patients. *Psychological Medicine, 16,* 431–438.

McGinn, L. K. & Young, J. E. (1996). Schema-focused therapy. In P. M. Salkovskis (Ed.), *Frontiers of cognitive therapy.* New York: Guilford.

McGorry, P. D., Chanen, A., McCarthy, E., van Riel, R., McKenzie, D., & Singh, B. S. (1991). Post traumatic stress disorder following recent onset psychosis. *Journal of Nervous and Mental Disease, 179,* 253–258.

McGorry, P. D., McFarlane, C., Patton, G. C., Bell, R., Hibbert, M. E., Jackson, H. J., & Bowes, G. (1995). The prevalence of prodromal features of schizophrenia in adolescence: A preliminary survey. *Acta Psychiatrica Scandinavica, 92,* 241–249.

McKenna, P. J. (1994). *Schizophrenia and related syndromes.* Oxford: Oxford University Press.

Maher, B. A. (1974). Delusional thinking and perceptual disorder. *Journal of Individual Psychology, 30,* 98–113.

Maher, B. A. (1988). Anomalous experience and delusional thinking: The logic of explanations. In T. F. Oltmanns & B. A. Maher (Eds.), *Delusional beliefs* (pp. 15–33). New York: John Wiley.

Manchester University (2000). *Cope initiative.* Manchester: Author.

Margo, A., Hemsley, D. R., & Slade, P. D. (1981). The effects of varying auditory input on schizophrenic hallucinations. *British Journal of Psychiatry, 139,* 122–127.

Marshall, R. (1990). The genetics of schizophrenia: Axiom or hypothesis? In R. P. Bentall (Ed.), *Reconstructing schizophrenia* (pp. 89–117). London: Routledge.

Meehl, P. (1962). Schizotaxia, schizotypia, schizophrenia. *American Psychologist, 17,* 827–838.

Menezes, P. R., Johnson, S., Thornicroft, G., Marshall, J., Prosser, D., Bebbington, P. E., & Kuipers, E. (1996). Drug and alcohol problems among individuals with severe mental illnesses in South London. *British Journal of Psychiatry, 168,* 612–619.

Meyer, H., Taiminen, T., & Vuori, T. (1999). Posttraumatic stress disorder symptoms related to psychosis and acute involuntary hospitalisation in schizophrenic and delusional patients. *Journal of Nervous and Mental Disease, 187,* 343–352.

Miller, L. J., O'Connor, E., & DiPasquale, T. (1993). Patients' attitudes to hallucinations. *American Journal of Psychiatry, 150,* 584–588.

Milton, F., Patwak, K., & Hafner, R. J. (1978). Confrontation vs belief modification in persistently deluded patients. *British Journal of Medical Psychology, 51,* 127–130.

Mlakar, J., Jensterle, J., & Frith, C. D. (1994) Central monitoring deficiency and schizophrenic symptoms. *Psychological Medicine, 24*, 557–564.

Morrison, A. P. (1998a). A cognitive analysis of the maintenance of auditory hallucinations: Are voices to schizophrenia what bodily sensations are to panic? *Behavioural and Cognitive Psychotherapy, 26*, 289–302.

Morrison, A. P. (1998b). Cognitive behaviour therapy for psychotic symptoms of schizophrenia. In N. Tarrier, A. Wells, & G. Haddock (Eds.), *Treating complex cases: The cognitive behavioural therapy approach* (pp. 195–216). London: John Wiley.

Morrison, A. P. (2001). The interpretation of intrusions in psychosis: An integrative cognitive approach to hallucinations and delusions. *Behavioural and Cognitive Psychotherapy, 29*, 257–276.

Morrison, A. P., & Baker, C. A. (2000). Intrusive thoughts and auditory hallucinations: A comparative study of intrusions in psychosis. *Behaviour Research and Therapy, 38*, 1097–1106.

Morrison, A. P., & Haddock, G. (1997a). Self-focused attention in schizophrenic patients with and without auditory hallucinations and normal subjects: a comparative study. *Personality and Individual Differences, 23*, 937–941.

Morrison, A. P., & Haddock, G. (1997b). Cognitive factors in source monitoring and auditory hallucinations. *Psychological Medicine, 27*, 669–679.

Morrison, A. P., & Wells, A. (2000). Thought control strategies in schizophrenia: A comparison with non-patients. *Behaviour Research and Therapy, 38*, 1205–1209.

Morrison, A. P., Haddock, G., & Tarrier, N. (1995). Intrusive thoughts and auditory hallucinations: a cognitive approach. *Behavioural and Cognitive Psychotherapy, 23*, 265–280.

Morrison, A.P., Bowe, S., Larkin, W., & Nothard, S. (1999). The psychological impact of psychiatric admission: Some preliminary findings. *Journal of Nervous and Mental Disease,* 187, 250–253.

Morrison, A. P., Wells, A., & Nothard, S. (2000). Cognitive factors in predisposition to auditory and visual hallucinations. *British Journal of Clinical Psychology, 39*, 67–78.

Morrison, A. P., Sharkey, C., & Johnson, R. (2002a). *Bullying and psychotic experiences in a non-patient population.* Manuscript in preparation.

Morrison, A. P., Beck, A. T., Glentworth, D., Dunn, H., Reid, G., Larkin, W., & Williams, S. (2002b). Imagery and psychotic symptoms: A preliminary investigation. *Behaviour Research and Therapy, 40(9)*, 1053–1062.

Morrison, A. P., Frame, L., & Larkin, W. (in press). Relationships between trauma and psychosis: a review and integration. *British Journal of Clinical Psychology.*

Mortensen, P. B., Pedersen, C. B., Westergaard, T., Wolfahrt, J., Ewald, H., Mors, O., Andersen, P. K., & Melbye, M. (1999). Effects of family history and place and season of birth on the risk of schizophrenia. *New England Journal of Medicine, 340*, 603–608.

Mueser, K. T., Goodman, L. B., Trumbetta, S. L., Rosenberg, S. D., Osher, F. C., Vidaver, R., Auciello, P., & Foy, D. W. (1998). Trauma and posttraumatic stress disorder in severe mental illness. *Journal of Consulting and Clinical Psychology, 66*, 493–499.

Mueser, K. T., Rosenberg, S. D., Goodman, L. A., & Trumbetta, S. L. (2002). Trauma, PTSD and the course of severe mental illness: an interactive model. *Schizophrenia Research, 53*, 123–143.

Mullen, P. (1979). Phenomenology of disordered mental function. In P. Hill, R. Murray & G. Thorley (Eds.), *Essentials of postgraduate psychiatry* (pp. 25–54). London: Academic Press.

Myhrman, A., Rantakallio, P., Isohanni, M., Jones, P., & Partanen, U. (1996). Unwanted-ness of preganancy and schizophrenia in the child. *British Journal of Psychiatry, 169*, 637–640.

Nayani, T. H., & David, A. S. (1996). The auditory hallucination: a phenomenological survey. *Psychological Medicine, 26*, 177–189.

Nelson, E. B., Saz, K. W., & Strakowski, S. M. (1998). Attentional performance in patients with psychotic and nonpsychotic major depression and schizophrenia. *American Journal of Psychiatry, 155*, 137–139.

Norman, R. M. G., & Malla, A. K. (1991). Dysphoric mood and symptomatology in schizophrenia. *Psychological Medicine, 21*, 897–203.

Nothard, S., Morrison, A. P., & Wells, A. (2002). *Safety behaviours and auditory hallucinations*. Manuscript in preparation.

Nuechterlein, K. H., & Dawson, M. E. (1984). A heuristic vulnerability-stress model of schizophrenic episodes. *Schizophrenia Bulletin, 10*, 300–312.

Nuechterlein, K. H., Parasuraman, R., & Jiang, Q. (1983). Visual sustained attention: Image degradation produces rapid sensitivity decrement over time. *Science, 220*, 327–329.

Oltmanns, T. F., & Neale, J. M. (1978). Distractability in relation to other aspects of schizophrenic disorder. In S. Schwartz (Ed.), *Language and cognition in schizophrenia* (pp. 117–143). Hillsdale, NJ: Lawrence Earlbaum Associates, Inc.

Orlinsky, D. E., Grawe, K. & Parks, B. K. (1994). Process and outcome in psychotherapy. In A. E. Bergin & S. L. Garfield (Eds.), *Handbook of psychotherapy and behaviour change*, (pp. 270–276). New York: John Wiley.

Oswald, I. (1974). *Sleep*. Harmondsworth: Penguin.

Padesky, C. A. (1993a). Schema as self-prejudice. *International Cognitive Therapy Newsletter, 5/6*, 16–17.

Padesky, C. A. (1993b). *Socratic questioning: Changing minds or guiding discovery?* Keynote address delivered at the European Congress of Behavioural and Cognitive Therapies, London, September.

Padesky, C. A. (1994). Schema change processes in cognitive therapy. *Clinical Psychology & Psychotherapy, 1*, 267–278.

Padesky, C. A. (1996). Developing cognitive therapist competency: Teaching and supervision models. In P. M. Salkovskis (Ed.), *Frontiers of cognitive therapy*. New York: Guilford.

Padesky, C. A., & Greenberger, D. (1995), *Clinician's guide to mind over mood*. New York: Guilford.

Paul, G. L., & Lenz, R. J. (1977). *Psychosocial treatment of chronic mental patients: Milieu vs social-learning programs*. Cambridge, MA: Harvard University Press.

Penn, D. L., Hope, D. A., Spaulding, W., & Kucera, J. (1994). Social anxiety in schizophrenia. *Schizophrenia Research, 11*, 277–284.

Persons, J. B. (1989). *Cognitive therapy in practice: A case formulation approach*. New York: Norton Press.

Peters, E. R., Joseph, S. A., & Garety, P. A. (1999). Measurement of delusional ideation in the normal population: Introducing the PDI (Peters et al. Delusions Inventory). *Schizophrenia Bulletin, 25*, 553–576.

Pilgrim, D., & Bentall, R. P. (1999). The medicalisation of misery: A critical realist analysis of the concept of depression. *Journal of Mental Health, 8*, 261–274.

Pitschel-Walz, G., Leucht, S., Bauml, J., Kissling, W., & Engel, R. R. (2001). The effects of family interventions on relapse and rehospitalization in schizophrenia. *Schizophrenia Bulletin, 27*, 73–92.

Posey, T. B., & Losch, M. E. (1983). Auditory hallucinations of hearing voices in 375 normal subjects. *Imagination, Cognition and Personality, 2*, 99–113.

Priebe, S., Broker, M., & Gunkel, S. (1998). Involuntary admission and posttraumatic stress disorder symptoms in schizophrenia patients. *Comprehensive Psychiatry, 39*, 220–224.

Prochaska, J. O., & DiClemente, C. C. (1992). In search of how people change. *American Psychologist, 47*, 1101–1114.

Rachman, S. J. (1997). A cognitive theory of obsessions. *Behaviour Research and Therapy, 35*, 793–802.

Rachman, S. J., & De Silva, P. (1978). Abnormal and normal obsessions. *Behaviour Research and Therapy, 16*, 233–238.

Ragin, A. B., Pogue-Geile, M., & Oltmanns, T. F. (1989). Poverty of speech in schizophrenia and depression during in-patient and post-hospital periods. *British Journal of Psychiatry, 154*, 52–57.

Read, J. (1997). Child abuse and psychosis: A literature review and implications for professional practice. *Professional Psychology: Research and Practice, 28*, 448–456.

Read, J., & Argyle, N. (1999). Hallucinations, delusions, and thought disorder among adult psychiatric inpatients with a history of child abuse. *Psychiatric Services, 50(11)*, 1467–1472.

Read, J., Perry, B. D., Moskowitz, A., & Connolly, J. (2001). The contribution of early traumatic events to schizophrenia in some patients: A traumagenic neurodevelopmental model. *Psychiatry: Interpersonal and Biological Processes, 64*, 319–345.

Reynolds, C. A., Raine, A., Mellingen, K., Venables, P. H., & Mednick, S. A. (2000). Three-factor model of schizotypal personality: Invariance across culture, gender, religious affiliation, family adversity, and psychopathology. *Schizophrenia Bulletin, 26*, 603–618.

Reynolds, M., & Tarrier, N. (1996). Monitoring of intrusions in post-traumatic stress order: A report of single case studies. *British Journal of Medical Psychology, 69*, 371–379.

Robins, C. J., Ladd, J., Welkowitz, J., Blaney, P. H., Diaz, R., & Kutcher, G. (1994). The Personal Style Inventory: Preliminary validation studies of new measures of sociotropy and autonomy. *Journal of Psychopathology and Behavioral Assessment, 16*, 277–230.

Robins, L. N., & Locke, B. Z. (Eds.) (1991). *Psychiatric disorders in America*. New York: Free Press.

Rochester, S., & Martin, J. R. (1979). *Crazy talk: A study of the discourse of psychotic speakers*. New York: Plenum.

Rodriguez-Solano, J. J., & Gonzalez de Chavez, M. (2000). Premorbid personality disorders in schizophrenia. *Schizophrenia Research, 44*, 137–144.

Rogers, C. (1957). The necessary and sufficient conditions of therapeutic personality change. *Journal of Consulting Psychology, 21*, 95–103.

Rogers, C. R., Gendlin, E. T., Kiesler, D. J., & Traux, C. B. (Eds.) (1967). *The therapeutic relationship and its impact: A study of psychotherapy with schizophrenics*. Madison, WI: University of Winsconsin Press.

Romme, M., & Escher, A. (1989). Hearing voices. *Schizophrenia Bulletin, 15*, 209–216.

Romme, M. A. J., Honig, A., Noorthorn, E. O., & Escher, A. D. M. A. C. (1992). Coping with hearing voices: An emancipatory approach. *British Journal of Psychiatry, 161,* 99–103.

Rosenhan, D. L. (1973). On being sane in insane places. *Science, 179*(4070), 250–258.

Ross, C. A., Anderson, G., & Clark, P. (1994). Childhood abuse and the positive symptoms of schizophrenia. *Hospital and Community Psychiatry, 42,* 489–491.

Rush, A. J., Beck, A. T., Kovacs, M., & Hollon, S. (1997). Comparitive efficacy of cognitive therapy and imipramine in the treatment of depressed outpatients. *Cognitive Therapy and Research, 1,* 17–37.

Saccuzzo, D. P., & Braff, D. L. (1981). Early information processing deficit in schizophrenia. *Archives of General Psychiatry, 38,* 175–179.

Safran, J. D. (1990a). Towards a refinement of cognitive therapy in light of interpersonal theory. I: Theory. *Clinical Psychology Review, 10,* 87–105.

Safran, J. D. (1990b). Towards a refinement of cognitive therapy in light of interpersonal theory. II: Practice. *Clinical Psychology Review, 10,* 107–121.

Safran, J. D., & Segal, Z. V. (1990). *Interpersonal process in cognitive therapy.* New York: Basic Books.

Safran, J. D., & Wallner, L. (1991). The relative predictive validity of two therapeutic alliance measures in cognitive therapy. *Psychological Assessment: A Journal of Consulting and Clinical Psychology, 3,* 22–37.

Salkovskis, P. M. (1985). Obsessional-compulsive problems: A cognitive behavioural analysis. *Behaviour Research and Therapy, 23,* 571–583.

Salkovskis, P. M. (1988). Phenomenology, assessment and the cognitive model of panic. In S. Rachman & J. Maser (Eds.), *Panic: Psychological perspectives.* Hillsdale, NJ: Lawrence Erlbaum Associates, Inc.

Salkovskis, P. M. (1990). Obsessions, compulsions and intrusive cognitions. In P. Peck, & C. Shapiro (Eds.), *Measuring human problems: A practical guide.* Chichester: John Wiley.

Salkovskis, P. M. (1991). The importance of behaviour in the maintenance of anxiety and panic: A cognitive account. *Behavioural Psychotherapy, 19,* 6–19.

Salkovskis, P. M. (Ed.) (1996a). *Frontiers of cognitive therapy.* New York: Guilford.

Salkovskis, P. M. (1996b). The cognitive approach to anxiety: Threat beliefs, safety-seeking behaviour, and the special case of health anxiety and obsessions. In P. M. Salkovskis (Ed.), *Frontiers of cognitive therapy* (pp. 48–74). New York: Guilford.

Salkovskis, P. M., Forrester, E., Richards, H. C., & Morrison, N. (1998). The devil is in the detail: Conceptionalising and treating obsessional problems. In N. Tarrier & A. Wells (Eds.), *Treating complex cases: The cognitive behavioural therapy approach* (pp. 46–80). New York: John Wiley.

Salkovskis, P. M., & Harrison, J. (1984). Abnormal and normal obsessions: A replication. *Behaviour Research and Therapy, 22,* 549–552.

Scheff, T. J. (Ed.) (1975). *Labelling madness.* Englewood Cliffs, NJ: Prentice Hall.

Schmucker, M. R., & Niederee, J. L. (1995). Treating incest related Post Traumatic Stress Disorder and pathogenic schemas through imaginal exposure and rescripting. *Cognitive and Behavioural Practice, 2,* 63–92.

Schmucker, M. R., Dancu, C., Foa, E. B., & Niederee, J. L. (1995). Imagery rescripting: A new treatment for survivors of childhood sexual abuse suffering from post traumatic stress. *Journal of Cognitive Psychotherapy, 9,* 3–17.

Schneider, K. (1959). *Clinical psychopathology.* New York: Grune & Stratton.

Sensky, T., Turkington, D., Kingdon, D., Scott, J. L., Scott, J., Siddle, R., O'Carrol, M., & Barnes, T. R. E. (2000). A randomized controlled trial of cognitive-behaviour therapy for persistent symptoms in schizophrenia resistant to medication. *Archives of General Psychiatry, 57*, 165–172.

Shaw, K., McFarlane, A., & Bookless, C. (1997). The phenomenology of traumatic reactions to psychotic illness. *Journal of Nervous and Mental Disease, 185*, 434–441.

Shorter, E. (1997). *A history of psychiatry*. New York: John Wiley.

Siegel, R. K. (1984). Hostage hallucinations: Visual imagery induced by isolation and life-threatening stress. *Journal of Nervous and Mental Disease, 172*, 264–272.

Siris, S. G. (1991). Diagnosis of secondary depression in schizophrenia, *Schizophrenia Bulletin, 17*, 75–98.

Slade, P. D. (1972). The effects of systematic desensitization on auditory hallucinations. *Behaviour, Research and Therapy, 10*, 85–91.

Slade, P. D., & Bentall, R. P. (1988). *Sensory deception: A scientific analysis of hallucination*. London: Croom-Helm.

Smari, J., Stefansson, S., & Thorgilsson, H. (1994). Paranoia, self-consciousness and social cognition in schizophrenics. *Cognitive Therapy and Research, 18*, 387–399.

Snaith, P. (1995). Depression: A need for new directions in practice and research. *Journal of Psychosomatic Research, 39*, 943–947.

Speilberger, C. D., Gorusch, R. L., Lushene, R. E., Vagg, P. R., & Jacobs, G. A. (1983). *Manual for the State-Trait Anxiety Inventory*. Palo Alto, CA: Consulting Psychologists Press.

Spencer, E., Murray, E., & Plaistow, J. (2000). Relapse prevention in early psychosis. In M. Birchwood, D. Fowler, & C. Jackson (Eds.), *Early intervention in psychosis: A guide to concepts, evidence and interventions*. New York: John Wiley.

Spitzer, M. (1997). A cognitive neuroscience view of schizophrenic thought disorder. *Schizophrenia Bulletin, 23*, 29–50.

Spitzer, R. L., & Fliess, J. L. (1974). A reanalysis of the reliability of psychiatric diagnosis. *British Journal of Psychiatry, 123*, 341–347.

Stein, M. B., Koverola, C., Hanna, C., Torchia, M. G., & McClarty, B. (1997). Hippocampal volume in women victimized by child sexual abuse. *Psychological Medicine, 27*, 951–959.

Strauss, J. S. (1969). Hallucinations and delusions as points on continual function. *Archives of General Psychiatry, 21*, 581–586.

Strupp, H. H. (1989). Psychotherapy: Can practitioners learn from the researcher? *American Psychologist, 44*, 717–724.

Suh, C. S., Strupp, H. H., & O'Malley, S. S. (1986). The Vanderbilt process measures: The psychotherapy process scale (VPSS) and the negative indicators scale (VNIS). In L. S. Greenberg & W. M. Pinsof (Eds.), *The psychotherapeutic process: Research handbook*. New York: Guilford.

Suomi, S. J. (1997). Long-term effects of different early rearing experiences on social, emotional, and physiological development in nonhuman primates. In M. S. Keshavan & R. M. Murray (Eds.), *Neurodevelopment and adult psychopathology* (pp. 104–116). Cambridge: Cambridge University Press.

Tarrier, N. (1987). An investigation of residual psychotic symptoms in discharged schizophrenic patients. *British Journal of Clinical Psychology, 26*, 141–143.

Tarrier, N. (1997). *The Manchester cognitive-behaviour therapy trial for chronic schizophrenia*. Paper presented at the British Association for Behavioural and Cognitive Psychotherapy Annual Conference, July, Canterbury.

Tarrier, N., Barrowclough, C., Vaughn, C. E., Bamrah, J. S., Porceddu, K., Watts, S., &

Freeman, H. (1988). The community management of schizophrenia: A controlled trial of a behavioural intervention with families to reduce relapse. *British Journal of Psychiatry, 153*, 532–542.

Tarrier, N., Beckett, R., Harwood, S., Baker, A., Yusupoff, L., & Ugarteburu, I. (1993). A trial of two cognitive-behavioural methods of treating drug-resistant residual psychotic symptoms in schizophrenic patients. I: Outcome. *British Journal of Psychiatry, 162*, 524–532.

Tarrier, N., Yusupoff, L., McCarthy, E., Kinney, C., & Wittkowski, A. (1998). Some reasons why patients suffering from chronic schizophrenia fail to continue in psychological treatment. *Behavioural and Cognitive Psychotherapy, 26*, 177–181.

Teasdale, J. D. (1983). Negative thinking in depression: cause, effect or reciprocal relationship. *Advances in Behaviour Research and Therapy, 5*, 3–25.

Teasdale, J. D. (1988). Cognitive vulnerability to persistent depression. *Cognition and emotion, 2(3)*, 247–274.

Teasdale, J. D. (1996). Clinically relevant theory: Integrating clinical insight with cognitive science. In P. M. Salkovskis (Ed.), *Frontiers of cognitive therapy*. New York: Guilford.

Teasdale, J. D., & Barnard, P. J. (1993). *Affect, cognition and change: Re-modelling depressive thought*. Hove, UK: Lawrence Erlbaum Associates Ltd.

Teasdale, J. D., & Fennel, M. J. (1982). Immediate effects on depression of cognitive therapy interventions. *Cognitive Therapy and Research, 6(3)*, 343–352.

Teasdale, J. D., Segal, Z. V., & Williams, J. M. G. (1995). How does cognitive therapy prevent relapse and why should attentional control (mindfulness) training help? *Behaviour Research and Therapy, 33*, 25–39.

Tien, A. Y. (1991). Distribution of hallucinations in the population. *Social Psychiatry and Psychiatric Epidemiology, 26*, 287–292.

Toomey, R., Faraone, S. V., Simpson, J. C., & Tsuang, M. T. (1998). Negative, positive and disorganized symptom dimensions in schizophrenia, major depression and bipolar disorder. *Journal of Nervous and Mental Disease, 186*, 470–476.

Torrey, E. F., Bowler, A. E., Taylor, E. H., & Gottesman, I. I. (1994). *Schizophrenia and manic-depressive disorder*. New York: Basic Books.

Trimble, M. (1996). *Biological psychiatry* (2nd ed.). Chichester: John Wiley.

Turkington, D., & Kingdon, D. G. (1996). Cognitive therapy with a normalising rationale in schizophrenia. In G. Haddock & P. D. Slade (Eds.), *Cognitive behavioural interventions in psychosis*. London: Routledge.

Van Os, J., Gilvarry, C., Bale, R., van Horn, E., Tattan, T., White, I., & Murray, R. (1999). A comparison of the utility of dimensional and categorical representations of psychosis. *Psychological Medicine, 29*, 595–606.

Van Os, J., Hanssen, M., Bijl, R. V., & Ravelli, A. (2000). Strauss (1969) revisited: A psychosis continuum in the normal population? *Schizophrenia Research, 45*, 11–20.

Varma, V. K., Wig, N. N., Phookun, H. R., Misra, A. K., Khare, C. B., Tripathi, B. M., Behere, P. B., Yoo, E. S., & Susser, E. S. (1997). First-onset schizophrenia in the community: Relationship of urbanization with onset, early manifestations and typology. *Acta Psychiatrica Scandinavica, 96*, 431–438.

Ventura, J., Nuechterlein, K. H., Subotnik, K. L., Gutland, D., & Gilbert, E. A. (2000). Symptom dimensions in recent-onset schizophrenia and mania: A principal components analysis of the 24-item Brief Psychiatric Rating Scale. *Psychiatry Research, 97*, 129–135.

Verdoux, H., Maurice-Tison, S., Gay, B., van Os, J., Salamon, R., & Bourgeois, M. L.

(1998). A survey of delusional ideation in primary-care patients. *Psychological Medicine, 28,* 127–134.

Vernon, J. (1963). *Inside the Black Room.* Harmondsworth: Penguin.

Vollema, M. G., & van den Bosch, R. J. (1995). The multidimensionality of schizotypy. *Schizophrenia Bulletin, 21,* 19–31.

Warner, R. (1985). *Recovery from schizophrenia: Psychiatry and political economy.* New York: Routledge & Kegan Paul.

Warner, R. (1994). *Recovery From Schizophrenia.* London: Routledge.

Warwick, H. M., & Salkovskis, P. M. (1990). Hypochondriasis. *Behaviour Research and Therapy, 28,* 105–117.

Weissman, A. N. & Beck, A. T. (1978). *Development and validation of the Dysfunctional Attitudes Scale.* Paper presented at the Annual Meeting of the Advancement of Behaviour Therapy, Chicago.

Weller, M. P. I. (1989). Mental illness: who cares? *Nature, 339,* 249–252.

Wells, A. (1995). Meta-cognition and worry: A cognitive model of generalised anxiety disorder. *Behavioural and Cognitive Psychotherapy, 23,* 301–320.

Wells, A. (1997). *Cognitive therapy for anxiety disorders.* London: John Wiley.

Wells, A. (2000). *Meta-cognition and emotional disorders.* Chichester: John Wiley.

Wells, A. and Davies, M. (1994). The thought control questionnaire: a measure of individual differences in the control of unwanted thoughts. *Behaviour Research and Therapy, (32),* 871–878.

Wells, A., & Hackmann, A. (1993) Imagery and core beliefs in health anxiety: Contents and origins. *Behavioural and Cognitive Psychotherapy, 21,* 265–273.

Wells, A., & Matthews, G. (1994) *Attention and emotion: A clinical perspective.* Hove, UK: Lawrence Erlbaum Associates Ltd.

Wells, A., & Matthews, G. (1996). Modelling cognition in emotional disorder: The S-REF model. *Behaviour Research and Therapy, 34,* 881–888.

Wells, A., Clark, D. M., Salkovskis, P. M., Ludgate, J., Hackmann, A., & Gelder, M. G. (1995). Social phobia: The role of in-situation safety behaviours in maintaining anxiety and negative beliefs. *Behavior Therapy, 26,* 153–162.

White, E. (1990). *The third quinquennial survey of community psychiatric nurses.* Manchester: Manchester University Press.

White, E. (1995). *The fourth quinquennial survey of community psychiatric nurses.* Manchester: Manchester University Press.

Williams, J. M. G., Watts, F., Macleod, C., & Mathews, A. (1997). *Cognitive psychology and emotional disorders* (2nd ed.). Chichester: John Wiley.

Wing, J. K., & Brown, G. W. (1970). *Institutionalism and schizophrenia.* London: Cambridge University Press.

Wing, J. K., Cooper, J. E., & Sartorius, N. (1974). *The measurement and classification of psychiatric symptoms* (Vol. 9). Cambridge: Cambridge University Press.

Woodruff, P. W. R., & Lewis, S. (1996). Structural brain imaging in schizophrenia. In S. Lewis & N. Higgins (Eds.), *Brain imaging in psychiatry.* Oxford: Blackwell.

World Health Organization (1973). *International Pilot Study of Schizophrenia.* Geneva: Author.

World Health Organization (1992). *ICD-10: International statistical classification of diseases and related health problems* (10th revision ed.). Geneva: Author.

Wright, J. H., Thase, M. E., Ludgate, J., & Beck, A. T. (1993). *Cognitive therapy with inpatients: Developing a cognitive milieu.* New York: Guilford.

Young, J. E. (1994). *Cognitive therapy for personality disorders: A schema-focused approach* (revised ed.). Sarasota, FL: Professional Resource Press.

Young, J. E., & Beck, A. T. (1980). *The cognitive therapy scale: Rating manual.* Unpublished manuscript, Centre for Cognitive Therapy, Philadelphia, PA.

Young, J. E., & Behary, W. T. (1998). Schema-focused therapy for personality disorders. In N. Tarrier, A. Wells, & G. Haddock (Eds.), *Treating complex cases: The cognitive behavioural therapy approach.* Chichester: John Wiley.

Young, J. E., & Brown, G. (1994). Young schema questionnaire. In J. E. Young (Ed.), *Cognitive therapy for personality disorders: A schema-focused approach.* Sarasota, FL: Professional Resource Press.

Zubin, J., & Spring, B. (1977). Vulnerability: A new view on schizophrenia. *Journal of Abnormal Psychology, 86,* 103–126.

Index